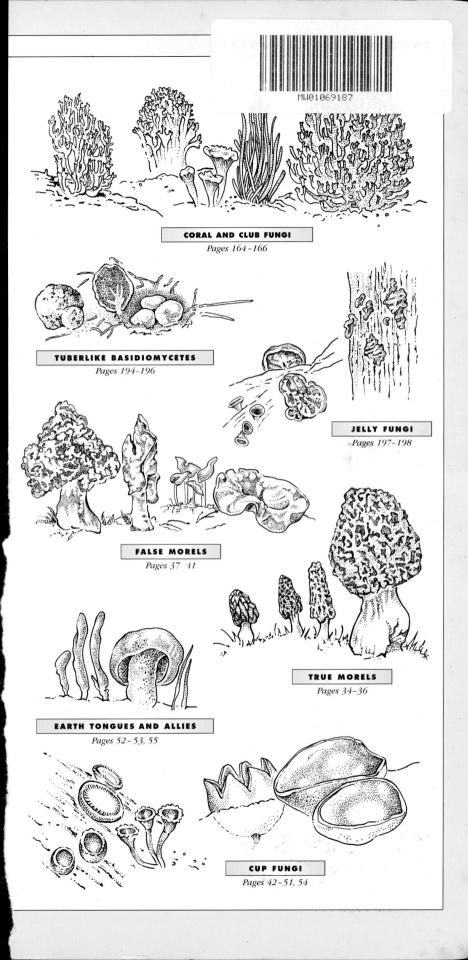

CORAL AND CLUB FUNGI
Pages 164–166

TUBERLIKE BASIDIOMYCETES
Pages 194–196

JELLY FUNGI
Pages 197–198

FALSE MORELS
Pages 37–41

TRUE MORELS
Pages 34–36

EARTH TONGUES AND ALLIES
Pages 52–53, 55

CUP FUNGI
Pages 42–51, 54

Mushrooms
of Colorado
AND THE SOUTHERN ROCKY MOUNTAINS

Vera Stucky Evenson

Denver Botanic Gardens
Denver Museum of Natural History
Westcliffe Publishers

All the species of wild mushrooms in this region have not yet been identified, described, or even discovered. And although many species of mushrooms are edible for many people, some species cause illness in some people. The author and the publishers cannot accept any responsibility for the identification of any mushroom or for the consequences of consuming wild mushrooms.

Project staff
Project developer: Betsy R. Armstrong
Managing editor: James T. Alton
Art director/Designer: Amy L. Thornton
Editor: Lori D. Kranz
Illustrator: Marjorie Leggitt
Production assistant: Danielle B. Okin
Proofreader: Caryl Riedel

Photo credits
All photographs by the author except as follows:
Athalie Barzee, p. 44; Robert Chapman, pp. 24, 162;
Karen Ruth Evenson, frontispiece, pp. 1, 19 top, 66;
Kenneth M. Evenson, pp. 14 top, 19 bottom,
102, 168, 178 bottom, 198; Monique Gardes, p. 10.

Cover: *Tricholoma flavovirens*
Frontispiece: *Boletus edulis*

Publisher's Cataloging in Publication
Evenson, Vera Stucky, 1933–
Mushrooms of Colorado and the southern
Rocky Mountains / Vera Stucky Evenson.
p. cm.
Includes index.
ISBN: 1-56579-192-4

1. Mushrooms—Rocky Mountain Region—
Identification. 2. Mushrooms—Colorado—
Identification. I. Title.

QK617.E84 1997   589.2'22'09788
                          QBI96-40770

International Standard Book Number: 1-56579-192-4
Text and photographs © 1997 by Denver Botanic Gardens
Structure, line art, and design © 1997 by Denver Museum of Natural History
All rights reserved.
Published by Denver Botanic Gardens, 909 York Street, Denver, Colorado 80206;
Denver Museum of Natural History, 2001 Colorado Boulevard, Denver, Colorado 80205;
and Westcliffe Publishers, Inc., 2650 South Zuni Street, Englewood, Colorado 80110.
Printed in Hong Kong by Palace Press International.

Dedication

I dedicate this book to the memory of my great friend, Sam Mitchel, an honest thinker with a very inquisitive mind. He found me (in his words) "already hooked" on mushrooms and then taught me his craft, his vision, and his joy in mycology. Sam's incisive and independent thinking, his great love of nature and its conservation, and his determined quest for knowledge combined to transform him—an amateur mushroomer and indefatigable collector—into an astute toxicologist and mycologist. Sam used his training as a medical doctor to understand fungi. He loved making a diagnosis, putting an unknown fungus into a taxonomic framework, and that love helped him become an international expert on Myxomycetes, the slime molds. His drive to satisfy his curiosity and understand everything about the natural world made him a great teacher whose inspiration sent many of us on a lifelong treasure hunt.

Sam led a thirty-year study of the mycoflora of Colorado, collecting and identifying new species and building the Herbarium of Fungi at the Denver Botanic Gardens. Among his many publications was a booklet entitled *Colorado Mushrooms,* first published by the Denver Museum of Natural History in 1966. This new book has its roots in that small but pioneering publication.

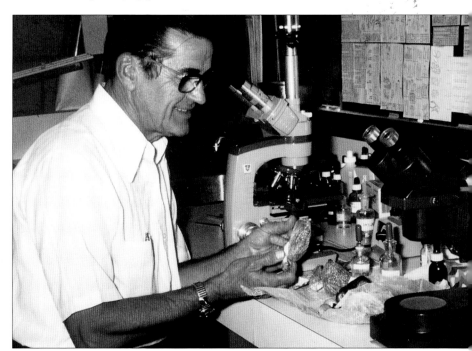

D. H. "Sam" Mitchel, M.D. (1917–1993)
Founder of the Colorado Mycological Society and
the Denver Botanic Gardens' Herbarium of Fungi

Acknowledgements

I want to thank my husband, Ken, for his constant support during the field work, photography, writing, and editing of this work. Kenny is the brains behind my photographs, the supplier of tea and encouragement, and the light of my life. I wish also to thank my four children: Sally, Grant, Carl, and Karen, who each in her or his own way added support, ideas, and enthusiasm. For my mother, Marie, I feel grateful for her patience during collecting trips. I thank Karen Schoen for her constancy and friendship, Larry Latta for his enthusiasm for the project, volunteers Rosa-Lee and Bob Brace for their friendly assistance, and Allein Stanley for her support. Others gave freely of their expertise during the writing and I thank each one: Nancy Weber, Marilyn Shaw, Joe Ammirati, Jack States, Gro Gulden, Rod Tulloss, and Hal Burdsall. I am grateful for the gentle skill of Jamie Alton, the editor who guided the project, and for the vision and talents of the book's art director/ designer, Amy Thornton.

Panaeolus semiovatus

Coprinus comatus

Contents

Close-up of *Cantharellus cibarius*

List of Figures

Photographs of Species

Almost all of the mushrooms pictured in this book are preserved in the Denver Botanic Gardens' Herbarium of Fungi. The DBG number listed below identifies the specimen in the herbarium.

FIGURES AND PHOTOGRAPHS

Lepiota clypeolaria

FIGURES AND PHOTOGRAPHS

Polyporus arcularius

Entoloma lividoalbum group

FIGURES AND PHOTOGRAPHS

Suillus lakei

Preface

*T*he word *mushroom* conjures up a great variety of responses in people's minds. Some react with a combination of loathing and suspicion usually reserved for earthy creatures such as snakes, worms, and slugs, whereas others with hunter-gatherer instincts immediately think of something good to eat. For most people, the beautiful colors and amazing shapes of wild mushrooms appeal to their sense of curiosity and wonder. Both children and adults want to know why mushrooms are growing where they are, how they so mysteriously appear and then suddenly vanish, what role mushrooms play in the grand scheme of the natural world, and how to tell them apart. This book is designed to answer those questions and more by attempting to satisfy the curious, inform the novice, and give pleasure to the artist and nature lover.

The stars of these pages are mushrooms the author found growing wild in Colorado's varied habitats. Because state boundaries mean nothing to a mushroom, you can expect many of the mushrooms featured here to occur throughout the Rocky Mountain region (or, in some cases, all over the world if habitats are similar). For example, mushrooms found near Colorado's treeline will be similar or identical to those found near Montana's more northern but lower treeline. Grassland mushrooms are similar throughout the West, in many cases because habitats are comparable. Correspondingly, "city mushrooms" among Denver's cultivated gardens will be very similar to those in urban lawns and parks throughout the region.

The most complete collection of scientific specimens of Colorado mushrooms is located at the Denver Botanic Gardens' Herbarium of Fungi. More than 1,700 species and about 250 genera make up the nearly 20,000 dried specimens presently kept and studied there. Almost all of the mushrooms pictured in this book are voucher specimens preserved in the herbarium and available for future study. However, the extensive collection at the Herbarium of Fungi does not contain even half the kinds of mushrooms and other fungi that could be found in our state. As more mycologists—scientists who study fungi— collect mushrooms in our varied habitats, more species new to science will be discovered.

Throughout Colorado's history, amateur mushroom hunters have asked, "What kind of mushroom is that?" while hiking in the woods or mountains or strolling through parks, backyards, and barnyards. Answers to their questions have come from many different sources: fellow mushroom hunters, university professionals, mushroom clubs, staff at the Denver Botanic Gardens, books, and newspapers. Along the way, our knowledge of mushrooms has grown, thanks to those determined amateurs who took note of intricate details, exclaimed over the colors and shapes, appreciated the variety, and then asked more questions.

I wrote this book for the amateur mushroom hunter in Colorado and the southern Rocky Mountain region. Use it to guide your hunts, and keep asking the question: "What kind of mushroom is that?"

CHAPTER ONE

Introducing Mushrooms

W e use the term *mushroom* to represent the fleshy, or relatively large fruiting body of a fungus, a good example being the button mushroom you can buy at the grocery store. Fungal fruiting bodies, often lasting only a few hours or days, produce the microscopic reproductive cells, the spores. The fruiting bodies of most fungi are too small for us to see without a microscope. Although these multitudes of tiny fungi are immensely important to us and the environment, they are not the subjects of this book. We will focus our attention on the higher fungi—those that produce relatively large fruiting bodies.

Fungi are not considered plants or animals but are classified in their own Kingdom of Fungi. They are characterized by having as their major structural unit a microscopic cylindrical cell called a hypha (plural, hyphae). These filamentous hyphae resemble long tubes many times smaller in diameter than a human hair. Hyphae growing and branching in a mass make up the mycelium, the body of the fungus organism. This three-dimensional network of hyphae may last for years, growing in soil or other organic matter. You know mycelium as the cobweblike mass of minute, whitish threads found in moist rotting logs, decaying leaf litter, or composting vegetable matter throughout the natural world.

Fungi differ from plants in that they have evolved without chlorophyll, the green pigment that allows plants to photosynthesize, or use the sun's energy to make carbohydrates. Nutritional requirements of fungi are in some ways similar to those of humans and other animals: Fungi need to utilize already formed organic material, such as living or dead plants, to obtain their energy.

Mycophagists, those who eat mushrooms, have developed a body of mushroom lore based on knowledge passed down through human history, our predecessors gradually learning to separate the edible from the poisonous, the hallucinogenic from the nourishing. Obviously this process was one of trial and error with many a bellyache involved! Successful foragers must have honed their skills of observation, learning to notice the most minute details of colors, shapes, textures, and specialized structures of the fruiting bodies.

As for our ancestors who gathered mushrooms for food or religious purposes, your greatest ally in any attempt to identify a wild mushroom is your power of observation. By being observant, keeping notes, using one or more good mushroom books, and going out with a knowledge-able collector or consulting an expert, you can learn to recognize many kinds of mushrooms on sight. If you plan to eat these mushrooms, absolute certainty of identification is necessary. There is no better protection against being poisoned than a combination of careful collecting, certain identification, and wise eating.

THE ANATOMY OF A MUSHROOM

Figure 1 illustrates the basic features and terms used by amateurs and professionals alike to describe mushroom parts. Most mushrooms have

Hygrophorus gliocyclus

a cap (also called a pileus) and a stalk (also called a stipe), although some lack the latter. The cap serves to protect the fertile surfaces (gills or tubes or other structures) on its underside. The stalk, if present, keeps the fertile surfaces out of the dirt, away from excess moisture, and up into the air for good spore dispersal. The shapes and surface features of the cap and stalk, the arrangement and attachment of the gills (also called lamellae), and the position of the stalk are important characteristics to note for identification.

Before the cap expands (like an umbrella), the underside bearing the gills or tubes is often covered with a thin tissue called a partial veil, which may stretch between the cap margin and the upper stalk. As the cap expands, the veil will eventually tear away, sometimes leaving pieces of its tissue as remnants on the cap margin or more commonly as a ring around the stalk. At the very young, or button, stage, some mushrooms are entirely enclosed by a different tissue called the universal veil, or volva, which is ruptured as the mushroom emerges (see inside back cover). Pieces of this universal veil may stick to the mature cap surface as warts, or scales, or patches. In some species the universal veil remains at the base of the stalk as a saclike cup or as scales or bands of tissue near the base of the stalk. Changes in shape, color, and surface features of all these parts of a mushroom are to be expected as it matures.

Specialized terminology used to describe parts of mushrooms is provided inside the back cover.

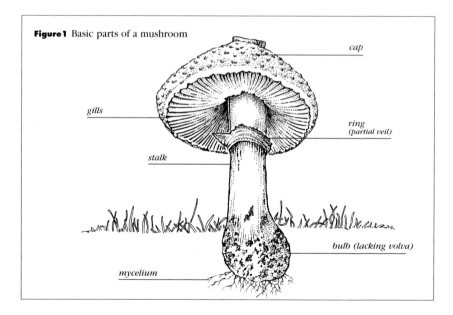

Figure 1 Basic parts of a mushroom

cap

gills

ring
(partial veil)

stalk

bulb (lacking volva)

mycelium

MUSHROOM NAMES

We name mushrooms so that we can distinguish one kind from another and in so doing show relationships between groups of similar ones. To arrange thousands of mushrooms in a scheme understood worldwide, we use the binomial system developed by the great Swedish naturalist, Carolus Linnaeus (1707-1778). Each kind of fungus is assigned a name comprised of two words: first, the name of the genus (which is capitalized), and second, a designation for the particular species (which is referred to as the specific epithet). These scientific names, or binomials,

Mycelium in a rotting log

appear in italics, for example, *Amanita muscaria,* commonly known as the Fly Agaric. (If a binomial appears repeatedly in text, the name of the genus is often abbreviated: *A. muscaria,* being an example.) There is only one distinct, carefully defined kind of organism known by this binomial, but there are many other species within the genus *Amanita,* such as *Amanita pantherina* and *Amanita bisporigera.* These species share many features and are known to be related. Similar genera are further grouped into families (ending in -aceae), similar families into orders (ending in -ales), and similar orders into classes (ending in -mycetes). Classes are grouped into subdivisions, which are all part of the largest group, the Kingdom of Fungi.

The most renowned author of mushroom names was a Swedish mycologist, Elias Magnus Fries (1794–1878). Mycologists worldwide continue to recognize Fries's concept of some species by listing his name after the binomial name—for example, *Marasmius oreades* Fries. In this same manner, every mushroom name has its author associated with it. In this book, authors' names will be included only at the beginning of each species description.

Latin, being an unchanging language, is used by the entire scientific community for describing a species for the first time and naming it thereafter. As most mushroom names incorporate Latin descriptions of some aspect of the fruiting body or its location, we can learn a lot about the mushroom from its name. For example, the specific epithet of *Boletus edulis* means "edible," which certainly describes this well-known esculent. Or take the name of the genus *Cortinarius: cortin-* is Latin for the English word *curtain,* and *-arius* means "pertaining to" in Latin. "Pertaining to a curtain" signifies that the members of the genus *Cortinarius* have distinct cobweblike veils known as cortinas. More information about the Latin names can be found in the individual species accounts.

Common names for mushrooms are often colorful, easy to remember, and quaintly descriptive, but they can also be confusing. Sometimes common names vary from locale to locale. At least three unrelated fungi are called the Beefsteak Mushroom in this country, one a potentially deadly poisoner! Another drawback to common names is that they often do not reflect relatedness, thus presenting an obstacle to communicating information about the mushrooms. In this book, only if a mushroom has a common name locally and that name has been incorporated into general use in this region is that name given.

Another commonly used but antique name for a mushroom— toadstool—is English in origin. The term often indicates a poisonous mushroom, although there is no scientific basis for the distinction. Perhaps the ancient beliefs that toads were poisonous, and therefore made mushrooms toxic if they sat on or under them, or the fact that both mushrooms and toads were mysterious in their sudden appearance after rains, have been responsible for the use of this quaint expression.

CHAPTER TWO

Using This Book to Help You Identify Your Mushrooms

As you seek to identify a mushroom, one of the first things to keep in mind is that you may not be able to positively name it using just one book. In fact, because no one knows all of the mushrooms that fruit every season in Colorado, you might not be able to conclusively identify it at all. Sometimes you will need more descriptions than can be provided in this introductory guide. Be prepared to consult the guides listed in the Suggested Reading that have color pictures and descriptions of additional species of mushrooms. However, beware of the temptation to go "window shopping" in field guides looking for a picture match. Sometimes you can be successful doing this, but you should read the whole description carefully, including habitat and sizes of mushroom parts—details that are not often obvious in a photo.

Colorful *Flammulina velutipes*

Let us assume you have found a mushroom. You have collected it carefully, noted colors and general shapes, determined the color of the spores by making a spore print, and kept it fresh so features of the fruiting body are still obvious (see Chapter 5). First compare your mushroom with the drawings in the Picture Key to Groups inside the front cover, looking for common features and overall aspect of the fruiting body. Once you have made a selection, follow the referrals to the pages that feature members of that group, read the keys, and compare the descriptions and photos.

For example, if your mushroom has gills, you will be directed to a dichotomous Key to Major Families of Gilled Mushrooms, in which you are asked to choose the most appropriate of two possible characteristics (example: spores brown or spores white). Select the one that best describes your mushroom and follow the directions to another section of the book or the next set of choices.

To key out your specimen in the Key to Major Families of Gilled Mushrooms, you must know the color of the spores. Sometimes you will have a successful spore print to examine, but if you did not obtain a spore print, you may have to make an educated guess by looking at the source of the spores, the mature gills. It is important to remember, however, that spores are not always the same color as the gills. Perhaps your field notes will remind you that the leaves or other mushroom caps all around the mushroom were colored from a dusting of spore powder. Sometimes the stalk and ring of your mushroom are moist enough to have retained a coating of fallen spores, as is often the case with the rusty-colored spores of the genus *Cortinarius*.

Once you reach the family or genus level, compare descriptions and photos of that group. Be sure to read the details of the descriptions thoroughly. Do not depend only on similarities with the photo. As you compare your unknown mushroom with the descriptions, be certain your mushroom fits in *all* details. The species concept is based on a "suite" of characters, not just one. For instance, *Amanita muscaria* and *Russula emetica* can both be described as bright red mushrooms with white stalks, white spores, and white gills, growing under conifers in subalpine ecosystems. But further reading about the universal veil alone, which is characteristic of all species of *Amanita* and absent in all species of *Russula,* will distinguish the two immediately.

If you are considering eating your mushroom, be absolutely certain of its identity. Read about the mushroom, its habitat, and growth habit in a second mushroom guide. Consult an expert, perhaps at a local university, botanic garden, or mycological society. In the Denver area, get the advice of experts associated with the Colorado Mycological Society. If you have any doubt about the identity of your mushroom, *do not eat it!* No gourmet meal is worth the risk of poisoning yourself and your friends or family. Chapter 6 provides more information about the wise consumption of wild mushrooms.

READING THE DESCRIPTIONS

The species descriptions in this book are headed by the Latin name and its original author. Underneath appears the order and family, the common name(s) (if there are any), and a statement about the mushroom's edibility. Next comes a brief description of the mushroom, then a more detailed "portrait" with the following information.

FRUITING BODIES Cap color and size (in centimeters [cm] and/or millimeters [mm]); shape noting variations in age and surface details; description of surfaces where spores are produced, such as gills or tube layer, if present, including colors in young and older mushrooms; nature of gill (or tube) attachment to stalk; obvious bruising reactions. **Stalk** color, size, shape, and surface details; special features, such as mycelium, attachments to substrate, or rootlike extensions; description of partial veil and universal veil, if present; staining or bruising reactions of stalk tissue. **Flesh** (of the cap tissue) texture, thickness, color, and color changes; odor and taste of crushed cap flesh. Note that taste means the result of a nibble of a tiny piece of the mushroom. This tiny piece should never be swallowed and should be spit out after a few moments. Beginners should refrain from this test until they have the skills to tell whether they might be tasting a poisonous mushroom.

SPORES Color in print, in mass, or under microscope; size in micrometers (one µm equals one/ten-thousandth of a cm), including ornamentation such as warts or apiculi unless otherwise noted; general shape; and, if applicable, color changes in Melzer's solution.

ECOLOGY/FRUITING PATTERN When and in which habitats the mushroom fruits in Colorado or the southern Rocky Mountain region; typical growth habit; mycorrhizal relationships—associations with specific trees and other plants; unusual features of the mushroom or its growth habit relating it to its ecosystem. Typical habitats rather than actual collecting sites are emphasized to protect vulnerable sites and to encourage the interested collector to explore new habitats.

OBSERVATIONS My interpretation of the meaning of the specific epithet; interesting facts about the species; information about comparing similar-looking or related mushrooms.

CHAPTER THREE

Reproduction and Lifestyles of Mushrooms

*T*he survival of any organism depends on its ability to adapt to a changing environment and to procreate—that is, to have as many offspring as possible and to place them in fertile environments. Fungi have mastered these activities for eons and hence are now found everywhere on land in a great variety of habitats.

MUSHROOM REPRODUCTION

The main body of a mushroom is the perennial organism, the mycelium. It reproduces vegetatively, absorbing and assimilating its food as it spreads outward through its food source. The mycelia of most mushrooms look very much alike, but the genetic information inside each kind of mycelium can produce very different fruiting bodies. The sexual stage of mushroom reproduction results in the fusion of compatible nuclei from different mycelia and the production of fruiting bodies that contain the reproductive cell, the spore.

A mushroom spore is microscopic in size and generally single-celled. Spores are produced in a dazzling array of shapes, sizes, and colors, each specific to the individual species. Several fascinating examples are shown in Figure 2. Because of these signature characteristics of mushroom spores, mycologists use microscopic features of the spores to aid in identifying species.

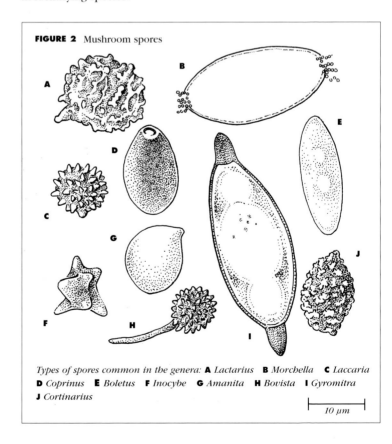

FIGURE 2 Mushroom spores

Types of spores common in the genera: **A** *Lactarius* **B** *Morchella* **C** *Laccaria* **D** *Coprinus* **E** *Boletus* **F** *Inocybe* **G** *Amanita* **H** *Bovista* **I** *Gyromitra* **J** *Cortinarius*

10 μm

FIGURE 3 Life cycle of a gilled mushroom

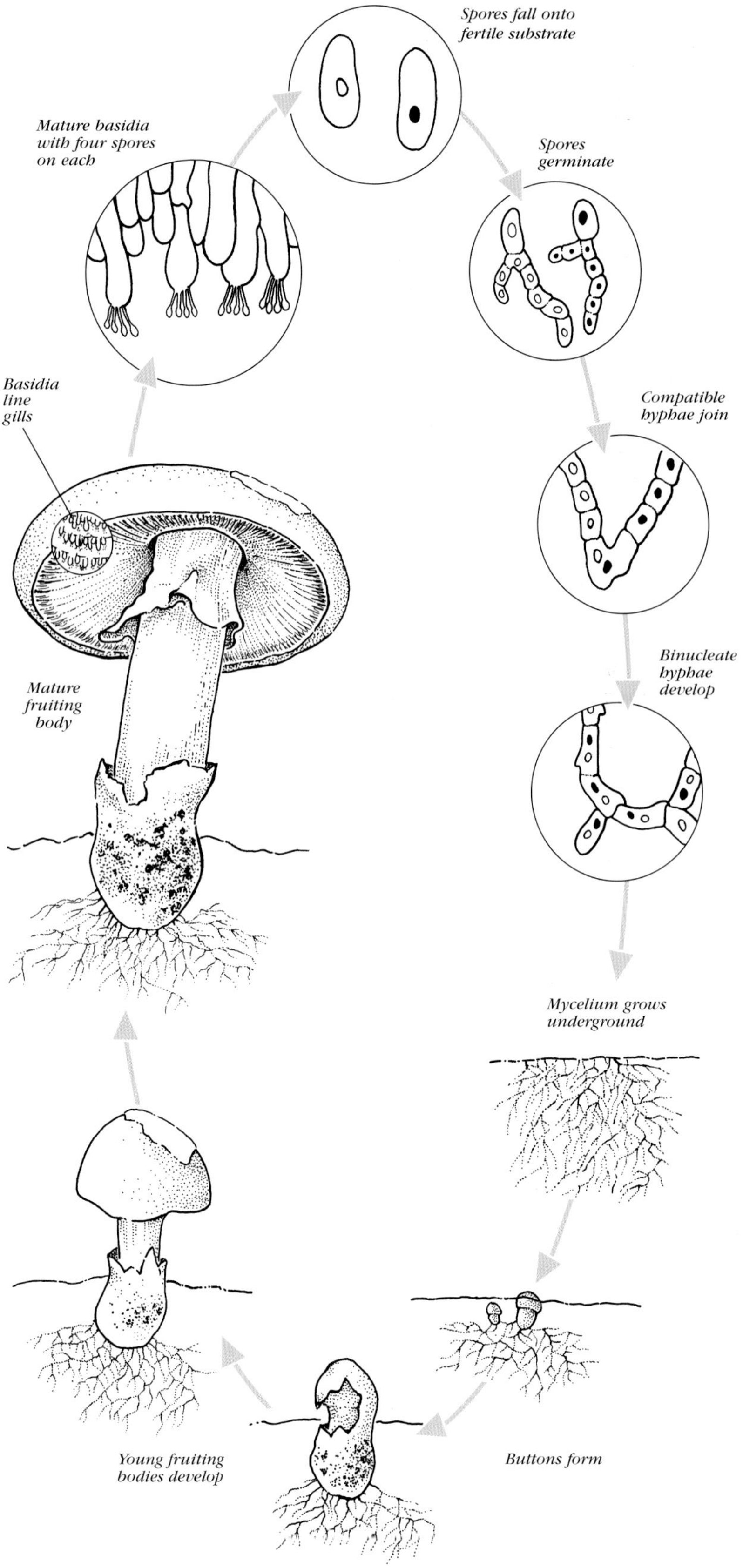

Spores fall onto fertile substrate

Mature basidia with four spores on each

Spores germinate

Basidia line gills

Compatible hyphae join

Binucleate hyphae develop

Mature fruiting body

Mycelium grows underground

Young fruiting bodies develop

Buttons form

Although some features of a mushroom vary according to age and growing conditions, spore color of a given mushroom species is usually very constant. Among the genera, spore colors span a broad range from white to cream to all shades of yellow, pink, lilac, greenish gray, yellow-brown, rusty brown to chocolate, purple-brown to smoky gray and black. Because colors of individual spores are often hard to determine

Clitocybe nuda

accurately under a microscope, we resort to assessing the color of the spore "powder" by allowing the fruiting body to mimic a natural spore release on a piece of white paper. Making a spore print is an easy activity and takes only a few minutes to set up (see Chapter 5). Knowing the spore color is a particularly valuable aid for the identification of mushrooms, many of which are difficult to tell apart without this additional information.

Spores are commonly produced in a layer known as the hymenium, which is located on the surface of or inside a variety of structures unique to specific kinds of mushrooms. For example, a spore-producing layer covers the edges and sides of gills in the gilled mushrooms, or it lines the inside of the tiny tubes of the fleshy boletes and the woody polypores. Other mushrooms have spore-bearing layers on projections such as teeth, veins, or tips of specialized branches. Some, notably members of the class Ascomycetes, have spore-bearing layers that line open cups, pits, or surface convolutions, or that are formed inside underground structures called truffles.

Many types of fungi do not produce spores in a hymenium on their outer surfaces. Members of the class Gasteromycetes (puffballs and their allies) develop and protect their spores inside "spore cases" whose "skins" protect them until a pore or slit develops or disintegration occurs and air currents disperse the spores. Learning where spores are produced on different mushrooms will aid you in making spore color determinations and will help you identify unknown mushrooms.

Mature spores are often dispersed by air currents, but the spores can also be eaten and passed through the guts of animals, washed away by raindrops, or projected some distance from their origins by expulsion. A simplified life cycle of a gilled mushroom is shown in Figure 3. The cycle begins when a fresh spore containing a single nucleus falls onto a proper substrate, such as moist leaf litter, soil, or other nutrient-rich material. If all conditions are ideal, a small germ tube will grow out of the spore to form a long, cylindrical hypha, which has a single nucleus. As that hypha reproduces vegetatively by taking in nourishment from its environment, it begins to lengthen and branch profusely, forming a tangled network of mycelium. If hyphae from two different but genetically compatible mycelia (or mating types) come into contact, they may join and form hyphae with two compatible nuclei in each cell. Entering into its sexual reproductive stage, the resulting mycelium now has genetic information from two "parents." It may grow vegetatively in this state for a while. When conditions are just right, the hyphae may gather to form tiny knots, which eventually grow to be visible. These knots are known in the mushroom growing industry as pinheads.

With adequate moisture and warmth, the pinheads form into immature fruiting bodies called buttons, which may develop quite quickly into mature mushrooms. The mushrooms are made up of the binucleate hyphae tightly packed together to form the cap, stalk, and other structures (such as gills and veils). As the gills develop, some of the hyphae form specialized cells called basidia. It is inside the basidia that the two nuclei fuse, combining the genetic information of both parents into a single nucleus. This nucleus then divides, reducing the genetic information in each of the "offspring" nuclei back to the former amount but now somewhat rearranged (through genetic recombination). Usually the two offspring nuclei reproduce in kind, resulting in four nuclei in each basidium. Spores, usually four of them, are then formed on the outside of each basidium and a single nucleus migrates into each. From here the spores are dispersed to begin the cycle all over again.

MUSHROOM LIFESTYLES

By means of their spreading hyphae, fungi live in intimate contact with their food source, whether it be soil, deadwood and leaves, insect carcasses, or live plant or animal tissue. Through these close associations, fungi play many specialized roles in their environment. Mycologists use an understanding of these roles to separate fungi into three groups with distinct lifestyles: saprophytes (fungi that feed on dead or decaying organic matter), mutualistic symbionts (fungi that live together with other organisms in a mutually beneficial relationship), and parasites (fungi that feed on a living host organism, which they usually injure).

Saprophytes act as the recyclers in our natural world. They break down dead organic materials into smaller molecules, which can then be used by plants. Through their very narrow hyphae, saprophytes exude digestive enzymes into their immediate environment and then reabsorb the resulting nutrients back into the mycelium for transport to the entire organism. This breaking down of organic matter is absolutely essential for the functioning of life on earth. If something were to happen to stop this decomposition by fungi, waste in all forms would accumulate and smother our planet.

Under natural conditions fungal cells die by the trillions and are released back into the environment for recycling. Materials thus produced, such as nitrates, carbon dioxide, water, and phosphates, are once again available for the creation of new organic matter by plants, which use those simpler inorganic materials along with the sun's energy to make carbohydrates through photosynthesis. At the end of the plants' lives, the fungi function once again to recycle that organic matter.

A familiar example of a saprophyte is *Agaricus campestris,* the Meadow Mushroom, which is often abundant in Colorado gardens, compost heaps, and fields. Other examples include genera such as *Coprinus,* the inky caps. These digesters of organic material serve our planet well by recycling animal and vegetable wastes.

Many of the saprophytes—primarily the polypores, or woody conks and bracket fungi—get their nourishment by breaking down the celluloses and lignin in wood. The large group of species known as the white-rot fungi can decompose the very resistant lignin along with the celluloses to yield carbon dioxide and water, turning the wood into a whitish spongy residue (hence the name white-rot). Brown-rot fungi, on the other hand, digest the celluloses but leave the lignin behind, turning the tissues into brownish, often cubic, brittle or crumbly pieces (hence the name brown-rot). Brown-rotting polypores are found mainly in conifer ecosystems, so they are common here in Colorado.

Having inhabited the earth for so many eons, fungi have had plenty of time to master cooperative living. Those fungi living in an arrangement that is beneficial to both parties are called mutualistic symbionts. Among the most ancient examples of this type of relationship are the toughest of all organisms, the lichens. Lichens are essentially "dual" organisms made of fungi and blue-green algae living together as an entirely new entity, the lichen thallus. The algae provide carbohydrates through photosynthesis, and the fungal component provides minerals, water, and physical strength to the union. Thousands of kinds of lichens in an amazing array of shapes and colors grow throughout Colorado, helping to turn rock into soil and breaking down mineral soils into materials usable by plants. Lichens are the true pioneers on this good green earth.

Always adaptable, fungi have also entered into another great cooperative union—this one with vascular plants and trees. Without this union, the natural world as we know it would not exist. Specialized swollen and branched fungus/root structures called mycorrhizae are formed when

Three different mycorrhizae on a pine rootlet

fungal filaments grow in dense sheaths around or within the superficial layers of the plant partner's roots. Taken together, the fungal hyphae have a much larger surface area for absorbing minerals from a greater volume of the surrounding soil than the plant could ever reach. Through the mycorrhizae, the fungus regulates the flow of minerals that go to the plant, supplying them when they are most needed. Through the intimate contact with the plant's tissues, fungal hyphae also serve to protect the roots of their symbiont plant from diseases. In return, the fungus gets the benefit of much-needed sugars and carbohydrates, which are produced by the green plant during photosynthesis, along with some nitrogen-containing compounds. Scientists believe that more than 90 percent of land plants have mycorrhizal associations with fungi—in some cases very specific fungi. Such plants are unable to achieve maximum growth or survive adverse conditions without their fungal partners. Because many Rocky Mountain mushrooms form mycorrhizal associations with conifers and broad-leaved trees, their fruiting bodies will always be found near these trees, a very important fact to keep in mind. For instance, the popular *Boletus edulis* is commonly found under or near Engelmann spruce in our subalpine forests.

Fungi exploit every possible food source, and many have developed parasitism as a lifestyle. Parasites feed upon their host, the organism on or in which they live, usually to the host's detriment. Some parasites, such as the wood-inhabiting Honey Mushroom, *Armillaria mellea*, actually destroy living trees by invading root systems and spreading throughout the tree, making them dangerous parasites in both coniferous and deciduous forests. Other parasitic mushrooms break down just the heartwood, causing the weakened trees to succumb to the wind.

Understanding the variety of fungal lifestyles will help you predict the habits and habitats of the mushrooms you seek. You will also gain a greater appreciation for the other fungi you see along the way.

CHAPTER FOUR

Colorado's Mushrooms: Where and When

*C*olorado's Rocky Mountains rise out of the plains to elevations of more than 14,000 feet, creating a diverse terrain that ranges from shortgrass prairies to dense forests. Such varied habitats allow for a mind-boggling degree of biodiversity, or diversity of life, to exist here— more than in any other inland state. Colorado's mushroom flora is no exception, with an amazing variety of species found throughout the state.

Like birds, mammals, plants, and soils, mushrooms are an integral part of every ecosystem in Colorado. An ecosystem is a recognizable grouping of plants, animals, environmental conditions, and the interactions among them. The Denver Museum of Natural History has developed a simplified classification of the state's major ecosystems. This classification defines eight ecosystems largely by their dominant plants.

GRASSLANDS Although the plains of Colorado appear flat, they really slope gently eastward. They cover roughly the eastern two-fifths of the state, forming a nearly treeless grassland. In Colorado, most grassland elevations are below 5,500 feet, but there are some mountain grasslands at elevations up to 8,000 feet, examples of which are the North Park, Middle Park, and South Park areas. Here the combination of precipitation, temperature, and soil conditions is not suitable for tree growth, but a wealth of grasses and prairie flowers flourishes. Without the presence of trees, grasslands do not have the variety of mushroom species found in other ecosystems. Mushroom fruitings in these regions are as

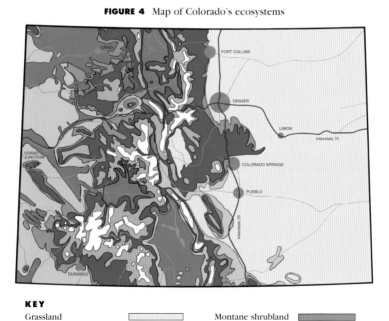

FIGURE 4 Map of Colorado's ecosystems

KEY

Grassland
Semidesert shrubland
Piñon-juniper woodland
Riparian land

Montane shrubland
Montane forest
Subalpine forest
Alpine tundra

Giant Western Puffball, *Calvatia booniana*

sporadic and unpredictable as the rainfall. However, huge puffballs are quite common, such as *Calvatia cyathiformis,* which has been found as giant fairy rings reported to be centuries old. Other saprophytes such as the Fairy Ring Mushroom, *Marasmius oreades,* are also often found in grazed and irrigated fields, which now occupy much of the former prairie. Other grassland mushrooms include members of the genera *Agaricus, Coprinus, Stropharia,* and *Panaeolus,* which break down organic materials and animal dung.

SEMIDESERT SHRUBLANDS Dominated by rabbitbrush, sagebrush, greasewood, and saltbush, semidesert shrublands are most commonly found along drainages in the plateau regions of western and south-central Colorado. Often called cool deserts, semidesert shrublands experience extremes of intense sun-baked heat in the summer, frigid cold in the winter, and arid conditions all year long. Like the shrubs and grasses that share the loose sandy soil, fungi are able to eke out just enough moisture from winter snows and an occasional summer thunderstorm to fruit sporadically here. Many of the same mushroom species found in the grasslands also thrive in these shrublands. The large fruiting bodies of the Giant Western Puffball, *Calvatia booniana,* can occasionally be found lying like huge overgrown eggs among the sagebrush.

PIÑON-JUNIPER WOODLANDS Rising somewhat higher than the semi-desert shrublands, piñon pine and juniper woodlands form huge sprawling evergreen forests in western and southern Colorado and an isolated one near Fort Collins. Often called pygmy forests because of the short stature of the trees, piñon-juniper woodlands are typically not quite as hot nor as dry as the regions below them.

Here mycorrhizal fungi begin to occur much more commonly, garnering scarce moisture and minerals from the coarse gravel soil. The fungi transport these nutrients to their tree symbiont's rootlets and receive sugars in turn. Although never plentiful, mycorrhizal species of the genera *Boletus, Leccinum, Suillus, Russula,* and *Lactarius* can be found in this ecosystem, especially after heavy rains. Stalked puffballs, species of *Tulostoma,* fruit in the poor soil here along with tiny bird's nest fungi, species of *Crucibulum* and *Cyathus,* that sometimes form clusters of lilliputian "nests" (or "splash cups") and "eggs" (spore cases) on deadwood. The splash cups aid these wood rotters in spore dispersal during rainstorms.

Crucibulum laeve

Rhizopogon species, hypogeous (fruiting underground) fungi, are characteristic inhabitants of this land. Their fragrant nutlike fruiting bodies serve as an important food source for the small mammals that can detect their odors.

RIPARIAN LANDS Colorado's rivers, streams, lakes, ponds, and marshes provide much-needed moisture to a thirsty land. Vegetation in riparian lands (meaning "adjacent to water") often contrasts dramatically with that in the drier landscapes nearby. Conditions in riparian lands encourage the growth of hundreds of species of higher fungi. Most of them are mycorrhizal fungi living symbiotically with trees. In lower elevations, cottonwoods and willows line the watercourses. These are the best places to find the elusive Common Morel, *Morchella esculenta,* which fruits in the spring in cottonwood groves, along with an assortment of cup fungi. In the mountains, riparian ecosystems feature conifers and aspens along bogs, streams, and lakes. Look for clusters of *Pleurotus populinus* during moist weather growing in shelving masses on aspens. Other common riparian mushrooms include *Lactarius deliciosus, Laccaria laccata, Russula emetica, Suillus brevipes,* and *Amanita muscaria.*

A cluster of aspen-loving *Pleurotus populinus*

MONTANE SHRUBLANDS

As the land rises to elevations of 5,500 to 10,000 feet in Colorado's foothills and mountains, coarse soils support the growth of dense-to-sparse discontinuous belts of deciduous shrubs, such as mountain-mahogany, sumac, and Gambel oak. Hot in the summer and very cold in the winter, montane shrublands are too arid to support many full-sized trees or their associated mycorrhizal fungi. The limited but interesting mushroom flora include several *Rhizopogon* species, which withstand the rigorous climate by developing underground. Visible on the soil surface are members of the Gasteromycetes, such as the true puffballs; some of the stalked puffballs, including *Tulostoma campestre;* and earthstars, such as *Astraeus hygrometricus.* Rotters of Gambel oak can also be found, such as *Polyporus arcularius.* Occasionally decomposers in the genera *Coprinus, Agaricus,* and *Agrocybe* will fruit after moisture saturates the loose soil.

MONTANE FORESTS

This type of ecosystem covers the mountains at elevations between 5,500 and 9,000 feet. The characteristic tree species are pines, both ponderosa and lodgepole, which are interspersed with groves of aspen and stands of Douglas-fir, especially on north-facing slopes. Meadows abundant with grasses and wildflowers, densely forested north-facing slopes, and more open south-facing slopes provide both dry and moist environments—a great variety of habitats for fungi. Mushrooms of all forms abound here throughout the collecting season, which begins when the snow melts in April or May and ends about mid-September when snow again covers the leafy debris.

Because of the predominance of conifers, all of which depend upon mycorrhizal fungi, there are great harvests of many mushrooms when the litter is moist and the atmosphere humid. They include the delectable *Boletus barrowsii,* the common sticky-capped *Suillus brevipes,* tiny umbrella *Mycena* species, goblet-shaped *Clitocybe* species, and pinkish-gilled *Laccaria.* The much sought-after *Tricholoma magnivelare,* the White Matsutake, and colorful *Hygrophorus, Cortinarius, Russula,* and *Lactarius* species also inhabit montane forests, along

13

with tiny wood-rotters such as *Marasmius thujinus,* polypores such as *Ganoderma applanatum,* and puffballs such as *Calbovista subsculpta.*

One of the most exotic-looking fungi in Colorado thrives here. The bright red-orange *Amanita muscaria* always gets attention because of its gaudy colors, evoking fairy tales, witches' brews, and primitive and modern hallucinogenic rituals. In late spring and early summer, the popular Black Morel, *Morchella angusticeps,* can occasionally be found among the aspens and conifers, amazingly well camouflaged to resemble wet pinecones scattered about the shadows.

Snowbank mushroom habitat

SUBALPINE FORESTS As the mountains rise above 9,000 feet, the dark, rich subalpine forest of spruce, subalpine fir, bristlecone pine, and aspen reigns supreme. Like the montane forests below, the vegetation here is diverse, depending on the steepness of the slope and the exposure to sun and weather. However, the temperatures are cooler, the moisture greater, and the snow cover lasts longer. Many kinds of mushrooms flourish in this ecosystem, but their fruiting season is short. Look for "snowbank mushrooms," such as the bright orange cups of *Caloscypha fulgens,* fruiting at the edge of melting snowbanks in the late spring. The sun's intense energy reflects off the glistening snowbanks and provides localized warmth. When combined with almost 100 percent humidity, these conditions encourage the growth of a few hardy mushrooms: flattened cup-shaped *Discina perlata* and the jelly fungus *Guepiniopsis alpinus,* which hangs like tiny orange gumdrops on dead twigs. Giant "brain fungi," *Gyromitra gigas,* can be found nearby, as can the silvery-colored gilled mushroom *Lyophyllum montanum.* Other subalpine forest mushrooms include the very poisonous *Galerina autumnalis,* gloriously colored species of *Ramaria* (the corals of the forest), tiny *Clavaria purpurea,* red-staining *Agaricus amicosus* and yellow-staining *Agaricus silvicola,* and members of the huge Cortinariaceae family, which form mycorrhizal associations with nearly every kind of tree here.

ALPINE TUNDRA As you climb out of the subalpine forest, you reach a boundary known as treeline. Here the rocky landmass thrusts upward so high that conditions become so cold, dry, and windy that trees can no longer grow. However, such adversities do not stop fungal growth entirely, and they certainly do not inhibit the lichens from clinging to rocks. Right at the edge of the alpine tundra—which is defined as the land above

Lyophyllum montanum, a typical western snowbank mushroom

the trees—live dwarf willows and *krummholz* (stunted and twisted conifers). They survive in these harsh conditions by forming mycorrhizal unions with fungi such as alpine *Cortinarius, Hebeloma,* and *Inocybe* species. Occasional fruitings of saprophytic puffballs, *Calvatia* species, can also be found. They eventually weather away, leaving their "footprints" in the tundra as dried, vase-shaped remains of the once rounded spheres.

WHEN MUSHROOMS FRUIT IN COLORADO

Two important factors are needed for conditions to be right for the mushrooms to begin fruiting: increasing temperatures and moisture. Often the very best time to find mushrooms is about a week after a warm dry spell has been abruptly ended by a heavy downpour or a few days of afternoon rains. The eager mushroomer's best reward for enduring hot dry weather is the joy of the "blooming" of the mushroom flora in a favorite habitat when moisture comes again.

The mushroom season in Colorado generally lasts from mid-April to the end of September. At higher elevations it is the short span of time between spring weather warm enough to melt the snowpack and the return of frigid conditions and snow in early fall. Some years a delightful warm spell in March or early April produces flushes of early fruiting mushrooms, such as *Agrocybe praecox, Pleurotus pulmonarius,* or *Peziza repanda,* along the Platte River drainages around Denver or in cottonwood groves in grassland areas. In the fall, continued warm weather or a late first frost makes excellent mushrooming possible in some habitats into early October. Local mushroomers generally consider late July until

Cantharellus cibarius, a golden delicacy

early September to be the most productive season in our montane and subalpine habitats, with August being the peak.

In Colorado, mushroom enthusiasts can extend the season simply by traveling to another elevation. If your favorite mushroom—say, a member of the *Pleurotus pulmonarius* group—produces abundantly in April and May at lower elevations, keep watching for it or a close relative, *Pleurotus populinus,* at higher elevations as spring changes to summer. You can essentially chase spring up the mountains. The high country may still be covered with snow when mushrooms such as the Yellow Morel, *Morchella esculenta,* are fruiting in May along the rivers below 5,000 feet. Then, when the plains begin to dry up in early summer, the warming air and moist snowmelt conditions of the montane and subalpine ecosystems begin to stir the mycelium into producing a great succession of mushrooms, such as the golden Chanterelle, *Cantharellus cibarius,* and many species of *Agaricus.* The fruiting of large quantities of the mushrooms favored by many collectors is usually dependent on the depth of the winter snowpack and, more importantly, the rain that comes with thunderstorms during the summer and early fall. If that rain soaks down into the soil and the late summer sun warms the earth, then conditions are ripe for a bountiful fruiting of mushrooms.

CHAPTER FIVE

Collecting Mushrooms

*I*n this high-tech world it is a joy to participate in the ancient rite of mushroom collecting. Only the simplest pieces of equipment are required. You will need a container to hold your mushrooms; a device to dig, cut, or trim the mushrooms; and some waxed paper or paper bags to isolate each kind you find.

The best container for collecting is an open basket with a flat bottom. It has the firm support necessary to keep your prizes from being crushed and a handle to facilitate picking it up and putting it down as you hunt. A backpack is much less handy because you have to keep taking it off and putting it on. Delicate specimens can easily be crushed in the process. A knife and a small brush are an ideal combination for neatly extracting your mushroom from its substrate and brushing off the debris that clings to it. An old soft toothbrush works well as a brush. Wrap each kind of mushroom in its own bundle using waxed paper or a paper bag. Do not use plastic bags because the moist mushrooms will begin to sweat and then will deteriorate very rapidly.

Collector with basket and equipment

A few other pieces of equipment can add to the mushrooming experience. You may want to take along a field guide (this book, or another listed in the Suggested Reading), a hand lens, a camera with close-up lenses, and, of course, any outdoor gear you usually carry when hiking (maps and compass, water, a snack, simple first-aid kit, and so forth).

Try to pick mature (but not old) specimens with expanded cap margins or opened cups. If there are young buttons, you may want to collect one to aid in identification. Remove the mushroom gently from its substrate so that you do not disturb the fungus's mycelium. Most collectors pry or rock and twist the mushroom from the substrate with their fingers or a knife. If necessary, cut the mushroom from its woody substrate. For proper identification you should get *all* of the fruiting body. Do not leave identifying features out in the woods, such as a cup at the base of the stalk, and then expect to name your specimen properly when you get home. Experienced foragers, who know their species well, often cut the mushroom off at its base in the field, but inexperienced mushroomers are warned against this practice. Dangerously poisonous *Amanita* species have been carelessly mistaken for edible species because the characteristic volva, the "death cup," was never even seen before the rest of the mushroom was brought home for dinner.

Separately wrap each kind of mushroom, including both young and mature members of the same fruiting. At this point it is a good idea to set up an expanded cap for a spore print right in your basket using white paper under the gills and a waxed paper wrapping. If you are foraging and know the species well, brush off the debris so that you arrive home with clean specimens. Be careful not to clean them so well that you eliminate important identification features. Even experienced foragers often want to review and compare their finds before eating them.

Proper identification requires all of the fruiting body.

Take some simple notes at the time of collection. A few pertinent facts about the location, the habitat, and the growth habit of your mushroom—jotted on a slip of paper and included with the packet—can be invaluable later on. Some mushrooms are always found on specific substrates, such as wood (lignicolous mushrooms), dung or manure (coprophilic mushrooms), moss, or sand. Often the mushroom cannot be positively identified unless the type of tree it was growing on or under is known. An easy way to remember the vegetation associated with your specimen is to slip a recognizable leaf or cone into the packet with the specimen. If you seek the assistance of an expert, she or he will most likely want to know where and how your mushroom was growing and with what vegetation it was associated.

A COLLECTING ETHIC

Fungi are essential elements of our ecosystems and should be protected and conserved like any other natural resource. Indiscriminate and constant picking of fruiting bodies can damage the perennial mycelium, from which the next fruiting will come. In addition, over-picking can remove so many fruiting bodies from a habitat that the processes of spore distribution and natural selection (the survival of the fittest) could be disrupted. On a larger scale, housing developments, poor mining practices, indiscriminate road building, invasion of vehicles, poor logging practices, overnitrification of fields, and pollution of soils and water have all been blamed for the loss of mushroom habitat, especially in Europe and the long-settled regions of our country. Here in the Rocky Mountains, these problems and others are damaging our native fungal populations. Besides defending our wild areas and mushroom habitats politically and socially, mushroomers should develop a personal collecting ethic.

If you are collecting, be selective about which ones you pick. It is possible to love and study mushrooms in their natural habitat without collecting bags and bags of them to later toss in the trash. Learn to notice whether your mushroom is dried up or too deteriorated to be valuable for either food or study. In our dry climate, mushrooms often quickly mature and shrivel, and as they then become difficult to identify, they should not be disturbed. Some fruiting bodies may be infested with larvae or may become mushy (What would you expect from a mushroom?!) and could cause food poisoning if eaten.

Choose mature but still fresh mushrooms that have probably already dropped or shot a large percentage of their spores. Also, avoid constant picking of buttons, as is too often done with the White Matsutake, *Tricholoma magnivelare.* This action endangers the viability of the whole fungal organism and thus the trees that depend on them.

Go gently into the mushrooms' habitats without disturbing every fruiting body you see! Try not to leave the area cluttered with the untidy remnants of your explorations and cuttings. Cover up the holes you make in leaf litter when searching for underground fungi. If you are curious about the beautiful underside of a mushroom but want to leave it in place, use a dental mirror. If you discover after picking a specimen that it is undesirable, try propping it up at a natural angle so that it can continue to disperse spores. Consider making sketches or taking photographs of your finds instead of collecting them, unless you are going to eat them or study them for identification or research purposes. By collecting wisely, we can help ensure that plenty of mushrooms will be around for future generations to enjoy.

Russula aeruginea, one of the few greenish mushrooms

YOUR MUSHROOM: UP CLOSE AND PERSONAL

Once you return home with your treasures, you may want to examine each one more closely. After observing colors and surface features (sticky, shiny, dry, or rough, for example), take careful measurements of the cap and stalk. You can use the ruler on the back cover of this book. Look for the often fragile features of the ring and/or volva, if present, noting whether the tissues are membranous, powdery, scaly, or hairy. Then cut your mushroom in half lengthwise, from the top of the cap through the entire stalk. Observing the cut surfaces is the best way to determine the gill attachment and to see the profile of the stalk and cap. At this point, a simple sketch will help you remember the details, and using a magnifying glass or hand lens will allow you to examine details, such as hairs or fibrils, spots, and scales. Watch for color changes of the tissues, particularly when the fresh specimen has just been cut. Certain species, such as some within the genus *Leccinum,* the orange caps, can be differentiated partly by color changes that occur when the flesh is cut. Watch for possible "bleeding" or so-called latex oozing from a cut, especially in the areas of the upper stalk or the gills. You may have a member of the genus *Lactarius,* which is characterized by latex production.

HOW TO MAKE A SPORE PRINT If you know where the spores are found on the fruiting body you are studying, and your mushroom is mature but still in good, fresh condition, you can make a spore print. A spore sprint reveals the color of the spores in mass. Sometimes the spore color is the same as that of the mature gills, but not always. For example, the gills of a young *Agaricus campestris,* the Meadow

Spore prints are easy to make and crucial for identification.

Mushroom, are pink until they turn chocolate-colored because of the spores. Many species of *Cortinarius* have lavender-colored young gills that turn rusty brown at maturity from the developing spores.

Making a spore print involves catching the dropping mature spores by placing a white, plain piece of paper under the gills, tubes, teeth, or branch tips of a fruiting body, depending on which part produces the spores. First remove the stalk (if present) so that the spore-producing area can rest directly on the paper. Then cover your specimen with a glass or bowl to avoid swirling air currents and leave it at room temperature for two to twelve hours. Too dry, overmature, or undermature specimens may not drop their spores, but you will usually be rewarded with a pretty pattern of the deposited spore "dust." If the spores are strongly colored, you will be able to see their color easily. If the spores are white or very lightly colored, you will have to hold the paper up to the light to catch the

A spore print

reflections. Slightly colored spore deposits all look alike on black paper, so resist the temptation to use it for spore color determination (but it does work well for art projects).

OTHER TESTS Experienced collectors will often pick up a mushroom and smell it. Detecting an odor does not determine whether one can eat the mushroom, but it does provide one more clue to the specimen's identity. If you crush a tiny bit of the edge of the cap or gills with your fingers and then smell, you can often detect a characteristic odor, such as anise, spice, phenol, radish, green corn, or a farinaceous (like fresh meal) odor. Tasting is also done, but it should be called nibbling.

A drop of KOH on the base of the *Agaricus xanthodermus* emphasizes the yellow staining.

Always immediately spit out the tiny bit you put on your tongue! Bitter, sweet, acidic, and burning are the major tastes you should note for identification. Learn to recognize the dangerous species and avoid nibbling on them at all.

Many amateurs get so hooked on mushrooms that they want to examine the microscopic details of their specimens. Spore shapes and sizes, reactions in certain solutions, and features of the hymenium and surfaces of the cap and stalk can be viewed with a compound microscope.

Two common chemical tests are used to study mushroom tissues: One uses an iodine solution called Melzer's solution, the other a dilute solution of potassium hydroxide (KOH). Formulas for both are provided in the Glossary. A small bottle of KOH can be handy when identifying some of the members of the genus *Agaricus*. For instance, a bright yellow reaction emphasized by KOH dropped on the cut stalk of the sickener *Agaricus xanthodermus* should warn you not to eat it.

Melzer's solution applied to mushroom spores under a microscope reveals starchy compounds by coloring the spores blue-gray to blue-black. Such a color change is called an amyloid, or positive, reaction. It helps determine the identity of numerous mushrooms, including some deadly species in the genus *Amanita*. Many nonpoisonous mushrooms also have amyloid spores, among them the edible *Lactarius deliciosus*. Some spores give red-brown color reactions, called dextrinoid reactions, with Melzer's, as is the case with the edible *Lepiota rachodes*. However, a great percentage of mushrooms has spores that show no color change when treated with Melzer's. Such spores are described as non-amyloid, as in the case of *Amanita muscaria*, the Fly Agaric.

You can also test for Melzer's reactions without a microscope. Make a spore print on a bit of glass or mirror and then scrape the spores together into a tiny pile. (Paper can be starchy, and scraping paper fibers into your test spores might alter the test results.) Using the tip of a knife, carefully move a tiny bit of the spore pile into a small drop of Melzer's solution and watch for a color change to amyloid or dextrinoid (or no change at all). The color change, if it happens, will occur within a few seconds. This Melzer's test is best observed with a magnifying lens.

CHAPTER SIX

Have Fungi ... But Be Careful!

*M*any of us who see mushrooms growing wild also envision something tasty to sauté or include in a luscious soup. Eastern Europeans and Asians have historically been avid consumers of wild mushrooms, and many of their descendants in this country draw upon their culture's traditional knowledge of mushrooms in their collecting. On the other hand, many Americans of primarily British descent are much more cautious about eating wild mushrooms, perhaps because of superstitions about the ephemeral and mysterious growth habits of mushrooms or their reputation for being poisonous.

Today Americans are slowly overcoming their reservations about eating wild mushrooms, and many clamber for information about distinguishing edible fungi from poisonous ones. Such information is crucial to have. Mistakes in identification, poisonous look-alikes, failure to use wise collecting techniques, and just plain foolhardiness result in numerous calls to emergency rooms and poison centers during the collecting season. Entire books have been written about the cooking and eating of wild mushrooms and about the toxic effects of mushrooms. The Suggested Reading lists several books on both topics. Should you decide to eat a wild mushroom, following the guidelines below will help you avoid a trip to the hospital.

TIPS FOR EATING WILD MUSHROOMS

Identify your prize. Do not eat any mushroom without getting an expert opinion on its identification and its reputation for edibility. Many foreigners and immigrants are victims of poisoning here in the United States because they bring with them folklore about mushrooms that does not apply to our different habitats and often different species. Do not believe old wives' tales about boiling your mushroom with a silver coin to determine edibility or that you can tell whether a mushroom is poisonous by where it grows. Do not take a stranger's opinion for a fact, no matter how believable she or he sounds. Depend instead on the knowledge of local experts at universities and botanic gardens. The Colorado Mycological Society can also provide help and classes in identification. Knowing the identity of the mushroom will bring you great peace of mind through the assurance that your prize is not one of the deadly few. Mushroom hunting should be a pleasure, not a nerve-wracking guessing game!

Do not depend on pictures alone. Picture matching from books has led many a mushroom eater to misidentify a meal. Often a photo or painting cannot be detailed enough to show identifying substrates or subtle colors. Sometimes details about a ring or color change written into the species description is the only indication you will have to look for that particular feature. When identifying a specimen, read one or more descriptions of possible candidates, and pay close attention to comparisons with similar mushrooms. Foreign or outdated guidebooks do not deal with many of the mushrooms that occur in our area. For example, a common, very poisonous mushroom, greenish-spored *Chlorophyllum molybdites,* which

often grows in large fairy rings in Denver, is not even described in European guidebooks, but a look-alike— white-spored *Lepiota procera*—is always pictured as a delectable edible. Although some species can be found worldwide, you should rely on information from guidebooks to North American fungi.

Chlorophyllum molybdites

Slice all puffballs from top to bottom. Some mushrooms, including the species in the dangerous genus *Amanita,* develop from a rounded button enveloped in a universal veil. These buttons emerging from the soil can look almost identical to white puffballs. Cut any puffball intended for the frying pan from top to bottom and carefully examine the cut surface, using a hand lens if possible, for the developing stalk and young gills of an *Amanita.* All puffballs should be homogenous and white inside if you plan to eat them.

Cook wild mushrooms well. Mushrooms are more digestible, more nutritious, and safer if they are cooked. Some mushroom toxins, perhaps even unknown ones, are vaporized or inactivated by heat, so it is always a good idea to cook wild mushrooms before consuming them. However, this caveat is useless with mushrooms containing deadly amanitins and many other toxins. Their dangers are not diminished by cooking or by other methods of preparation, such as removing the skin first.

Eat moderately. Just like strawberries, peanuts, and shrimp, some mushrooms known to be edible for most people cause problems for a few others. When first trying a wild mushroom, eat only a small amount of it cooked—perhaps a tablespoon or so—and then observe your reaction to it. If you experience no ill effects, you can try a larger amount the next day. Some mushrooms, such as the Black Morel, *Morchella angusticeps,* should not be eaten in large amounts for several days in a row; certain toxins may accumulate and eventually cause problems. Overeating of any food product can cause illness, and mushrooms are no exception. Also, when you eat a wild mushroom for the first time, do not drink alcohol. Some individual reactions to mushrooms are exacerbated by the presence of alcohol in the blood.

Do not swallow when you do a taste test. If you nibble a mushroom to help identify it, do not swallow! Spit it out after a few moments, and do not swallow the juices. Beginners should learn to recognize poisonous genera. Never taste them.

Eat only fresh mushrooms. Just as you would not eat wormy or mushy apples, do not eat mushrooms in this condition. Any deteriorated food product can cause food poisoning. Collectors should take care to keep their mushrooms cool until they are eaten. Mushrooms should not be collected for the table from sites where toxic materials, such as automobile exhaust, pesticides, or chemical pollutants, may be present.

Eat only one kind of mushroom at a time. Mixing different species of wild mushrooms together in a dish can be risky. The diner may react differently to each. Many poisonings, often serious ones, have involved consuming mixed mushrooms, one of which was poisonous. Mixing your mushrooms makes the job of your doctor and the poison center especially difficult and could complicate or confuse the diagnosis and treatment.

Save a specimen and make a spore print. Set aside in the refrigerator one unwashed, untrimmed specimen of every kind of mushroom you eat. Also set one up for a spore print at room temperature. If you get sick, your doctor can more easily decide if it is the result of eating the mushroom. An authority can then identify the saved specimen, and appropriate treatment can be instigated.

If you suspect a poisoning, get help immediately!
If you have been poisoned, medical treatment can usually prevent further injury. Often a call to your local poison center will reveal that no serious aftereffects will be likely. In the Rocky Mountain region, the excellent, knowledgeable staff at the Rocky Mountain Poison Center is available twenty-four hours a day by calling (303) 629-1123 in the Denver metro area and 1-800-332-3073 outside the metro area. Proper treatment for a mushroom poisoning depends largely on a rapid identification of the type of poisoning at hand. A sample of the offending mushroom can hasten this process considerably. Consequently, the patient or family members should supply a general description of the mushroom eaten, where it was found, and, most importantly, the time elapsed between eating and the first appearance of symptoms. Remember to save a specimen for examination by an expert.

MUSHROOM TOXINS

Medical researchers and mycologists generally divide mushroom toxins into eight groups based on the toxins involved, the symptoms presented, and the time of onset of the symptoms after ingestion. Each group can then be placed into one of four categories: 1) toxins with delayed onset affecting cells in vital organs; 2) toxins affecting the autonomic nervous system with rapid onset; 3) toxins affecting the central nervous system with rapid onset (the psychoactive mushrooms); and 4) miscellaneous toxins (usually gastrointestinal irritants).

CELLULAR TOXINS WITH DELAYED ONSET Three of the eight groups of mushroom toxins fall into this most deadly type of poisoning. Life-threatening damage to major organs occurs at the cellular level while symptoms do not appear for hours or even days. The three groups of toxins are the amanitins, found in some species of the genera *Amanita, Galerina, Lepiota,* and *Conocybe;* orellanine, found in several members of the huge genus *Cortinarius;* and gyromitrin, from certain false morels in the genera *Gyromitra* and *Helvella.*

Amanitins Amanitins are complex molecules called cyclopeptides. When ingested, they cause the destruction of liver and kidney cells by inhibiting the production of essential proteins. Amanitin poisoning is often called phalloides syndrome because of one of the worst offenders, *Amanita phalloides.* The poisoning is recognized by a long latent period, then serious gastrointestinal disturbances, and eventual liver and kidney damage. The onset of symptoms is typically delayed for six to twenty-four hours (ten to fourteen hours on average) after ingestion. Initial symptoms include nausea, severe vomiting, abdominal pain, and diarrhea, which usually last one to three days and often require hospitalization. The symptoms may subside long enough for the patient to go home, but the typical victim then has a relapse with severe abdominal pain, jaundice, kidney failure, liver deterioration, and convulsions. These conditions often lead to death in a matter of days. Rapid diagnosis and immediate treatment can save a life, but organ damage usually begins even before the initial symptoms appear.

Cooking does not inactivate amanitins, and the ingestion of as little as half of a poisonous mushroom can cause death, especially in the very young, the infirm, or the elderly. Obviously, learning to recognize the main field characters of the genera *Amanita, Galerina, Conocybe,* and *Lepiota,* and their poisonous species, could be a matter of life and death. A wise mushroom hunter learns which mushrooms to avoid before ever collecting for the table.

A Destroying Angel, *Amanita bisporigera,* found in the south-western United States

The Death Cap, *Amanita phalloides;* its close relatives, the Destroying Angels, *Amanita virosa* and *Amanita bisporigera;* and other look-alikes are responsible for a large percentage of deaths from mushrooms worldwide. These beautiful, stately-appearing species are found in various habitats in many parts of North America but so far have not been reported in Colorado. With proper instruction and field experience, collectors can learn to recognize these infamous mushrooms and appreciate them only for their beauty, photogenic qualities, or sinister reputations. These most dangerous of all higher fungi have the following combination of characters in common:

- Universal veil (volva) present on stalk. Basal bulb rounded with volva as membranous, saclike cup. Cup often half-buried in soil, and easily ignored or broken and discarded.

- Partial veil present, first covering developing gills and then clinging skirtlike to top of stalk as white ring. May be lost with age or during careless collecting.

- Cap white (to pale green or brownish olive), infrequently with one or more whitish patches of universal veil stuck to cap surface.

- Gills free (not attached) or very narrowly attached to stalk, white to whitish.

- Fruiting bodies solitary to scattered in soil.

- Spore print white, spores globose (nearly spherical) to elliptical (to narrowly cylindrical in one species); amyloid (blue-gray) in Melzer's solution.

Color illustrations of the deadly *Amanita* species can be found in most of the guidebooks listed in the Suggested Reading. All mushroom collectors should become familiar with them.

Even though none of the deadly *Amanita* species with all the aforementioned characters has been verified as growing in Colorado so far, they have been reported in nearby states. Mushroomers should develop good collecting techniques that would not ignore their telltale signs. Throughout time immemorial, fungi have pioneered new habitats. We can expect these *Amanita* species to be found fruiting here eventually in some habitat. Of real concern is the possibility that they will be brought on soil and roots as mycorrhizal associates of transplanted trees in our parks and yards. Such an occurrence is believed to have brought *Amanita phalloides,* the Death Cap, to the Pacific Northwest and California, where it had not been known before the 1940s.

Much smaller than members of the genus *Amanita* but equally as deadly per weight are some members of the genera *Galerina* and *Conocybe.* A few species in both genera contain amanitins. Particular attention should be paid to *Galerina autumnalis,* which fruits in Colorado every season on rotting conifer wood. *Conocybe filaris,* much less common but potentially as deadly, has been documented in Colorado growing in grassy habitats. Both of these species and their close relatives have small yellowish brown, orange-brown, to brown caps; ringed stalks; pale brown gills; and rusty to cinnamon

Galerina autumnalis, a deadly LBM found in Colorado

brown spore prints. Falling into the category of Little Brown Mushrooms (LBMs), both genera are rather nondescript and fragile-looking and therefore not tempting for the mycophagist. However, small children put most anything in their mouth. The extensive use in yards of forest wood mulch, which could bring with it wood-inhabiting *Galerina* species, raises a new concern.

Although many other LBMs are not poisonous, the folk warning not to eat LBMs should be heeded because of the possibility of picking these dangerous genera. Hallucinogenic-mushroom seekers should pay particular attention to this warning. They often hunt for small brownish mushrooms growing in the wild. There are documented cases of deaths by *Galerina* poisoning in just such situations.

Some small to medium-sized members of the genus *Lepiota* have been involved in amanitin poisonings in Europe and the United States. These *Lepiota* species superficially resemble *Amanita* species in their free, white to creamy gills; often fragile ring on the stalk; and white spores. However, their shaggy cap cuticles, lack of a universal veil, and resultant lack of a volva distinguish *Lepiota* species from *Amanita* species. Although some very large *Lepiota* species are quite common and often eaten in Colorado, collectors should avoid the less common smaller species because of the danger of deadly amanitins.

Orellanine Another category of cellular poison is orellanine, a complex of closely related toxins that inhibit essential enzymes and eventually destroy the kidneys. Found in several members of the genus *Cortinarius,* orellanine has a particularly odious characteristic: The time between consumption of the mushroom and the onset of symptoms can be as long as three to fourteen days, with an average delay of eight days! Orellanine poisoning produces symptoms of kidney damage, such as dryness of the mouth, intense thirst, pain in the abdominal and lumbar regions, nausea, and vomiting. Kidney and liver failure and death may result without proper medical care.

The culprits found to contain orellanine are *Cortinarius orellanus,* *C. speciosissimus* (known also as *C. rubellus*), *C. orellanoides,* and possibly *C. rainierensis.* As the genus is more thoroughly studied, more toxic species may be identified.

Although none of these *Cortinarius* species has yet been found in Colorado, a relative suspected of having similar poisons, *Cortinarius gentilis,* is reported here every year. You should consider it a seriously poisonous mushroom. Common in Colorado as mycorrhizal associates of many kinds of trees, members of the genus *Cortinarius* are fairly easy to recognize in the field. However, the great size and variability of the genus—with nearly 2,000 species known worldwide—require a specialist to positively identify a specimen to the species level. Therefore none is recommended for the table because of the reputation of a deadly few. The orellanine-containing species fall into the category of LBMs, with fairly small, red-brown to orange-brown, dry caps; cinnamon to rusty brown mature gills; rusty spores; and cobwebby partial veils. Again, heed the warning not to eat LBMs!

Gyromitrin Although collected and sold in Europe for centuries as an edible mushroom, one of the false morels, *Gyromitra esculenta,* has caused many deaths there and serious poisonings in the United States.

Traditional methods of preparation, supposedly to drive off any toxins, involve parboiling and discarding the water or drying the mushrooms before cooking, but poisonings still occur. No *Gyromitra* species are recommended as edibles.

People working near *Gyromitra esculenta* being cooked in kitchens or canneries have also been poisoned. This fact led researchers to realize that the toxic ingredient is volatile. The poison gyromitrin is easily converted by heat (or being eaten) to monomethylhydrazine, or MMH. The toxic effects of MMH have been well researched because it is used by the U.S. space program as a rocket propellant. MMH is not only extremely poisonous to humans and other animals but is a suspected carcinogen as well. MMH interferes with the utilization of vitamin B_6, causes hemolysis of the blood, and damages the central nervous system and the liver. Symptoms typically appear two to twelve hours (an average of six to eight) after ingestion and begin with a bloated feeling, followed by nausea, vomiting, diarrhea, and abdominal pain. In severe cases, liver damage ensues, accompanied by convulsions, high

Gyromitra esculenta from Colorado

fever, and often death. Stories about some people being unaffected by eating the same meal of *Gyromitra* that seriously poisoned others have been explained by a curious "all-or-none" effect. A narrow margin may exist between a possibly lethal dose of MMH and an apparently harmless one. There are reports of a cumulative effect of MMH on some people, suggesting that repeated meals of toxic mushrooms can suddenly result in full-blown poisonings.

Brown-headed *Gyromitra esculenta* is related to the true morels in the genus *Morchella*. It is distinguished from them by its lobed, brainlike cap surface and its sturdy convoluted stalk. *Gyromitra esculenta* fruits occasionally in Colorado's conifer habitats, as do several members of the genus *Helvella*, some of which are suspected of containing gyromitrin. The *Gyromitra gigas* group, the Snowbank False Morel, is more common in the Rockies and is consistently found in spring and early summer at high elevations, often fruiting near melting snow. Some research indicates that the *G. gigas* group has little or no MMH content in the western United States. Nevertheless, because of the possibility of confusing *G. esculenta* for *G. gigas,* the geographical variation of the latter species, and the dangers of improper detoxification prior to eating, no *Gyromitra* (or *Helvella*) should ever be collected for the table, especially when edible mushrooms with less sinister reputations are fruiting at the same time.

TOXINS AFFECTING THE AUTONOMIC NERVOUS SYSTEM WITH RAPID ONSET Coprine Imagine enjoying a savory soup made from fresh inky cap mushrooms found in your yard. The next day you participate in a wine tasting with friends. Within half an hour, you find yourself experiencing a frightening toxic reaction that you later

Coprinus atramentarius

discover was not the result of the wine or yester-
day's soup. It was the combination of the two.
The so-called inky caps were *Coprinus atramentarius,* an infamous sickener because it contains
the chemical compound coprine.

Coprine is an unusual amino acid that blocks the
mechanism by which alcohol is broken down in
the body, allowing toxic acetaldehyde to accumulate. Symptoms of this particular mushroom
poisoning occur thirty to sixty minutes after the
mushroom eater has an alcoholic drink and
include hot flushes of the face and neck, tingling
of the arms and legs, a metallic taste in the mouth,
racing heartbeat, nausea, and vomiting. The symptoms persist until the blood alcohol level drops
and may recur if more alcohol is consumed as
many as five days later. The poisoning is reported
to have no serious aftereffects, save a healthy respect for the combination of alcohol and *Coprinus atramentarius,* the Alcohol Inky Cap. The
compound disulfiram, prescribed to make alcoholics sick if they drink,
produces an almost identical effect, but it differs chemically from
coprine. Collectors should learn to differentiate *Coprinus atramentarius* from the common, fairly large Shaggy Mane, the edible *Coprinus
comatus.* The Alcohol Inky Cap is generally smaller, has a grayer, furrowed (not shaggy) cap, and is more likely to grow on or near wood.

Muscarine Many species of mushrooms, especially those in the genera
Clitocybe and *Inocybe,* contain the compound muscarine. Some contain amounts large enough to cause serious but usually not life-threaten-

Inocybe sororia

ing poisonings. Muscarine is a heat-stable
toxin, so its poisonous properties are not
affected by cooking. In the body, muscarine
overstimulates the parasympathetic nervous system, producing uncontrollable
perspiration, salivation, and tears, beginning
five to thirty minutes after ingestion.
Nausea and vomiting, constriction of the
pupils and blurred vision, difficulty in
breathing, and slowing of the heart rate
may also occur, depending on the amount
eaten and the muscarine content of the
offending mushroom. If properly diag-
nosed, this kind of poisoning can be suc-
cessfully treated with the drug atropine.
A rapid recovery can usually be expected.
However, a few deaths from muscarine
poisoning have been reported in Europe, and children, the elderly, or
the infirm could be seriously poisoned.

Muscarine-containing mushrooms reported from Colorado include
many members of the genus *Inocybe*, such as *I. geophylla, I. fastigiata,
I. mixtilis,* and *I. sororia.* Like *Cortinarius,* the genus *Inocybe* is quite
easy to identify in the field but often hard to identify to species.
Recognized by their small to medium-sized, generally brownish, concial
to knobbed caps with fibers radiating from the center; mycorrhizal
associations with many kinds of trees (including those found in yards);

and dull brown spores, no *Inocybe* should ever be gathered for the table. The warning against eating LBMs certainly applies to this genus.

Clitocybe dealbata and *Clitocybe dilatata,* found occasionally in Colorado, also contain muscarine. These whitish-capped, small to medium-sized mushrooms have pale gills attached to the stalk and grow singly to clustered on the ground, often in grass. *Clitocybe dealbata* has caused muscarine poisoning when it was accidentally picked from grassy areas along with the edible Fairy Ring Mushroom, *Marasmius oreades.* The somewhat larger *C. dilatata* grows in large, compact masses in the ground along roads or disturbed sites in the West. Small amounts of muscarine may also be found in *Mycena pura,* a small, white to pale lavender, gilled fungus that occurs quite commonly in certain Colorado habitats.

TOXINS AFFECTING THE CENTRAL NERVOUS SYSTEM WITH RAPID ONSET (Psychoactive Mushrooms) **Ibotenic acid and Muscimol**

Causing a type of poisoning referred to as inebriation syndrome are two closely related compounds, ibotenic acid and muscimol. Both are found in the common Colorado mushrooms *Amanita muscaria* and *Amanita pantherina. Amanita muscaria,* known worldwide as the

Amanita muscaria var. *flavivolvata*

Fly Agaric, is perhaps the most spectacular Colorado mushroom, delighting nature lover and artist alike with its red-orange caps decorated with a scattering of white spots. But *A. muscaria* and the related pale to brownish *A. pantherina* also have a darker side: They are responsible for a fairly large percentage of the serious mushroom poisonings in the Rocky Mountain region.

Ibotenic acid and muscimol interfere with the normal utilization of some important amino acids, producing toxins that affect the central nervous system and motor function. The result of consuming these compounds is known as inebriation syndrome because the effects are similar to drunkenness. The severity of the effects are dose dependent, so consuming many mushrooms containing these toxins can be life threatening. Symptoms begin to appear thirty to ninety minutes (and even up to three hours) after ingestion. These include mumbling, staggering, and confused or manic behavior, such as strong urges for intense physical activity or running and leaping over small objects as if they were much larger. Tremors, muscle spasms, nausea, and vomiting may also occur. Then the person falls into a comalike sleep, from which most recover with no ill effects. Victims may not remember what happened, or they may report delusions of superhuman strength, extreme anxiety, distortions in space and time, and sensations of floating.

Ibotenic acid/muscimol poisonings in Colorado generally occur when a mycophagist misidentifies or a small child accidentally ingests a poisonous mushroom. Purposeful eating of *Amanita muscaria* to escape from reality can also lead to the reality of a serious poisoning. Like kids, cats and dogs can be attracted to these mushrooms and seriously poisoned; their small bodies are greatly affected by the level of poison even in one mushroom cap. Mistakes in identification can happen: *Amanita muscaria*'s bright red colors can fade, and mature fruiting bodies of *A. pantherina* often have uncharacteristically light-colored caps in our area, making them look like edible *Agaricus* species. Mushroom hunters may also mistake young buttons of either of these *Amanita* species for puffballs. Puffball eaters are warned to ensure that they have an edible puffball, not an *Amanita* button, by cutting their puffballs from top to bottom and looking for signs of a developing stalk and young gills. Any puffball will be white and homogeneous throughout at the edible stage.

Psilocybin and Psilocin Since the 1950s much attention has been given in some circles to the psychoactive qualities of two closely related compounds, psilocybin and psilocin. Many species of *Psilocybe* and some species of *Gymnopilus, Pluteus,* and *Panaeolus* contain these toxins. Because psilocybin and psilocin are controlled substances, unauthorized possession of any mushroom containing them is illegal. Currently no reliable information exists about the frequency of illicit recreational use of these so-called magic mushrooms, but the Rocky Mountain Poison Center has received reports of accidental poisonings — the result of a "bad trip."

The effects of consuming these mushrooms are quite noticeable within thirty to sixty minutes. As it enters the body, psilocybin is quickly converted to psilocin, which stimulates the autonomic nervous system and depresses motor functions. Initial symptoms may include numb lips, confusion, light-headedness, and giddiness. Soon these symptoms may progress to unusual visual effects, color images stimulated by sound, uncontrolled laughter, decreased concentration, and sleepiness. Accidentally poisoned small children may experience convulsions and often require hospitalization, but adult subjects usually return to normal four to twelve hours after ingestion.

Psilocybe species occur very infrequently in the natural world in Colorado. *Psilocybe coprophila,* sometimes reported to be weakly hallucinogenic, has been documented here. The grass-inhabiting Haymaker's Mushroom, *Panaeolus foenisecii,* occurs more commonly. Individual specimens of this species may or may not contain small amounts of hallucinogens.

Unless they are experienced collectors, seekers of hallucinogenic mushrooms run the risk of mistaking dangerous LBMs or even amanitin-containing *Galerina* species for their "recreational" mushrooms. At least two deaths from misidentifying species of *Galerina* as hallucinogenic mushrooms have been reported in the United States.

MISCELLANEOUS TOXINS AND GASTROINTESTINAL IRRITANTS Here we find a heterogeneous assortment of unknown mushroom toxins and irritants. Some cause only temporary misery, some affect only a fraction of the people who consume them, and some are potentially deadly. The symptoms usually appear fifteen minutes to four hours after ingestion and normally include nausea, stomach pains, and vomiting, or just a bout of diarrhea. Usually the symptoms abate by the time the offending mushrooms are ejected by vomiting or passing through the digestive tract. Hypersensitive or allergic reactions can elicit other symptoms, depending on the individual. Even well-known edibles such as *Boletus edulis,* the orange-capped species of *Leccinum, Morchella angusticeps,* and

Russula emetica

Cantharellus cibarius have caused adverse reactions in a few people. Some of the miscellaneous poisons are undoubtedly heat sensitive, so the advice to cook all wild mushrooms thoroughly should be heeded.

A few well-known poisonous mushrooms with unknown toxins are consistent offenders, such as the green-spored *Chlorophyllum molybdites.* This attractive, large mushroom is responsible for a good percentage of violent but usually not life-threatening poisonings in urban settings, such as Denver. Others with "tainted" reputations are yellow-staining *Agaricus* species, *Ramaria formosa* and others with gelatinous bases, *Boletus* species with red (rather than olive or brownish) tube mouths, *Hebeloma crustuliniforme* and other *Hebeloma* species, peppery-tasting species of *Lactarius,* and the complex of species closely related to *Russula emetica.* Additional sometimes poisonous or suspect mushrooms include *Hypholoma fasciculare, Pholiota squarrosa, Armillaria mellea* group (especially if eaten raw), *Gomphus floccosus, Scleroderma* species, *Sarcosphaera coronaria,* and some *Tricholoma* species. The *Entoloma lividoalbum* group, *Tricholoma pardinum,* and *Russula nigricans* also contain unknown toxins that can cause very serious poisonings. *Paxillus involutus* has been implicated in hemolytic anemia poisonings, which occur when susceptible people eat consecutive meals of this fungus. In rare cases these poisonings can be fatal. *Amanita smithiana* has been suspected of containing unknown toxins causing serious damage to the kidneys. Although the presence of this mushroom has not yet been documented in Colorado, similar species have been recorded, and collectors should learn to recognize the characters of the genus and avoid it.

31

The True Fungi

*T*wo subdivisions of the true fungi, Eumycota, are Ascomycotina and Basidiomycotina. They include the fleshy mushrooms that are the subject of this book. With experience, one can usually distinguish between these two groups by noticing gross field characters of their fruiting bodies. More precise, however, is the fundamental microscopic difference in their spore-bearing structures, which gives the two groups their names.

Ascomycotina, or ascomycetes, develop their spores inside tiny saclike mother cells called asci (see pages 33–55).

Caloscypha fulgens, an example of an ascomycete

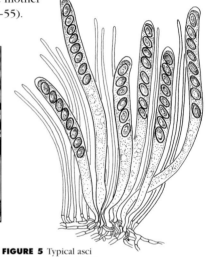

FIGURE 5 Typical asci with spores on the inside

Basidiomycotina, or basidiomycetes, bear their spores on the outside of minute cells called basidia (see pages 56–198).

Ramaria largentii, an example of a basidiomycete

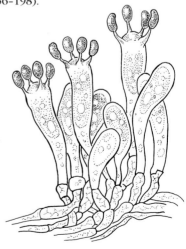

FIGURE 6 Typical basidia with spores on the outside

The Ascomycetes

Ascomycetes are by far more numerous and ubiquitous than basidiomycetes, but most of them are too small to be noticed by the casual observer. However, their size does not diminish their importance to nature's web of life or to humankind. Many thousands of different species of ascomycetes live with algae to form lichens; many kinds have established mycorrhizal relationships with higher plants, and thousands are parasitic or saprophytic on practically every substrate in nature. You are looking at an ascomycete when you see the common bread mold, you benefit from an ascomycete when you take penicillin, you consume ascomycetes known as yeasts (or their by-products) when you eat bread or drink wine or beer, and you may find ascomycetes as powdery mildews in your garden. If you are fortunate enough to taste the delectable and expensive truffles of Italy and France, you are sampling an ascomycete. Indeed, the ascomycetes are an exceedingly diverse group of fungi.

Most of the representative fleshy ascomycetes included in this guide are members of the orders Pezizales and Leotiales, which collectively belong in the class Discomycetes. Discomycetes are distinguished by having a microscopic palisade layer of asci on the exposed spore-bearing surfaces. This layer may be inside the pits of morels, on the surfaces of the wrinkled tops of false morels, on the concave surfaces of cup fungi, or within the convoluted interiors of tuberlike underground fruiting bodies known as truffles. Another group of ascomycetes is the class Pyrenomycetes, an example being the mushroom parasite, the Lobster Mushroom, which has asci that line the inner surface of minute, flask-shaped structures known as perithecia.

Within Discomycetes, members of the Morchellaceae family, the true morels, have heads composed of ridges and pits, asci that do not turn blue when treated with Melzer's solution, and smooth-appearing spores that lack oil droplets. In contrast, members of the genera in the Helvellaceae family, the false morels, have a cap or head that is wrinkled to nearly smooth or saddle-shaped, and (with one or two exceptions) have spores with one or more distinct oil droplets at maturity. In addition, many Helvellaceae genera have asci that turn blue in Melzer's solution, and the spores are distinctly ornamented in many species.

Discina perlata, a beautiful example of an ascomycete

ORDER
Pezizales
FAMILY
Morchellaceae
COMMON NAMES
Yellow Morel, Blond Morel,
Sponge Mushroom
EDIBILITY
Edible, choice

Medium-sized to large, rounded head with light yellow to tan pitted surface, distinct light-colored ridges, head continuous with whitish stalk; fruiting bodies hollow at maturity.

FRUITING BODIES Head light yellowish brown to honey-colored; oval to elongate; surface with rounded tan pits with light gray to whitish (never black) ridges, irregularly arranged; head broader than stalk, 3–8 cm wide x 5–9 cm high; attached to stalk without forming a skirt; solid when very young, hollow at maturity. **Stalk** whitish to creamy yellow; 3–5 cm high x 1.5–3 cm wide; cylindrical or larger at base, often longitudinally depressed; hollow; surface dry, granulose-roughened. **Flesh** brittle, thin; odor and taste mild.

SPORES Produced in asci, which line the pits; dingy yellow in mass; 21–25 x 12–16 μm; elliptical; smooth, homogeneous.

ECOLOGY/FRUITING PATTERN Fruits in soil in the spring, often before the vegetation gets very high; late April to early May at lower elevations under cottonwoods; along rivers and streams, in undisturbed meadows and parks near trees, in old orchards, and in burned-over ground; at times a bit later in mixed woods at higher elevations. Easily recognized but rarely ever abundant. Morels are apparently not mycorrhizal, but have a complicated life cycle involving a resting stage called a sclerotium.

OBSERVATIONS *esculenta:* an esculent, edible (Latin). A close relative, the Black Morel, *Morchella angusticeps,* differs from *Morchella esculenta* by its overall darker fruiting bodies with distinct blackening ridges surrounding the pits at maturity, a generally smaller stature, and a conical shape.

False morels, such as the poisonous *Gyromitra esculenta,* differ from true morels by having wrinkled or brainlike heads without pits on their surfaces. *Verpa bohemica* has a bell-shaped, wrinkled head, which is attached only at the top of the stalk; it has caused poisonings. *Morchella semilibera* has an extensive free "skirt" at the bottom of the pitted head;

its ridges darken with age. Beginners often confuse the common Stinkhorn, *Phallus impudicus,* with the Yellow Morel because of superficial similarities in its pitted-looking head. The Stinkhorn, however, fruits during summer and fall in backyards and disturbed areas. Close examination will reveal great dissimilarities between the mushrooms, including a disgusting odor from the Stinkhorn's slimy head.

A much larger blond morel, *Morchella crassipes,* is often called Bigfoot because of its large thick stalk and massive size. It is often found late in the morel season. This giant is sometimes considered to be either a larger variety of *Morchella esculenta* or one that develops from a particularly vigorous mycelium and, left unpicked, grows extra large.

The Bigfoot shown below measured 25 cm high (about 10 in) when it was found near the Dolores River in southwest Colorado in June.

Morchella crassipes

ORDER
Pezizales
FAMILY
Morchellaceae
COMMON NAME
Black Morel
EDIBILITY
Edible

Small to medium-sized, narrowly conical, honey-combed cap, blackish ribs; whitish stalk; head and stalk continuous and hollow.

FRUITING BODIES Head and stalk firmly grown together but without a "skirt" at juncture; hollow at maturity. **Head** shaped like blunted cone, 2–7 cm long x 2–5 cm broad, occasionally larger; dull brown pits with gray-brown ridges, ridges blackish in age, angular-vertical or ladderlike. **Stalk** 2–5 cm long x 1.5–3 cm wide; cylindrical, often with slit at base; creamy white; surface granular. **Flesh** brittle; odor and taste mild.

SPORES Cream-colored in mass, 20–25 x 12–14 µm, elliptical, smooth, homogeneous.

ECOLOGY/FRUITING PATTERN Solitary to gregarious; late May to late June around 8,000–9,000 feet, into July higher in the subalpine regions; under mixed aspen and pine or Douglas-fir. In spring a year after a forest burns, black morels are often some of the first signs of new life to rise out of the charred remains. They are rarely plentiful in any Colorado habitat except for burns, where they may be abundant for a season or two.

OBSERVATIONS *angusticeps:* from Latin, *angustus* (narrow) and *ceps* (head). Resembling dark pinecones, the "blacks" are hard to spot. Black morels in Colorado may represent a complex of species or may be different growth forms of a single species. *Morchella conica* and *Morchella elata* (*elatus* means "tall" in Latin) are European names also used, often to describe those with larger fruiting bodies and/or larger spores than found in *Morchella angusticeps*. Until more work is done on the genetics of the black morels, it is probably simplest to refer to them by the American name, *Morchella angusticeps,* or their common name.

    Morchella semilibera is similar, but it has a semifree skirt at the juncture of the head and stalk. *Verpa bohemica* has a dark, wrinkled, nonpitted, thimble-shaped head attached only at the top of the stalk.

ORDER
Pezizales
FAMILY
Helvellaceae
COMMON NAME
Pig's Ear
EDIBILITY
Not recommended

Yellow-brown to red-brown, flattened, fleshy cups with wrinkled surfaces and solid stubby bases, or stalkless; in spring near recently melted snowbanks.

FRUITING BODIES Cup or flattened disc, 3–9 cm across; thick fleshy margin rolled under or turned down; upper surface various shades of yellow-brown, cinnamon, red-brown to darker brown; wrinkled or veined especially toward center, which is often depressed; underside much paler than upper, brownish gray to whitish. **Stalk** short, solid, up to 2 cm long x 1–3 cm thick, or absent with simple point of attachment to substrate. **Flesh** thick, brittle.

SPORES Whitish in mass; 25–35 x 10–16 µm, including pointed ends; elliptical; minutely warty; three oil drops.

ECOLOGY/FRUITING PATTERN Scattered to clustered on rotting wood or wet soil; common in spring and early summer at higher elevations near recently receded snowbanks under conifers and occasionally aspen.

OBSERVATIONS *perlata:* meaning "very broad" in Latin. Slow to mature in the cool environment, these typical snowbank fungi may persist for two weeks or more. Several very similar *Discina* species occur under similar conditions, but they must be differentiated microscopically on spore characters. Because of their similarity to poisonous *Gyromitra* species, which have convoluted heads and multichannelled or hollow stalks, *Discina* species are not recommended for consumption.

The name Pig's Ear is sometimes used for an entirely unrelated species, *Gomphus clavatus* (another example of the disadvantages of using common names). A more useful name for the *Discina perlata* group might be "thick cup," which helps to distinguish the genus *Discina* from *Peziza* species; the latter have a much thinner and more fragile flesh and amyloid asci, in contrast to a non-amyloid Melzer's reaction of the asci in the genus *Discina*.

ORDER
Pezizales
FAMILY
Helvellaceae
EDIBILITY
Unknown

Small, smooth, brownish to grayish brown, saddle-shaped head on white slender stalk.

FRUITING BODIES **Head** grayish tan to gray-brown, smooth; 1–4 cm across; saddle-shaped with distinct, rather sharp depression in center where head is attached to stalk; lobes of head flared outward, but edges curved under slightly; undersurface smooth and whitish. **Stalk** white to cream-colored, smooth; cylindrical to tapered upward, often flattened, but without grooves or fluting; 2–5 cm high x 5–7 mm wide. **Flesh** thin, flexible but not rubbery.

SPORES Whitish in mass; 17–22 x 11–13 µm; thin-walled, smooth, or rarely warted; one large and several small oil drops when fresh.

ECOLOGY/FRUITING PATTERN Late summer until fall, often in groups; on soil or rarely on rotting wood; in moist areas near conifers or hardwoods.

OBSERVATIONS *elastica:* flexible. *Helvella stevensii* is quite similar to *Helvella elastica* in colors and stalk features, but its cap margin, which curves over the cap surface with age, and a hairy undersurface distinguish it. *Helvella crispa* and *Helvella lacunosa* also have saddle-shaped caps and are quite common in Colorado (the latter near Douglas-fir), but they both have distinctly fluted or ribbed stalks with conspicuous elongated pits. *Helvella crispa* has whitish caps attached to the apex of the stalk only, whereas *H. lacunosa* has gray to blackish (rarely whitish) caps with attachment to the stalk at several points.

ORDER
Pezizales
FAMILY
Helvellaceae
COMMON NAME
Hooded False Morel
EDIBILITY
Poisonous

Reddish brown, lobed to saddle-shaped cap attached to unbranched, lighter-colored stalk; often on or near rotting wood.

FRUITING BODIES Head cinnamon brown to red-brown, 2–5 cm broad; saddle-shaped or with two or three irregular lobes that rise above level of top of stalk, margins often fused with stalk in several places; surface smooth to slightly bumpy, but neither brainlike nor pitted; undersurface lighter colored and not ribbed. **Stalk** 3–6 cm high x 1–2 cm in diameter; slender in relation to cap, equal in diameter to slightly enlarged at base; interior hollow to stuffed; surface smooth or with one or more grooves; light pinkish brown to red-brown, usually paler than cap color; often with whitish mycelium over basal area. **Flesh** thin, brittle.

SPORES White in mass, 19–23 x 8–10 μm, narrowly elliptical, smooth, two oil drops.

ECOLOGY/FRUITING PATTERN Single to a few together; on rotting wood or soil in aspen groves and subalpine mixed forests throughout the Rocky Mountains; late summer and fall.

OBSERVATIONS *infula:* shaped like a priest's hood (Latin). *Gyromitra infula* may contain monomethylhydrazine (MMH) and is suspected to be dangerously poisonous. Because of its often saddle shape, *G. infula* could be confused with some *Helvella* species, but the red-brown cap colors and the relatively thick, nonfluted stalk are good field characters for *G. infula.* The similar-looking *Gyromitra ambigua* fruits in the same habitats and season, but it has pronounced lavender to violet tones on the hymenium, smaller fruiting bodies, and larger spores than *G. infula.*

ORDER
Pezizales
FAMILY
Helvellaceae
COMMON NAMES
Lorchel, Conifer False
Morel, Beefsteak Morel
EDIBILITY
Poisonous

Large, red-brown caps with highly wrinkled, brainlike folds; lighter-colored, compressed or simply folded stalk; on ground often under conifers; spring to early summer.

FRUITING BODIES Head outer surface bay brown to red-brown with tints of orange-brown; 4-10 cm across and high; folded, wrinkled, to convoluted, but not pitted; margin attached in several places to stalk; undersurface creamy tan. **Stalk** pale pinkish tan, never pure white; 3-8 cm long x 2-3 cm wide; enlarged somewhat just at base; at times grooved or fluted; cross-section round with single channel or compressed, but no multiple channels inside. **Flesh** thin, brittle; lightly aromatic.

SPORES Pale yellowish in mass; 21-24 x 10-12 μm; football-shaped, lacking conspicuous sharp ends; smooth; two oil drops.

ECOLOGY/FRUITING PATTERN Single to scattered near conifers; montane and lower subalpine ecosystems; often in sandy loose soil; late May into early summer. Fruiting bodies can last for many days before decaying and, according to some authorities, may become more toxic as they age.

OBSERVATIONS *esculenta:* meaning "edible" (but now known to be poisonous). Although *Gyromitra esculenta* has been eaten for centuries both in the United States and in Europe, many serious poisonings and deaths have occurred because it contains the toxin monomethylhydrazine (MMH). *Gyromitra gigas,* the Snowbank False Morel, has a much bulkier white stalk with multiple internal channels and larger spores with projections at each end. The poisonous *Gyromitra infula* and its look-alike *Gyromitra ambigua* have much less wrinkled caps and later fruiting times. Both of the false morels, *G. esculenta* and *G. gigas,* are distinguished in the field from the edible morels in the genus *Morchella* by their bulkier aspect and lack of pits on the caps.

ORDER
Pezizales
FAMILY
Helvellaceae
COMMON NAME
The Brain,
Snowbank False Morel
EDIBILITY
Poisonous

**Reddish brown, lobed
to saddle-shaped cap
attached to unbranched,
white stalk; often on or
near rotting wood.**

FRUITING BODIES Head strongly convoluted with brainlike folds, neither pitted nor obviously lobed; butterscotch yellow-brown, darkening to medium brown with age; 5-18 cm across; interior chambered; fused to massive, fleshy stalk. **Stalk** 3-14 cm long, well over half as thick; with several internal chambers; exterior whitish; folded or with rounded ridges. **Flesh** brittle, whitish; odor and taste mild.

SPORES Pale yellowish in mass, 24-36 x 10-15 µm, oval to broadly elliptical with small projections at each end, wrinkled at maturity, one large and several small oil drops.

ECOLOGY/FRUITING PATTERN Single to gregarious in cool spring weather; on soil or rotting wood near melting snowbanks or where snow has receded in coniferous forests; June and early July.

OBSERVATIONS *gigas:* gigantic (Latin). Because beginning mushroomers may confuse *Gyromitra gigas* with *Gyromitra esculenta,* which has caused serious, even fatal, poisonings (in spite of its specific epithet), neither is recommended for the table. *Gyromitra esculenta* has more red-brown colors and finer wrinkles and a relatively slender pinkish stalk. Although *G. gigas* in the West is reported to contain very little monomethylhydrazine, a toxin found in many species of *Gyromitra,* mycophagists should be cautious about eating the Snowbank False Morel because of the danger of chronic poisoning from cumulative effects. Because the literature is replete with contradictory statements about the edibility of *Gyromitra* species, and not all the indigenous species are yet known, it would be wise to avoid eating any member of the genus and simply appreciate them for their amazing presence in our mountains.

   Gyromitra montana and *Gyromitra korfii* are look-alikes that cannot be distinguished without a microscopic examination. In the United States, they are often lumped together as *G. gigas,* a European name. *Gyromitra montana* is found in the West and has padlike projections on its spores, whereas *G. korfii* has distinct knoblike ends on its spores and is found more often in eastern North America.

ORDER
Pezizales
FAMILY
Helvellaceae
COMMON NAME
Pine Fire Fungus
EDIBILITY
Inedible

Brown, crustlike fungus spreading stalkless over recently burned soil; attached to substrate by pale yellowish, rootlike structures.

FRUITING BODIES Reddish brown, flat, stalkless crusts spreading over substrate; irregularly undulating, light buff margins when young; indeterminate in size; 4–12 cm across, but sometimes individuals flow together to cover large patches of soil; upper spore-bearing surface chestnut brown to blackish, dull to shiny; undersurface dirty yellowish and floccose, attached directly to substrate by numerous whitish to pale yellow, rootlike outgrowths that anchor fruiting body to soil. **Flesh** brittle-spongy, becoming leather-hard, thin.

SPORES White in mass, 30–40 x 7–10 μm, spindle-shaped with pointed ends, smooth, two or more oil drops.

ECOLOGY/FRUITING PATTERN Most commonly found on the ground in early summer the next year or two after a fire spreads through a conifer forest. These strange-looking fungi fruit on the top of charcoal-laden soil, occasionally spreading onto burned wood. They can be parasitic on the roots of young conifer seedlings, especially pines.

OBSERVATIONS *undulata:* undulating, which describes the cap surface and margin. Also known as *Rhizina inflata*. Because of the specialized habitat and the distinctive fruiting bodies, this unusual ascomycete could hardly be mistaken for anything else. In some of the West's extensive forest fire areas, it can be abundant but not very noticeable amid the charcoal and blackened soil.

ORDER
Pezizales
FAMILY
Pezizaceae
EDIBILITY
Not recommended

Medium-sized, tan to light shallow cups with undulating margins; fruiting on rotting wood or nearby soil.

FRUITING BODIES Cups buff-tan to brownish, 3–10 cm across, broadly cup-shaped and flattening with age, with recurved or turned-down margins at maturity; smooth inner surface with whitish to cream-colored, minutely roughened exterior. **Stalk** absent, but often with central knot of tissue attaching fruiting body directly to substrate. **Flesh** thin and brittle; odor and taste mild.

SPORES White, 14–17 x 8–10 μm, rough, elliptical, no oil drops.

ECOLOGY/FRUITING PATTERN Usually clustered; saprophytic on humus and rotting hardwood; fruiting commonly on or very near cottonwoods and aspen wood; late spring and summer.

OBSERVATIONS *arvernensis:* from a locale in France (*-ensis* in Latin means "belonging to" and indicates place of growth or origin). Also known as *Peziza sylvestris*. In the Rocky Mountain region, there are several other brown cups similar to *Peziza arvernensis,* with subtle color and microscopic differences. The common *Peziza repanda* has similar brown cups with undulating margins at maturity, its flesh appears distinctly stratified when fresh (use a hand lens), and its spores are smooth and slightly larger than *P. arvernensis. Peziza badia* and its relatives have darker reddish brown cup colors. *Peziza violacea* has violet-brown cup interiors and fruits on burned ground and old campfires. Species of *Peziza* could be confused with *Discina* species, which fruit in similar habitats in early spring and summer, but the flesh of *Discina* species is much thicker and less fragile. Microscopically, the tips of *Discina* asci do not turn blue in Melzer's solution, as happens with members of the genus *Peziza.*

ORDER
Pezizales

FAMILY
Pezizaceae

COMMON NAME
Pink Crown

EDIBILITY
Not recommended,
possibly poisonous

Large, violet to pinkish
lavender, deep, crown-
shaped cup; partially
buried; margin splitting
into star-shaped rays
above ground level; stalk
absent or very short.

FRUITING BODIES **Cup** underground, at first a whitish hollow ball 3–10 cm across, buried near soil surface; as it emerges from soil surface, the wall of the top of ball splits into seven to nine pointed segments, giving fruiting body a crownlike shape; interior surface smooth and lovely violet to pinkish lavender at maturity, sometimes fading to brownish lavender; whitish exterior surface minutely felty. **Stalk** often absent or very short and stubby. **Flesh** white, thick, fragile.

SPORES Pale yellowish in mass, 15–18 x 8–9 µm, elliptical with blunted ends, smooth, usually two oil drops.

ECOLOGY/FRUITING PATTERN Barely emerging from soil and leaf litter under deciduous or conifer trees; fairly common in some seasons; fruiting solitarily to clustered from July through August in Colorado's montane and lower subalpine ecosystems; sometimes in grass-covered or shrubby areas, but usually associated with conifers.

OBSERVATIONS *coronaria:* pertaining to a crown (Latin). Also known as *Sarcosphaera crassa* and *Sarcosphaera eximia,* this interesting fungus sometimes looks like a deep violet hole in the ground. Because of its large size, unusual growth habit, and characteristic colors, it is unlikely to be confused with any other species. Specimens that are dug up and not yet split open could be confused with truffles, but the hollow interior with its beautiful colors should distinguish *Sarcosphaera coronaria.* It is not recommended as an edible, for there are reports of poisonings.

ORDER
Pezizales
FAMILY
Otideaceae
EDIBILITY
Unknown

Medium-sized, brown, fuzzy, irregularly spherical fungus with greatly convoluted interior; buried or partially buried; under conifers.

FRUITING BODIES Yellow-brown to darker brown, roughly spherical, 2–8 cm across; subterranean or partially buried with no obvious point of attachment; thin outer covering fuzzy from many fine dark hairs, unevenly furrowed; interior greatly convoluted and made up of meandering partitions, the folded layers often touching each other but leaving irregular channels in between. **Flesh** solid and brittle, whitish with ochre staining; odor of fermented cider, taste mild.

SPORES Colorless under microscope, 20–25 x 12–15 μm, elliptical, smooth, one oil drop or additional small oil drops at ends.

ECOLOGY/FRUITING PATTERN Found from July to September near conifers, *Geopora cooperi* may be more common than records show; its subterranean habit makes it difficult to find. Truffle hunters looking for hypogeous (underground) fungi sometimes discover it growing close to the soil surface. Rodents often unearth it for food. This remarkable fungus has been found as far north as Alaska, where it fruits near aspen.

OBSERVATIONS *cooperi:* named for J. G. Cooper, collector. Loosely referred to as a truffle because of its hypogeous habit, *Geopora cooperi* is classified with the cup fungi, the Pezizales, because the spores are shot from the asci, as in the latter group. Although not known as poisonous, *G. cooperi* does not have the delectable odor and flavor of the famous true truffles, members of the genus *Tuber,* which are so popular in Europe. A relative, *Geopora arenicola,* also occurs in Colorado's montane habitats; it is smaller and hollow, with an opening at maturity just at ground level, giving it its nickname, "hole in the ground."

ORDER
Pezizales
FAMILY
Otideaceae
COMMON NAME
Eyelash Cup
EDIBILITY
Inedible

Tiny, red to red-orange, flattened cups clustered on rotting wood; sharply pointed, eyelashlike, blackish hairs projecting from edge of cups.

FRUITING BODIES Cups tiny, 3–15 mm across; brilliant reddish orange to near cherry red; nearly spherical at first but finally flattening to discs, margins turned up and decorated with long, blackish brown, sharp-tipped, straight, eyelashlike hairs; exposed upper surfaces smooth, undersurface with few scattered eyelash-like hairs. **Stalk** absent; cups attached directly to substrate. **Flesh** very thin.

SPORES White in mass, 18–20 x 10–12 μm, elliptical, roughened, many small oil drops when young.

ECOLOGY/FRUITING PATTERN These tiny saprophytes are quite common throughout the growing season, usually in very moist environments and generally in subalpine ecosystems. They are sometimes solitary but typically grow in groups on rotting wood of many kinds. They may also be found on nearby moist soil or various kinds of plant debris.

OBSERVATIONS *scutellata:* like a small shield (Latin). The discovery of the Eyelash Cup is always a great pleasure. If you have a hand lens and can observe the beauty of the eyelashes close up, you will never forget these charming little fungi. Colorado's red-orange Eyelash Cups probably represent a complex of very similar species, distinguishable by the nature of the hairs, spore differences, and growth substrates. There are other less common *Scutellinia* species in the region, usually with paler colors, sometimes growing on soil, and differing microscopically.

ORDER
Pezizales
FAMILY
Otideaceae
COMMON NAME
Orange Peel Fungus
EDIBILITY
Not poisonous

Compact clusters of small, bright orange, shallow cups with no stalks; fruiting on mineral soil.

FRUITING BODIES **Cups** shallow, nearly rounded, often distorted by mutual pressure; up to 6 cm wide; striking bright orange to red-orange smooth interior; exterior pale orange and frosted-looking; margins hairless, often folded in on one side or split. **Stalks** absent. **Flesh** thin, whitish, brittle; odor and taste mild.

SPORES Whitish in mass, 14–17 x 8–9 μm, ornamented with a coarse network, elliptical, projections on ends up to 2 μm long, two small oil drops.

ECOLOGY/FRUITING PATTERN Often in clusters of dozens covering bare soil in open areas, roadcuts, and disturbed ground of landslides. As saprophytes, they fruit occasionally in late summer and fall in the Rocky Mountains and are often mistaken for discarded orange peels.

OBSERVATIONS *aurantia:* orange-colored (Latin). *Aleuria aurantia* is quite easy to recognize because of its distinctive color, lack of a stalk, and habit of growing directly on the soil. *Caloscypha fulgens* also has bright orangish cups, but the exterior stains blue to olive or blackish blue, and it fruits at high elevations early in the spring in Colorado's montane coniferous regions around melting snow. *Scutellinia scutellata* has much smaller, red to orange-red, shallow cups with blackish hairs on the margins. Some species of *Otidea* could be mistaken for the Orange Peel Fungus, but the earlike "cups" of *Otidea* are elongated and more erect.

ORDER
Pezizales
FAMILY
Otideaceae
EDIBILITY
Unknown

Bright orange, little cups with bluish green stains; on soil near recently receding snowbanks in spring and early summer.

FRUITING BODIES **Cups** orange to yellow-orange; often lopsided or cracked on one side; margins at first inrolled, but by maturity usually spreading or undulating somewhat; 1–4 cm across; inner surface smooth and evenly intensely orange to orange-yellow; outer surface frosted- or powdered-looking, orangish, but always staining some combination of dull olive, bluish green, intense indigo blue, to blackish blue, depending apparently on conditions of age, habitat, or light. **Stalk** absent. **Flesh** very brittle, thin.

SPORES White in mass, globose, 5–7 µm, smooth, no oil drops.

ECOLOGY/FRUITING PATTERN Singly or in groups in conifer duff where winter snowbanks have just receded. Considered to be parasitic on the seeds of conifers in subalpine ecosystems, *Caloscypha fulgens* is a characteristic member of the "snowbank flora" of Colorado.

OBSERVATIONS *fulgens:* from the Latin *fulgeo,* meaning "shiny." Before spring flowers bloom, these mushrooms can brighten the paths of hikers as they skirt around the melting snowbanks on their way up to the higher peaks. I have collected *Caloscypha fulgens* in the Indian Peaks Wilderness in the first week of June, and as late as early August above 10,000 feet in the Little Annie ski area near Aspen. *Caloscypha* translates from Latin as "beautiful cup." Another beautiful cup fungus, *Aleuria aurantia,* has quite similar bright orange colors, but its exteriors do not stain blue-green, its cups are often tightly clustered, and it does not fruit as early or near snowbanks as does *C. fulgens.*

ORDER
Pezizales

FAMILY
Otideaceae

EDIBILITY
Inedible

Small, ochre to red-brown, goblet-shaped cups with slender stalks occurring sometimes by the thousands in the charcoal of a burned area.

FRUITING BODIES **Cup** deep and shaped like tiny urn; 2–15 mm across and high; inner surface smooth and ochre-brown to brick red–brown; margin roughened with small whitish scallops, remaining curved inward even at maturity; outer surface roughened, somewhat lighter than inner surface. **Stalk** short, 2–10 mm long, very slender, off-white, roughened at base where embedded in substrate. **Flesh** thin, brittle.

SPORES Whitish in mass, 13–19 x 7–9 μm, smooth, homogeneous, no oil drops.

ECOLOGY/FRUITING PATTERN One of the most common pioneers on burned ground, masses of its fruiting bodies often blanket the charred earth and charcoal remains of forest fires in spring and early summer in montane and subalpine regions.

OBSERVATIONS *carbonaria:* pertaining to charcoal (Latin). I saw *Geopyxis carbonaria* by the millions the year after the 1988 fires in Yellowstone National Park. They fruited there along with other small burn-site cups and are probably responsible for the breakdown of organic material, thus beginning the long process of reforestation. Look for these tiny fungi in old campfires in the conifer regions throughout the summer season, usually scattered among the cinders. The photo shows the cups much larger than life-size.

ORDER
Pezizales
FAMILY
Sarcoscyphaceae
EDIBILITY
Unknown

Tiny, scarlet, flower-shaped, clustered cups; long rooting stalks attached to buried sticks; early spring at high elevations.

FRUITING BODIES Cups 1–2 cm across, goblet-shaped; buttons globelike with tiny center pore; at maturity interior scarlet to pinkish red, smooth, gelatinous; margins scalloped to fringed, pale pinkish; outer surface apricot pink, pallid below, clothed with soft whitish hairs. **Stalks** arising from hard, rootlike structure attached to buried wood and roots, often branching; slender, more or less equal, elongated to 4–6 cm; pallid above, dingy brown below; slightly hairy; hard, fibrous. **Flesh** brittle, thin.

SPORES Slightly yellowish in mass, 24–45 x 10–14 μm, elongated/elliptical, smooth, many small oil drops.

ECOLOGY/FRUITING PATTERN Rare, gregarious to clustered, attached to buried sticks and roots; in moist wooded sites, often under alder, willow; spring and early summer; reported in northern or high alpine areas.

OBSERVATIONS *protracta:* meaning "extending" in Latin (referring to the extended stalks). Resembling tiny flowers, this remarkable, rare little fungus is shown here to celebrate the diversity of Colorado fungi. Reported in several subalpine Colorado sites, it has also been photographed in northern regions in Canada and Alaska. Reports to me of its range in the Rocky Mountain region (or a photograph) would be greatly appreciated, but its mycelium should not be disturbed.

Microstoma floccosa, an apparently more common look-alike from eastern regions of the continent and elsewhere, has a very heavy coating of white hairs on the outside of the cups. Similarly colored scarlet cups in the related genus *Sarcoscypha* have shorter stalks and smooth nonscalloped cup margins and differ microscopically.

ORDER
Pezizales
FAMILY
Sarcosomataceae
EDIBILITY
Unknown

**Black, goblet-shaped,
little cups with long stalks
attached to woody debris;
at high elevations near
snowmelt in spring.**

FRUITING BODIES **Cup** dark olive-gray to black; margins remain curved inward, not flaring until very old; interior surface smooth; outer surface slightly roughened and grayish black; 1-1.5 cm across. **Stalk** black, fleshy, cylindrical, not brittle; up to 5 cm long, tapering toward base, which is embedded in woody debris and attached to buried sticks by blackish mycelium and hairs; with age, long blackish hairs may cover lower third of stalk. **Flesh** thin, solid, blackish gray.

SPORES White in mass, 23-28 x 11-14 µm, elliptical, smooth, numerous tiny oil drops.

ECOLOGY/FRUITING PATTERN Spring and early summer; single or in small groups attached to wet dead twigs and woody debris near melting snow or cold streamsides at high elevations in subalpine habitats. Rare even in these specialized habitats.

OBSERVATIONS *nannfeldtii:* named for Swedish mycologist J. A. Nannfeldt. You have to look carefully for these charming little black mushrooms because they are so easily camouflaged. The type collection from which the species was described was made in the early 1900s in Boulder Canyon, Colorado, by Dr. L. O. Overholts. It was later renamed by F. H. Seaver from the New York Botanical Garden. Both scientists made many valuable contributions to early Colorado mycology while visiting the old Mountain Laboratory of the University of Colorado at Tolland, Gilpin County, during the summers around 1915.

Another similar-looking, blackish, stalked cup, *Helvella corium,* also fruits in the spring, but can be distinguished by its spreading to lobed cups frequently with whitish margins, its lower height, its often fluted and roughened stalks, and its smaller spores.

ORDER
Neolectales
FAMILY
Neolectaceae
COMMON NAME
Earth Tongue
EDIBILITY
Inedible

Small, tapered, clublike fungus; bright to pale yellow above, whitish below; on soil under conifers.

FRUITING BODIES   2–3.5 cm tall; bright to pale yellow, elongated head confluent with short stalk. **Head** or fertile upper portion irregularly club-shaped to spoon-shaped, occasionally bluntly forking; fleshy, stuffed to hollow; smooth to coarsely wrinkled. **Stalk** or lower portion 3–6 mm wide above, tapering and rooted into substrate; much lighter-colored than head, whitish to pale yellowish; covered with white downy hairs. **Flesh** soft; odor and taste mild.

SPORES   Whitish in mass, 5.5–8.5 x 3–4 μm, smooth, oval to elliptical, often budding in ascus to produce small round conidia.

ECOLOGY/FRUITING PATTERN   Sometimes common in summer and fall; subalpine ecosystems around 9,000–10,000 feet; on soil scattered among conifer needles, mosses.

OBSERVATIONS   *vitellina:* from Latin, *vitellinus,* meaning "yellow." Formerly known as *Spragueola vitellina.* Members of the genus *Neolecta* differ from other similarly colored earth tongues by the lack of a sharply differentiated head, but the fruiting body top may be broadened, flattened, lobed, or branched.
   Neolecta irregularis is usually brighter orange-yellow, its heads are more highly lobed and branched and thus wider, and its spores and asci are somewhat larger. *Mitrula elegans* has a very distinct head that is orange to apricot-colored, a whitish stalk set off from the head, and differing microscopic features including longer cylindrical spores. Similarly colored simple coral fungi in the unrelated family Clavariaceae often fruit in small clusters, do not have broadened fertile heads, and bear their spores on basidia instead of inside asci.

ORDER
Leotiales
FAMILY
Geoglossaceae
EDIBILITY
Suspected of
being poisonous

Clustered; small drab-colored heads with convoluted nongelatinous upper surface; undersurface smooth without gills; distinctly stalked.

FRUITING BODIES Consisting of rounded head and stalk. **Head** 0.5–1.5 cm across; irregularly rounded and flattened, sometimes with central depression; upper (spore-bearing) surface wrinkled to convoluted, not sticky, ochre to dull tan; margins strongly incurved and not flared in age; underside more or less smooth. **Stalk** 2–6 cm long x 3–6 mm thick; equal to slightly thicker below; hollow with age; pinkish tan to drab and darker near base, overall somewhat darker than cap; attached to conifer needles and litter by (sometimes dense) yellow mycelium. **Flesh** cartilaginous, not gelatinous.

SPORES Whitish in mass, 30–40 x 2–3 µm, needle-like with multiple transverse septa, smooth.

ECOLOGY/FRUITING PATTERN Gregarious to clustered, sometimes as fairy rings; saprophytic in subalpine coniferous forests on needle litter; August and September.

OBSERVATIONS *circinans:* bent or circular (Latin), describing the cap shapes. By blowing across a cluster of mature caps of *Cudonia circinans,* which results in a little puff of "smoke," I have enjoyed watching the asci on the surfaces of the heads shoot their spores in unison. This example of an earth tongue could be mistaken for a small *Helvella,* but the field characters of the rounded, nonlobed caps and the clustered growth habit should distinguish *C. circinans.* A close relative, *Cudonia monticola,* found more commonly in the Pacific Northwest mountains, has larger fruiting bodies, pinkish cinnamon caps, much smaller spores, and fruits in the spring.

ORDER
Leotiales

FAMILY
Leotiaceae

EDIBILITY
Inedible

Tiny, bright yellow cups; usually stalkless; fruiting in troops on dead logs and twigs in late summer and fall.

FRUITING BODIES Cup very small, saucer-shaped, 2–4 mm across; both upper and undersurface smooth and bright lemon to egg-yolk yellow; edge of cup smooth, hairless. **Stalk** absent, or less commonly present with tiny stalk attached directly to decaying wood. **Flesh** very thin but quite firm.

SPORES Colorless under microscope, 10–14 x 3–5 µm, elliptical, often divided by cross-wall by maturity, two oil drops.

ECOLOGY/FRUITING PATTERN Sometimes common in late summer when there is enough moisture and cool conditions for fruiting; covers the surfaces of barkless dead branches and trunks, usually of deciduous trees; often numbering in the hundreds. This fungus decomposes and recycles wood in many of Colorado's forested ecosystems.

OBSERVATIONS *citrina:* from *citrin* (Latin), meaning "lemon yellow." You may find *Bisporella citrina* in a dried-up condition as dull, orangish brown, wrinkled spots scattered on twigs and logs. It is an example of the hundreds of species of inoperculate (having asci without lids) discomycetes, which occur in Colorado as decomposers of leaves, twigs, and logs. Their fruiting bodies come in boundless colors and forms, but are usually too small or dull-colored to get much attention except from some mycologists who love to study them. Collectively, however, they are of great importance as recyclers.

ORDER
Hypocreales
FAMILY
Hypocreaceae
EDIBILITY
Unknown

Bright greenish yellow, bumpy, moldlike growth covering gills and stalk of fresh specimens of Russulaceae mushrooms.

FRUITING BODIES Not a mushroom, *Hypomyces luteovirens* is a fungus parasite that completely covers and transforms the surface of the gills and most of the stalk of its host mushroom into a thin, green, bumpy layer. As it matures, the parasite layer changes from yellowish to bright yellow, then yellow-green to dark green, and finally blackish green. The pimplelike bumps in the green layer represent the perithecia, specialized structures in which the asci bear the spores of the *Hypomyces*. **Flesh** of the parasite is a firm layer 2–3 mm thick; flesh of the host mushroom is transformed into a very solid consistency.

SPORES Colorless under microscope, 32–35 x 4.5–5.5 µm, nonseptate, spindle-shaped with pointed ends, nearly smooth to warty.

ECOLOGY/FRUITING PATTERN Always an unusual find, this parasite could occur anywhere Russulaceae species (especially *Russula*) fruit, particularly after rain in forests during the summer and fall.

OBSERVATIONS *luteovirens:* yellow-green (Latin). Other species of *Hypomyces* have similar parasitizing habits but very different colors. *Hypomyces lactifluorum* transforms some species of *Russula* (often *Russula brevipes*) and some species of *Lactarius* into beautiful, orange-red fruiting bodies, producing the so-called edible Lobster Mushroom. Many mycologists express concern about eating the Lobster unless an identification of the host has been made. Another interesting relative is *Hypomyces chrysospermus,* which parasitizes members of the Boletaceae in a three-stage process, with color changes from white to yellow to finally reddish brown. Often it is impossible to discern the identity or edibility of the host in *Hypomyces* infections, and therefore eating these parasitized mushrooms is not recommended.

The Basidiomycetes

The vast majority of large mushrooms found in forests and fields are members of the subdivision Basidiomycotina, usually called basidiomycetes. They include most of the mushrooms collected for the table, such as the gilled mushrooms, boletes, puffballs, chanterelles, corals, jelly fungi, and teeth fungi, as well as the stinkhorns, the bird's nest fungi, and the woody conks and polypores.

Calbovista subsculpta, one of the nongilled basidiomycetes

These mushrooms all produce their spores on the outside of club-shaped fertile cells called basidia. More noticeable to the nature lover and mushroom forager, however, is the great variety of shapes and lifestyles of basidiomycetes. Anyone with an eye for the beauty of nature can appreciate this diversity by walking through a Colorado forest in the peak of the mushroom season. There you may find orange coral mushrooms, red and white Fly Agarics, tubby *Boletus,* pure white *Clitocybes,* clusters of the Devil's Snuffbox (*Lycoperdon* puffballs), troops of pinkish *Mycenas,* rubbery earlike *Auricularia* species, wood-rotting conks and brackets, and many others. In addition to their natural beauty and culinary use, these fungi are important ecologically because of their vital recycling activities and mycorrhizal associations.

Basidiomycetes are grouped by the location of the spore-producing surfaces on the fruiting bodies, which may be on the outside surfaces of gills, spines, folds, or branch tips; inside the lining of tubes; or inside the enclosed fruiting body.

Mushrooms with gills are found in every season and every habitat in Colorado and constitute some of our most interesting, edible, and poisonous species. Basidia on the gill surfaces will drop their spores at maturity and form a spore print, providing an essential clue to the identification of gilled mushrooms. Spore color is featured in the following key.

Coprinus micaceus, a gilled basidiomycete

Key to Major Families of Gilled Mushrooms

SPORE COLOR FROM PRINT   **KEY**

- Pale colors: white to yellow or tinted lilac,
  gray-green, pinkish buff   **A**

- Pink: pinkish brown to salmon-colored   **B**

- Brown: yellow-brown, orange-brown, rusty
  brown, dull brown, cinnamon brown   **C**

- Chocolate brown to purple-brown   **D**

- Dark: smoky gray to black   **E**

KEY A   Spores pale colors
1. Gills free from stalk.....2
1. Gills attached to stalk.....3
   2. Universal veil (volva) present as cup, patches,
      or warts at base; ring present or not   **Amanitaceae p. 58**
   2. With no volva of any kind; ring present   **Lepiotaceae p. 62**
   3. Flesh brittle; stalk breaks with a snap;
      spores with amyloid ornamentation   **Russulaceae p. 70**
   3. Not with above features.....4
     4. Gills waxy, thick, soft, often
       decurrent; on soil   **Hygrophoraceae p. 65**
     4. Gills not waxy or thick;
       growing on wood, soil, or dung   **Tricholomataceae p. 82**

KEY B   Spores pink: pinkish brown to salmon-colored
1. Gills free   **Plutaceae p. 116**
1. Gills attached   **Entolomataceae p. 116**

KEY C   Spores brown: yellow-brown, orange-brown, rusty brown, dull brown, cinnamon brown
1. Spores orange-brown, rusty brown, dull brown,
   cinnamon brown; gills not decurrent   **Cortinariaceae p. 118**
   (If lignicolous and smooth–spored, go to Key D)
1. Not as above.....2
   2. Spores yellow-brown to nearly chocolate
      brown; gills decurrent   **Paxillaceae p. 153**
   2. Spores bright yellow-brown; gills
      not decurrent   **Bolbitiaceae p. 144**

KEY D   Spores chocolate brown to purple-brown
1. Gills free   **Agaricaceae p. 146**
1. Gills attached   **Strophariaceae p. 138**

KEY E   Spores dark: smoky gray to black
1. Gills decurrent, thick   **Gomphidiaceae p. 151**
1. Gills not decurrent, sometimes inky   **Coprinaceae p. 130**

Family Amanitaceae

Of the two genera in this family, only the larger, *Amanita,* is featured here. It is represented here by a small group of species ranging from brilliantly colored to pale, from toxic to merely nonpoisonous. All have white (or pallid) spores and the gills are free from the stalk or nearly so. The genus is characterized by a layer that envelops the young button mushroom. This layer ranges from membranous tissue to powdery-crumbly tissue. As the button expands and the cap pushes upward, parts of this tissue, called the volva or universal veil, may be carried on the cap surface as warts or patches. Some or all of it remains at the base of the stalk as patches, concentric rings, or a membranous saclike cup. The universal veil may be fused to the stalk in various ways or may be so fragile that it adheres to fungal hyphae in the soil and is lost during collection. Some *Amanita* species also have a partial veil that extends from the cap edge to the stalk and that may eventually cling to the stalk as a skirtlike ring. One group within the genus *Amanita* does not have a partial veil and therefore lacks a ring.

Amanita muscaria var. **flavivolvata** (Singer) Jenkins

ORDER
Agaricales

FAMILY
Amanitaceae

COMMON NAMES
Fly Agaric, Sacred Mushroom

EDIBILITY
Poisonous

Medium-sized to large, bright red-orange to faded cap with scattered pale, cottony warts; white, free gills; whitish stalk with skirtlike veil and bulbous base; yellowish cottony scales in bracelets around base.

FRUITING BODIES Cap 5-20 cm wide; hemispheric as button, then expanding to convex or flattened; bright red to orange-red, fading to pale yellowish orange to dull pinkish orange where exposed to sunlight; buttons densely covered with yellowish crumbly, soft tissue, forming pale yellowish warts at maturity; margin at first yellowish and cottony, soon smooth, faintly striated; when fresh, red cuticle between warts feels tacky. **Gills** free, white to cream, crowded, broad, edges roughened. **Stalk** 7-14 cm long x 1.5-3 cm thick; white to creamy white; ring superior, skirtlike, creamy white, membranous with thickened edge and yellowish undersurface; stalk enlarging below into bulb and encircled in its lower part by three to five yellowish, concentric volval rings. **Flesh** of cap thick, white to yellowish with red-orange below cuticle, not staining; odor not distinctive, taste not recorded.

SPORES White in print, 9–12.5 x 6.5–8.5 µm, elliptical, smooth, non-amyloid.

ECOLOGY/FRUITING PATTERN Common and widely distributed; single, gregarious, to clustered in duff under mixed conifers, lodgepole and ponderosa pine, Douglas-fir, Engelmann spruce; July through September; foothills to subalpine ecosystems in Colorado.

OBSERVATIONS *muscaria:* pertaining to flies (Latin). *Amanita muscaria* variety *flavivolvata,* with its yellowish universal veil remnants, is the most common member of the *A. muscaria* group in Colorado. It is similar to *A. muscaria* var. *muscaria,* which usually has whiter universal veil remnants, smaller spores, and other microscopic differences; is found in other regions of North America; and is equally toxic. Called the Fly Agaric because of its early use as a fly poison, it is one of the most famous mushrooms in the world and the subject of myths and fairy tales. Its toxins can cause bizarre psychological experiences, which has made it a source of interest since prehistoric times. *Amanita muscaria* has been analyzed for more than two centuries. In fact, the first identified mushroom toxin, muscarine, was named for it, although it was later proven that the main toxins in *A. muscaria* are ibotenic acid and muscimol.

In Colorado this is the mushroom most talked about, admired, and photographed by the nature lover. Such an exotic-looking fungus growing along a hiking path in Colorado's high country is a spectacular sight.

Beware of confusing *Amanita* buttons for puffballs. Cutting *A. muscaria* buttons in half lengthwise will reveal a reddish pigment just under the universal veil (volva), along with the outline of the developing stalk and gills. In contrast, puffballs are white and homogeneous throughout in the fresh edible stage.

ORDER
Agaricales

FAMILY
Amanitaceae

COMMON NAME
The Panther

EDIBILITY
Poisonous

Cap medium-sized, creamy white, often pale brownish yellow at center, with white cottony warts; white, free gills, creamy stalk with white skirtlike ring; white rolled collar at top of basal bulb.

FRUITING BODIES **Cap** 3-11 cm across; convex to plano-convex; creamy to nearly white, often with pale brownish yellow disc; small, white, crumbly to powdery warts scattered over viscid cuticle; striated near margin. **Gills** white, free, crowded, moderately broad, edges roughened; in young, covered with white, membranous partial veil. **Stalk** 4-11 cm long x 1.5-2 cm wide; white, surface smooth above and roughened by fine white scales below superior ring; ring white, membranous, thick-edged, drooping and soon collapsing; stalk gradually enlarged downward to oval bulb; typically hollow; bulb topped by white, cottony, rolled collar. **Flesh** white; odor mild, taste not recorded.

SPORES White in print, 9-12 x 6.5-8.5 μm, elliptical-oval, smooth, non-amyloid.

ECOLOGY/FRUITING PATTERN Common after summer rains in June to September; solitary or scattered in mixed woods, commonly under ponderosa pine and Douglas-fir in montane regions; widely distributed under spruce in subalpine ecosystems.

OBSERVATIONS *pantherina:* resembling a panther. Older books use the name *Amanita cothurnata* for the mushroom now called *Amanita pantherina* var. *multisquamosa.* A somewhat darker member of the *Amanita pantherina* group with brownish caps and white warts has been found in many areas of Colorado. The more common variety, pictured here, is distinguished by its creamy pale yellowish caps and lightly squamulose or scaly stalk surface. The whitish warts are easy to miss because the light cap colors do not provide as much contrast as those of the darker, browner members of the group. In some seasons the pale Panther fruits in abundance. Mistaking it for an edible *Agaricus* or other mushrooms, or in its button stages for a puffball, has caused many serious poisonings in the Rocky Mountain region.

ORDER
Agaricales
FAMILY
Amanitaceae
COMMON NAME
Grisette
EDIBILITY
Not recommended

Gray to gray-brown, striated cap, often knobbed; white free gills; nonbulbous base; ring absent; white, saclike volva.

FRUITING BODIES Cap 4–9 cm broad; nearly conical, then flattening; often knobbed; dished, margins splitting with age; some shade of gray: delicate pale gray, mouse gray, lead gray, to dark gray-brown, darker on disc; striated up to one-third distance to center; sticky to shiny, smooth, rarely with adhering patch of whitish universal veil remnant. **Gills** white, broad, free, close to crowded, edges often minutely roughened. **Stalk** white to grayish; 8–15 cm long x 1–1.5 cm wide; cylindrical to club-shaped, without bulb; surface often covered with mealy flecks, often in zones; ring absent; base enclosed by fragile, whitish, membranous, loose sac with lobed, free margin. **Flesh** soft, thin, white; odor mild, taste not recorded.

SPORES White in deposit, 9–13 µm, globose, non-amyloid, smooth.

ECOLOGY/FRUITING PATTERN Widely distributed; under mixed aspen and conifers, also spruce/fir in subalpine ecosystems; solitary to gregarious; July through September.

OBSERVATIONS *vaginata:* sheathed (Latin), describing the volval sac. Often mentioned as edible, this mushroom and its ringless look-alikes are not recommended because of the possibility of confusing them with dangerous *Amanita* relatives. Only experts should take the risk of eating any *Amanita* species.

There are several very similar *Amanita* species in this region, some as yet unnamed, which have varying cap colors, but all of which have cap striations, no ring, and a saclike volva sheathing a nonbulbous stalk base. *Amanita fulva* is similar but has a tawny to orangish brown cap. *Amanita ceciliae* (formerly called *Amanita inaurata*) has a yellowish brown to brownish gray, striated cap with distinct grayish warts; the upper portion of its volva forms grayish, scaly zones girdling the lower part of the stalk.

Family Lepiotaceae

Often distinctive because of their size, members of this family have free gills and their stalks and caps are cleanly separable. Typically they have a ring or annular zone but no universal veil; hence a volva or cup is lacking. The spores are generally white to buff, but one, *Chlorophyllum molybdites,* has greenish spores. Lepiotaceae species are saprophytic on soil or plant remains.

Two genera, *Lepiota* and *Chlorophyllum,* are included here, representing both edible and poisonous species.

Lepiota clypeolaria (Bulliard) Kummer

ORDER
Agaricales
FAMILY
Lepiotaceae
EDIBILITY
Poisonous

Small, shaggy, yellowish brown to tawny caps with darker center; free, creamy gills; shaggy-wooly stalk; on ground, usually in woods.

FRUITING BODIES Cap 2–5 cm across, bell-shaped to expanded-knobbed; margin ragged from partial veil; cuticle yellowish brown to reddish brown, continuous over disc, splitting to form erect brown scales; surface whitish between scales. **Gills** free, creamy, close, broad, edges even. **Stalk** 3–10 cm long x 3–8 mm wide, equal, fragile; silky above, shaggy below; with poorly defined, loose, white ring often disappearing; lower stalk sheathed in pale yellow-brown scales and zones; cup or volva lacking. **Flesh** soft, white, not staining appreciably; odor and taste mild.

SPORES White in print; 13–18 x 4–4.5 μm; elongated, spindle-shaped; smooth; dextrinoid.

ECOLOGY/FRUITING PATTERN Single to scattered; under conifers, especially Douglas-fir; fruiting in late summer and fall in montane and subalpine ecosystems.

OBSERVATIONS *clypeolaria:* pertaining to a shield (Latin). This is a highly variable species and may represent a complex of similar species. Some species of *Floccularia* and *Cystoderma* superficially resemble small shaggy species of *Lepiota,* but their gills are attached. As there are several small species of *Lepiota* that are suspected of containing deadly amanitin toxins, collectors are warned not to taste or eat small *Lepiota* species.

ORDER
Agaricales

FAMILY
Lepiotaceae

COMMON NAME
Shaggy Parasol

EDIBILITY
Edible

Large, whitish to tan cap with coarse, pinkish to cinnamon brown scales; free white gills; white ring on club-shaped stalk; cut flesh turns yellow-orange.

FRUITING BODIES **Cap** large, 5-18 cm broad; buttons hemispheric, expanding to broadly convex; at first with tan to reddish brown cuticle that breaks up into large fibrous scales, often concentrically arranged on mature caps with white flesh showing through; margins shaggy. **Gills** free, close, broad, white at first, dingy brown with age. **Stalk** 6-20 cm long x 2-4 cm wide; clavate to bulbous; persistent double-edged ring is bandlike and movable; stalk interior solid, immediately staining yellow-orange when cut; exterior white above ring and dingy red-brown to dull brown below; volva absent. **Flesh** solid, white, turning yellow-orange where bruised; odor and taste mild.

SPORES White in print, 6-10 x 5.5-7 μm, short elliptical, smooth, thick-walled with pore at tip, dextrinoid.

ECOLOGY/FRUITING PATTERN Solitary to gregarious in soil, often near deciduous trees; in humus, compost piles, or gardens, along roads; quite common in late summer and fall in cities, plains, and foothills.

OBSERVATIONS *rachodes:* from the Latin *rhacodes*, meaning "shaggy." Another variety, *Lepiota rachodes* var. *hortensis*, reported rarely in Colorado growing in grass, is similar but distinguished by its large, sharply margined, bulbous base. It is reported to cause gastric upset in some people. Collectors are warned to become familiar with the very poisonous look-alike, the greenish-spored *Chlorophyllum molybdites,* before considering eating any large, scaly-capped *Lepiota* species. *Chlorophyllum molybdites* often grows in rings in grassy places and is easily confused with the Shaggy Parasol at the button stages, when the spores of the former have not yet developed enough to show the characteristic greenish spore print.

FRUITING BODIES Cap large, 6–30 cm broad; buttons oval to hemispheric, expanded caps broadly convex; cuticle pinkish tan, remaining intact on disc as cap expands and breaking up into pinkish tan scales elsewhere, exposing white flesh underneath. **Gills** free, broad, close, white in early stages, at times with dark margins, finally dull greenish gray from spores. **Stalk** 5–25 cm long x 1–2.5 cm thick, up to 5 cm across at base; often bulbous, volva absent; hairless; white to brownish pink; dingy brown over base; interior white, reddish brown when cut; ring thick-edged, fringed, can be moved up and down like a napkin ring. **Flesh** thick, white, discoloring to dingy reddish brown; odor mild, taste not recorded (but collectors are warned that even a small bite can cause serious vomiting).

SPORES Dull green-gray in print, 9.5–12 x 6.5–9 μm, elliptical, thick-walled with germ pore, smooth, dextrinoid (red-brown in Melzer's solution).

ECOLOGY/FRUITING PATTERN Common; in grassy places as fairy rings and arcs; found in Denver and other metropolitan areas in June and throughout the summer, into the fall after rains.

OBSERVATIONS *molybdites:* from the Greek *molybdos,* or lead, alluding to the greenish gray color of the mature gills and spores. Because the gills may remain white into maturity, a spore print is essential to identify this seriously poisonous mushroom. It is also known as *Lepiota molybdites.* The edible *Lepiota rachodes* has a white spore print and its stalk stains saffron (yellow-orange) at injuries. *Agaricus* species have young pinkish gills that eventually turn chocolate brown from spores. The edible *Coprinus comatus* has a more elongated cap, the flesh of its stalk is chalky white and does not change color when cut, and the gills soon become black and inky at maturity.

Family Hygrophoraceae

This is a family of often colorful or white to gray, small to medium-sized mushrooms, typically terrestrial under trees. Their gills are thick, widely spaced, waxy-feeling, clean-looking, and usually adnate to short decurrent. The smooth, non-amyloid spores are white and formed on very long basidia. Traditionally, all members of the family were placed in one genus, *Hygrophorus,* which is the only one treated here. Other genera have been segregated mainly by microscopic characters of the gills.

Hygrophorus chrysodon (Fries) Fries

ORDER
Agaricales
FAMILY
Hygrophoraceae
EDIBILITY
Nonpoisonous

Medium-sized, sticky white cap with tiny golden granules scattered over margin and at top of stalk; decurrent distant gills.

FRUITING BODIES Cap up to 7 cm across; white with distinctive tiny golden granules or flakes at margin; convex, becoming flattened with age, margin thin and wavy; surface smooth and slimy-viscid. **Gills** white, decurrent, rather narrow, waxy-feeling, distant. **Stalk** 3–7 cm long x 1–2 cm thick, equal, hollow; white with satiny sheen, golden pigment granules scattered on top in a zone. **Flesh** white, soft, not staining; taste mild or slightly bitter, odor mild.

SPORES White in print, 7–9.5 x 3.5–4.5 μm, elliptical, smooth.

ECOLOGY/FRUITING PATTERN Widely distributed; quite common after summer rains, July to September; often gregarious; montane to subalpine ecosystems; under conifers.

OBSERVATIONS *chrysodon:* golden tooth (Latin). It is always a pleasure to find this lovely little fungus with its sprinkling of gold. Once you know its field characters it is easy to recognize.

ORDER
Agaricales

FAMILY
Hygrophoraceae

EDIBILITY
Inedible

Medium-sized, white, very slimy cap and stalk; pale yellowish gills; no ring; under pines in fall.

FRUITING BODIES Cap 4-10 cm across; creamy buff with yellowish shading near center; convex to finally flattened, at times with low knob; smooth surface with thick, pale yellowish slime layer in young when moist, finally drying smooth and shiny. **Gills** waxy-feeling, thick, subdistant, decurrent; at first white, maturing to ivory yellow. **Stalk** 3-5 cm long x 1.5-3 cm thick, somewhat wider in middle; solid; white, sheathed below by pale yellowish, glutinous veil that ends in glutinous ring; above ring, stalk is white, lightly fibrillose. **Flesh** thick, white, not staining; taste and odor mild.

SPORES White in print, 8.5-11 x 5.5-6 μm, elliptical, smooth, non-amyloid.

ECOLOGY/FRUITING PATTERN In soil under lodgepole and ponderosa pines; scattered to numerous, sometimes in large clusters; late summer and early fall, even after the first frosts in the high country. Because of the slimy layer, the caps are often covered with needle debris when collected.

OBSERVATIONS *gliocyclus:* from the Greek *gli* (glue) and *kyklos* (circle), describing the cap. *Hygrophorus subalpinus* is a stocky, white relative, but it fruits in spring near snowbanks and has a distinct fibril-lose veil with a viscid but not slimy cap. *Hygrophorus eburneus* also has a sticky to glutinous cap and grows under conifers, including piñon pine in the southern part of the state, but it is pure white overall and has a longer, more slender stalk and smaller spores.

ORDER
Agaricales
FAMILY
Hygrophoraceae
EDIBILITY
Unknown

Medium-sized pink caps streaked with wine-colored fibrils; pink, distant gills with pinkish red spots; stalk with wine-colored streaks, bruising yellow.

FRUITING BODIES Cap 5-8 cm across; convex, becoming plane, with low hump in some; in young, margin inrolled and often beaded with moisture; surface pinkish with wine-colored streaking, margin lighter; surface glutinous to viscid. **Gills** pale pinkish to shell-pink, distant, medium broad, decurrent, soon spotted pinkish red. **Stalk** 4-7 x 0.5-1.5 cm; apex white, pale pink with fine wine-colored scales and streaks elsewhere; often with drops of moisture; at times yellowish where bruised; ring absent. **Flesh** thin on margin but thick on disc; odor not distinctive, taste mild.

SPORES White in print, 7-11 x 5-6 µm, elliptical, smooth, non-amyloid.

ECOLOGY/FRUITING PATTERN Common in some seasons in August and September at high elevations; gregarious in soil under conifers, especially spruce and pine.

OBSERVATIONS *erubescens:* becoming red (Latin). One variety, *Hygrophorus erubescens* var. *gracilis,* has a very long, slender stalk. Other similar *Hygrophorus* species fruit in our mountain areas and could be confused with this species. *Hygrophorus russula* has slightly viscid to dry caps and crowded *Russula*-like gills, and does not bruise yellow. *Hygrophorus amarus* looks similar, has buff yellow colors, and is very bitter-tasting. *Hygrophorus purpurascens* has darker, conspicuous, red to purplish streaks in a radial pattern over the larger caps; smaller spores (5.5-8 x 3-4.5 µm); and a distinctive fibrillose partial veil on the apex of the stipe.

ORDER
Agaricales
FAMILY
Hygrophoraceae
EDIBILITY
Inedible

Medium-sized to large, pinkish buff cap on long white to pinkish stalk; apex of stalk finely scaly; gills decurrent.

FRUITING BODIES Cap 5-12 cm across; convex, then flattening somewhat with margins inrolled and minutely downy; pale buff to pinkish buff, pinkish orange toward center; surface smooth, viscid in moist weather. **Gills** creamy to pinkish buff, not spotting, adnate to decurrent, narrow, distant, waxy. **Stalk** long and stout, 4-9 cm x 1-2.5 cm, equal or tapering downward; white to pinkish tinged; dry, upper part white and finely scaly or tufted, tufts turning reddish brown with age or drying and bright yellow-orange in KOH; ring absent. **Flesh** firm, thick; whitish, tinged with pink, but not staining yellow; odor mild, taste mild to resinous.

SPORES White in print, 6-9.5 x 4-5.5 µm, elliptical, smooth, non-amyloid.

ECOLOGY/FRUITING PATTERN This is one of the characteristic species of late summer and early fall mycoflora in the Rocky Mountains, fruiting in abundance after moisture under spruce and fir, sometimes in boggy areas; scattered to gregarious.

OBSERVATIONS *pudorinus:* blushing (Latin). This robust *Hygrophorus* is quite easy to recognize by its good size, pinkish buff colors, and the finely scaly stalk apex. Try the spot test with a drop of KOH, and you will cinch your identification and bring out the beautiful coloration of the tiny scales. The cooked mushroom is said to be edible (if the turpentine taste is not strong), but some variants are unpalatable.

ORDER
Agaricales
FAMILY
Hygrophoraceae
COMMON NAME
Witch's Hat
EDIBILITY
Not recommended

Small, pointed, bright red to yellow caps; gills yellow, staining blackish; stalk straight, greenish yellow to black; no ring; on soil under conifers.

FRUITING BODIES Cap 1.5–4.5 cm across; conical, sometimes convex with sharp conical knob; viscid, faintly streaked with fibers to smooth; scarlet red to red-orange, fading to orangish near margin, often with greenish olive tints; entire cap turns black with age; margin frequently lobed or cracked. **Gills** nearly free, broad, close, creamy white at first, soon olive-yellow to pale yellow-orange, staining blackish where bruised; edges uneven. **Stalk** straight, equal, 3–8 cm long x 4–9 mm wide; base whitish, remainder reddish, yellow, or greenish yellow, turning black at bruises or with age; hollow; fragile; smooth or with longitudinal striations; ring absent. **Flesh** thin, fragile, same color as cap surface, blackening; odor and taste mild.

SPORES White in print, 9–12 x 5.5–6.5 μm, elliptical, smooth, non-amyloid.

ECOLOGY/FRUITING PATTERN Not common but found in most seasons; gregarious in soil under conifers; subalpine ecosystems; August through September.

OBSERVATIONS *conicus:* conical, referring to cap shape. Also known as *Hygrocybe conica*. The pointed, brightly colored caps and the black staining throughout the fruiting body are good field characters. It is possible to find all ages and several colors of the Witch's Hat in one collection. Perhaps because of its blackening qualities or its association with witches, this beautiful little mushroom was once considered poisonous. The fruiting bodies are little and fragile and found in Colorado in such small quantities that they are hardly worth considering as food.

Family Russulaceae

One of the most interesting, colorful, and important families of mushrooms in Colorado's forests, members of the Russulaceae all have a characteristic brittle, crumbly texture to their flesh, stalk, and gills. They all lack veils. Their white to pale yellow or ochre spores are ornamented with various warts and ridges that turn blue-black in Melzer's solution. There are two genera: *Lactarius* species are often called milky caps because their flesh oozes a milky, clear, white, or colored latex when cut. *Russula* species do not have latex and their caps are usually colorful, often with great variation of shadings in one collection. The subtleties of spore color are also vital to their identification.

Russula decolorans Fries

ORDER
Agaricales
FAMILY
Russulaceae
EDIBILITY
Edible

Medium-sized to large, copper to dull reddish orange caps; brittle flesh, whitish gills, and stalk turn ash-colored upon injury; under pines.

FRUITING BODIES Cap orange-red to copper, often with bronzed red at center; 3–11 cm across; hemispheric in young, soon convex to slightly dished; cuticle smooth, sticky in wet weather, peels at margin only. **Gills** broad, close, adnate, forking in a few gills; white, soon yellowish buff, staining gray with age. **Stalk** often long and firm, white, staining ash gray at injury and with age, especially inside; 4–10 cm long x 1.5–2.5 wide, often thicker below. **Flesh** firm; white, turning gray with age or injury; odor mild, taste mild to slowly peppery in young gills.

SPORES Pale yellow in print, 9–12 x 7–10 μm, broadly elliptical, amyloid warts.

ECOLOGY/FRUITING PATTERN Common; fruiting in small groups in late summer and fall under lodgepole pines and perhaps other conifers; usually at 9,000–10,000 feet.

OBSERVATIONS *decolorans:* Latin for changing colors. There are some other very similar *Russula*s, all forming a closely related complex around Colorado's species. The attractive red-orange colors of the cap, the graying of the flesh and stalk surface, and a habitat under pine are good field characters.

70

ORDER
Agaricales
FAMILY
Russulaceae
EDIBILITY
Edible

Medium-sized, greenish to yellow-green, smooth, tacky caps; yellowish gills; brittle flesh; pale stalk.

FRUITING BODIES **Cap** 3–10 cm across; at first cushion-shaped, then flattened somewhat, broadly dished with age; yellow-green to gray-green, center darker green; smooth and sticky when fresh; shiny, not cracked with age; flesh at edge thin and furrowed, skin peels halfway. **Gills** crowded, barely attached, narrow to broad, brittle, sometimes forking near stem, white to creamy yellow. **Stalk** 3–7 cm long x 1–2 cm wide, cylindrical, white to slightly yellow, dull, smooth, often with rusty spots at base. **Flesh** white, brittle; odor and taste mild.

SPORES Creamy yellow in print, 6–8 x 6–7 μm, globose to short oval, amyloid warts and ridges.

ECOLOGY/FRUITING PATTERN On soil in scattered to small groups; often quite common among mixed conifers and aspen; late summer and fall; subalpine ecosystems.

OBSERVATIONS *aeruginea:* Latin *aeruginus,* color of tarnished copper, greenish. Members of the *Russula* genus are easy to recognize in the field but often difficult to name specifically; this is one of the easier ones found in the Rockies because of its distinct yellow-green, smooth caps and light yellow spore print. *Russula olivacea* has purple-red cap tones shading into greenish olive and a deep ochre spore print. *Russula cyanoxantha* has caps with mixed colors, from lavender to greenish, but with white spores.

ORDER
Agaricales
FAMILY
Russulaceae
COMMON NAME
Emetic *Russula*
EDIBILITY
Poisonous

Bright scarlet to red-orange cap with white gills, stalk, and spores; acrid taste; under conifers.

FRUITING BODIES **Cap** bright scarlet to red-orange; 2.5–7 cm broad; cushion-shaped to convex, finally flattening with age, margins even; surface sticky, smooth, cuticle peels partway from margin. **Gills** snow-white to slightly creamy, adnate, moderately broad, forking at times, close. **Stalk** 3–8 cm long x 1–2 cm wide, pure white, clavate to equal, longitudinally slightly grooved. **Flesh** brittle, white, pinkish just under cap cuticle; odor mild, taste acrid.

SPORES White in print, 7–10 x 6.5–7.5 μm, subglobose to broadly elliptical, amyloid warts joined by amyloid reticulum.

ECOLOGY/FRUITING PATTERN Single to small groups; on humus and soil often surrounded by mosses; associated with conifers; fairly common in moist areas of Colorado's subalpine ecosystems; summer and early fall.

OBSERVATIONS *emetica:* an emetic (a sickener). There are several closely related red *Russulas* with white gills, white spores, an acrid taste that fruit in the Rocky Mountains, together often called the *Russula emetica* group. The prototypical *Russula emetica* is usually found in sphagnum bogs under conifers or in mixed woods. It has slightly larger fruiting bodies and slightly larger spores than the specimens pictured here, which were found in mixed conifers at over 10,000 feet. *Russula rosacea* also has red caps and an acrid taste, but its stalk is tinged with pink or red and the gills and spores are pale yellow. *Russula montana,* the type specimen of which is from Colorado, has red caps suffused with gray-brown, very pale yellowish spores, white stalks, and an acrid taste; it fruits on duff or rotten wood among conifers.

ORDER	**FRUITING BODIES Cap** colors variable, deep red-
Agaricales	dish to purplish brown, in center often purplish
FAMILY	black, sometimes with bronze shadings; often large,
Russulaceae	5-15 cm across; at first convex but often flattening
COMMON NAME	or dish-shaped; viscid when wet, drying with age,
Shrimp *Russula*	skin peels only at margin. **Gills** attached, broad,
EDIBILITY	moderately close to almost distant; buff, becoming
Edible	orangish yellow to brownish with age. **Stalk** thick,
	5-9 cm long x 2-5 cm wide; often enlarged at base;
Medium-sized to large,	white flushed pinkish, staining yellow-brown; dry,
dark wine-red with purple	grooved surface. **Flesh** thick, white, at first, all parts
shades; yellowish gills;	slowly turning yellow-brown when cut or bruised;
flesh stains yellow-	odor may be mild at first but soon develops charac-
brown; shrimp odor.	teristic smell of shrimp or fish, particularly notice-
	able when drying; taste mild to pleasant.

SPORES Yellow to deep ochre-orange in print, 8-11 x 7-8.5 μm, elliptical, amyloid warts.

ECOLOGY/FRUITING PATTERN Scattered to gregarious on soil under conifers and in mixed woods; montane and subalpine ecosystems; late summer and fall; quite common.

OBSERVATIONS *xerampelina:* Greek *xer* means "dry"; Latin *ampelinus* means "of the vine" (wine-colored). This fairly large *Russula* is eaten in some circles. Its fishy taste often disappears when cooked.

   Russula xerampelina is a variable species or a complex of species in this region, but the combination of shrimplike odor, the brown stain-ing of the cut flesh, and a green reaction of the flesh when spotted with $FeSO_4$ (iron sulphate) are good field characters.

ORDER	**FRUITING BODIES** **Cap** thin, fragile, 2-5 cm broad;
Agaricales	convex, often with a knob, flattening, then
FAMILY	depressed; color variable, usually with mixture of
Russulaceae	shades of purple, grayish violet, olive greenish, often
EDIBILITY	fading; center distinctly darker, olivaceous to purple-
Inedible	black; surface smooth to sticky, marginal area with
	furrows, cuticle peels easily. **Gills** white to creamy,
Small fragile cap, varying	narrow, close, adnate to notched, edges even. **Stalk**
from purplish to violet,	white, fragile, 3-5 cm long x 1-1.5 cm wide, nar-
often with mixture of	rowly clavate. **Flesh** thin, very fragile; odor mild to
colors, center darker;	slightly fruity; taste slowly burning, finally acrid.
gills white to very pale	
cream; stalk white;	**SPORES** White to very pale creamy in print, 6-9 x
taste soon hot.	5-7 µm, broadly elliptical to subglobose, amyloid
	warts.

ECOLOGY/FRUITING PATTERN Gregarious in soil, humus, or rotten wood under conifers and aspen; August and September; montane and subalpine ecosystems; at times fairly common but often overlooked.

OBSERVATIONS *fragilis:* fragile (Latin), describing the fragile tissues. This attractive, hot-tasting little *Russula* varies greatly in cap color, but the dominance of gray- to purple-violet shades with darker centers, together with its fragility, very pale creamy gills and spores, and white stalk, help distinguish it. In Colorado's varied habitats, there are probably other similarly colored look-alikes that represent a complex of species.

ORDER
Agaricales
FAMILY
Russulaceae
EDIBILITY
Not recommended

Large red caps with orange to ochre shading; gills yellowish; white stalk tinted pink; taste usually mild.

FRUITING BODIES **Cap** 5–13 cm broad, convex to slightly depressed; strong red colors, fading to orange shades in places; surface viscid. **Gills** cream-colored even in young, soon pale yellowish ochre; close, adnate, moderately broad, often strongly inter-veined near stalk. **Stalk** robust, 4–12 cm long x 2–3 cm wide; cylindrical; white, often flushed pink; surface with low longitudinal ridges. **Flesh** white, staining slightly to dull grayish; firm; odor mild; taste mild, slightly acrid when young.

SPORES Pale ochre in print, 8–11 x 7–9 μm, broadly elliptical, amyloid warts.

ECOLOGY/FRUITING PATTERN Scattered, sometimes gregarious and often common; boggy, mossy areas in conifer forest; montane and subalpine ecosystems; late summer into fall.

OBSERVATIONS *paludosa:* of the bog (Latin). The mild taste, large size, long stalk, creamy gills, and yellow spores distinguish this mushroom from the *Russula emetica* group. Although *Russula paludosa* is not reported as poisonous in the literature, eating reddish-colored *Russula* species is not recommended because not all of Colorado's species are known, and some *Russula* species with red caps are definitely poisonous.

ORDER
Agaricales
FAMILY
Russulaceae
EDIBILITY
Nonpoisonous
but disagreeable

Large, funnel-shaped, dirty white cap; decurrent gills; short stalk; all parts stain brownish; deep in soil, often erupting partly through needle litter.

FRUITING BODIES Cap 5–14 cm across, broadly convex, depressed in center with age; dingy white, staining dull yellow-brown; surface feltlike, dry, not striated. **Gills** decurrent; white with blue-greenish reflections, staining cinnamon brown with age; close to crowded and often forked near stem, narrow. **Stalk** distinctly stubby, 3–6 cm long x 2–3 cm wide, equal, dry, smooth, dull white with brownish stains. **Flesh** firm; white, staining brownish, without latex; odor mild to slightly disagreeable, taste very peppery (hence the variety name).

SPORES Pale cream-colored in print; 8–11 x 6.5–8.5 µm, broadly elliptical; amyloid warts and ridges.

ECOLOGY/FRUITING PATTERN Quite common in montane ecosystems with conifers, especially lodgepole pines; July through September; solitary or two or three together. In dry periods the fruiting bodies develop under pine needles and can often be spotted under mounds of needles.

OBSERVATIONS *brevipes:* Latin *brevi* means "short"; *pes* means "foot" (stalk). Some *Lactarius* species may seem similar to *Russula brevipes,* but they exude a milky latex when cut. Other white-capped *Russula* species that could be confused with this one are *Russula albonigra* and *Russula nigricans,* but their tissues turn distinctly black upon injury or with age. Fruiting bodies of *R. brevipes* are often parasitized by the fungus *Hypomyces lactifluorum.* The parasite transforms a disagreeable-tasting mushroom into the well-known and popular edible, the bright orange Lobster Mushroom.

ORDER
Agaricales
FAMILY
Russulaceae
EDIBILITY
Not recommended

Large, dingy white caps with dull pink stains; pinkish gills; short stalk; white, unchanging latex; under aspens.

FRUITING BODIES Cap 4–20 cm broad; convex, becoming depressed to vase-shaped; margin inrolled, zoned, in young with short hairs; dingy white with lavender to dull pink tinges, sometimes in concentric bands; surface slimy to tacky, soon dry. **Gills** distinctly pale pink to pale vinaceous; narrow, very close, adnate to decurrent; latex white, unchanging. **Stalk** short, 2.5–7 cm long x 1.5–3 cm wide; white, dry to the touch; ring absent. **Flesh** firm, white; odor mild, taste slowly but strongly burning-acrid.

SPORES Pale pinkish cream in print, 6–7.5 x 4.5–5 µm, elliptical, amyloid warts.

ECOLOGY/FRUITING PATTERN On moist soil; mycorrhizal with aspens and willows; montane to subalpine ecosystems; gregarious to single; late summer through September.

OBSERVATIONS *controversus:* controversial (Latin). The pinkish gills, white unchanging latex, and robust fruiting bodies, along with its mycorrhizal associates, make *Lactarius controversus* a fairly easy species to recognize. Watch for it in moist swampy areas in aspen groves in Colorado's high country. The pinkish gills are often quite lovely. An acrid-tasting relative, *Lactarius torminosus,* looks similar (with white, unchanging latex), but it has a distinctive, densely bearded cap margin, whitish to cream-colored gills, and larger spores (7.5–10 x 6–7.5 µm).

ORDER
Agaricales
FAMILY
Russulaceae
COMMON NAME
Delicious Milky Cap
EDIBILITY
Edible

Orange to dull pinkish orange caps and gills, staining greenish; short pale stalk; orange latex, turning blue-green.

FRUITING BODIES **Cap** dull orange-red to paler, with or without indistinct zones of dull pinkish brown, staining dull greenish; 5–14 cm broad; smooth, convex when young, becoming depressed at center; margin inrolled when young; viscid, soon dry. **Gills** light orange, staining greenish, especially with age; crowded, adnate to decurrent, narrow. **Stalk** 2–5 cm long x 1–3 cm wide, equal, soon hollow; surface dry, light orange with darker spots; cut surface at base revealing scanty, carrot-colored latex line, eventually slightly redder, finally blue-green. **Flesh** creamy yellow; cut surface oozing scant orange latex, staining greenish; firm to crumbly or brittle; odor mild to fruity, taste mild.

SPORES Yellowish buff in print, 7–9 x 6–7 µm, broadly elliptical, low amyloid warts.

ECOLOGY/FRUITING PATTERN Scattered to gregarious under mixed conifers, especially pine; montane to subalpine; common and often abundant; late summer to fall.

OBSERVATIONS *deliciosus:* Latin for delicious. Although a popular edible in other countries, Colorado's varieties of this species are not always delicious. However, they are most flavorful when young and very fresh.

    There are several varieties of *Lactarius deliciosus* differentiated on subtle field characters and distinct microscopic differences; all are edible but of varying quality. *Lactarius deliciosus* var. *areolatus* is a common variety in Colorado. It lacks special sterile cells called pleurocystidia on its gill surfaces, has slightly larger spores (8–11 x 7–8 µm), and the cap surface is soon dry and cracked. *Lactarius deliciosus* var. *deterrimus* also occurs in Colorado. Its cap surface does not usually become cracked, its cut surfaces turn orange then wine-red before they turn green, its spores measure 7.5–9 x 6–7 µm, and it lacks pleurocystidia. *Lactarius rubrilacteus* has duller, less orange gills, and its latex is dark orange-red to bloodred in young specimens when first exposed.

ORDER
Agaricales
FAMILY
Russulaceae
EDIBILITY
Poisonous

Medium-sized to large, smooth, sticky orange caps with concentric zones; funnel-shaped with age; white latex; acrid taste.

FRUITING BODIES **Cap** 6-14 cm across; various shades of orange with narrow concentric zones of alternating apricot to orange-buff; convex with depressed disc, becoming funnel-shaped with age; smooth, viscid, not hairy at margins. **Gills** white, becoming light buff; latex white and acrid, not discoloring, but gills turn orange-rust at bruises; close, narrow, adnate, finally somewhat decurrent. **Stalk** nearly equal, 4-6 cm long x 1.5-3 cm thick, whitish with white bloom and nonpitted surface. **Flesh** white, staining rusty; odor mild, taste of flesh and latex acrid.

SPORES Buff in print, 7.5-11 x 7-9 μm, broadly elliptical, amyloid ornaments as isolated warts with short ridges.

ECOLOGY/FRUITING PATTERN Sometimes quite common in late summer and early fall; usually gregarious in spruce/subalpine fir forests of subalpine ecosystems.

OBSERVATIONS *olympianus:* recognizing the Olympic Mountains of Washington State, where the type specimen was collected. *Lactarius olympianus* is a common montane species of the western mountains of North America. The details of the spore ornamentation are important in its identification. The common orange-colored *Lactarius deliciosus* has similar cap colors and grows in similar habitats but differs by its mild taste, orange latex, and blue-green staining on all parts. *Lactarius alnicola* is also a conifer-lover with white acrid latex and a nonbearded, pale yellow-ochre, often zoned cap; however, its stalk is usually pitted with conspicuous spots.

ORDER Agaricales
FAMILY Russulaceae
EDIBILITY Poisonous

Large, pale golden yellow, bearded caps; copious white latex discoloring cut surfaces purple-lilac; stalk heavy, hollow with spotted surface.

FRUITING BODIES Cap large, 6-16 cm across, convex-depressed, pale golden yellow; surface shaggy under layer of slime; margin bearded with long hairs, inrolled in young; white latex quickly turns cut surfaces purple; latex mild to slightly acrid. **Gills** close, decurrent, broad, buff, oozing white latex, staining purple. **Stalk** 4-9 cm long x 1.5-4 cm wide; bulky-looking; pale yellowish, staining purple; sticky to dry; sometimes spotted with small pits; hollow. **Flesh** firm, whitish, staining dull purple-lilac; odor mild, taste bitter to slightly acrid.

SPORES Pale yellowish in thick deposit, 8-11 x 6.5-8 µm, elliptical, amyloid warts and ridges.

ECOLOGY/FRUITING PATTERN Scattered or in groups in late summer and fall in conifer zones, where it is a common associate of spruce. This is a northern species occurring at higher elevations of the West and north to the conifer areas of Alaska.

OBSERVATIONS *repraesentaneus:* well represented (Latin). Lilac-staining *Lactarius* members are considered poisonous and should not be eaten. This species could be confused with the poisonous *Lactarius scrobiculatus,* because they both fruit in similar habitats and at similar times in our region and have bearded margins and similar sizes. However, the white latex of *L. scrobiculatus* is very acrid and quickly turns yellow (not lilac) when exposed, and the stem is more distinctly spotted with yellow pits.

ORDER
Agaricales
FAMILY
Russulaceae
EDIBILITY
Poisonous

Purple drab to mottled gray-brown, sticky cap; creamy gills with copious white latex; all tissues staining dull lilac at injury.

FRUITING BODIES Cap 3-9 cm across; pale purple drab to vinaceous drab; some caps lightly zonate; staining dull purple to wine-colored where injured; convex, becoming depressed in center; surface moist, sticky, soon dry; surface stains green with KOH. **Gills** creamy, bleeding copious milk-white latex that stains gills lavender to finally dark wine-colored at injury; close, narrow, adnate. **Stalk** 3-9 cm long x 1.5-2.5 cm wide; dry, not viscid; clavate to equal, hollow in basal area; pallid, staining drab lilac. **Flesh** pallid, staining wine-colored to vinaceous brown where injured; odor mild; taste resinous, but not bitter or acrid.

SPORES Pale yellow in print, 8.5-10.5 x 7-8 μm, broadly elliptical, amyloid ornamentation with partial reticulum and scattered warts.

ECOLOGY/FRUITING PATTERN Gregarious on edges of high alpine boggy areas; near conifers and willows; quite common late July through September; montane and subalpine ecosystems.

OBSERVATIONS *uvidus, montanus:* Latin *uvidus* means "wet"; *montanus* means "of the mountains." This variety is distinguished from other varieties of *Lactarius uvidus* by its darker, drier cap; its sturdier stalk; and the mild, resinous, but not bitter taste. The drab lilac to vinaceous staining of injured flesh, gills, and stalk is characteristic of all varieties of *L. uvidus*. All purple- to lilac-staining *Lactarius* species are considered poisonous.

Family Tricholomataceae

Tricholomataceae is a huge "catchall" family with dozens of genera of white to very light-spored mushrooms with gills, only some of which can be included in this guide. Tricholomataceae includes those genera that do not fit in the other four families of light-spored gilled mushrooms (Amanitaceae, Lepiotaceae, Hygrophoraceae, and Russulaceae). The family is characterized by:

- **Spore prints usually white, but varying from white to creamy to pale pinkish, grayish or violaceous, never deeply or brightly colored; spores smooth or seldom ornamented.**
- **Cap and stalk not easily or cleanly separable.**
- **Gills attached (if stalk is present) or rarely free, not waxy.**
- **Stalks central, off-center, or lacking.**
- **Typically without universal veil; volva absent.**

Most collectors learn to recognize the various genera in this big family by a combination of eliminating "what it is not" and recognizing key field characters of "what it probably is." Of the dozens of genera in the family, some are common in Colorado. Several very popular edible mushrooms belong to the Tricholomataceae family, as well as some poisonous ones. Key field characters of nineteen genera are given.

ON WOOD (LIGNICOLOUS); STALK ABSENT, OFF-CENTER, OR CENTRAL:

Armillaria Stalk central, typically clustered, tough, often with ring; black rhizomorphs produced; cap with bristlelike hairs on disc; gills decurrent; spores white, smooth, non-amyloid, pp. 84–85. (Nonlignicolous *Armillaria* species, known as *Floccularia,* are also included here.)

Flammulina Stalk central, rooting, dark brown, velvety; cap yellow, smooth, sticky; spores white, smooth, p. 92.

Tricholomopsis Stalk central, gills attached/notched; cap often brightly colored; fibrillose, fibrils different color than flesh; gills brightly colored like cap, edges roughened, often discolored; spores white, smooth, non-amyloid, p. 93.

Xeromphalina Small fruiting bodies; stalk central, usually with yellow to dark hairs at base; cap small, convex to plano-convex; gills decurrent; lignicolous or on forest litter; spores white, smooth, amyloid, p. 95.

Heliocybe, Neolentinus (also known as *Lentinus*) Stalk central or off-center; gill edges saw-toothed; cap fleshy, becoming tough, persistent; spores white, non-amyloid, go to p. 111.

Phyllotopsis Stalkless; cap surface hairy, bright orange, dry; gills orange; odor unpleasant; spores pale pink, go to p. 111.

Pleurotus Stalk off-center, central, or absent; gills decurrent; edges even; cap fleshy; spores white or grayish lilac, go to p. 111.

TYPICALLY ON SOIL (HUMUS, LEAF LITTER, OCCASIONALLY ON VERY ROTTED WOOD, ROTTING MUSHROOMS); STALKS TYPICALLY CENTRAL:

Clitocybe Small to large fruiting body, typically depressed to vase-shaped, margin incurved; variously colored cap; gills often pale, not waxy-looking; generally decurrent to subdecurrent; without veils; spores white, yellowish, to pale pink, pp. 86–88.

Collybia Cap margin incurved, becoming decurved; cap dry, often dull, convex to plane, not reviving after drying; gills adnexed to adnate, never decurrent; stalk not hairlike; spores white to cream-colored, pp. 89–91.

Melanoleuca Cap surface leatherlike and smooth; cap convex or plane, often knobbed, gills adnate/notched, crowded, usually white; stalk typically straight, narrow; striated longitudinally; spores white or cream, rarely buff, warty, amyloid, p. 94.

Lyophyllum Flesh and gills often bruising blackish or dark gray; cap fleshy, white or dull-colored, gray, grayish brown, or blackish; spores white, non-amyloid, p. 95.

Leucopaxillus Thick, fleshy stalk with mass of white mycelium binding substrate at its base; cap dry, smooth, thick-fleshed, typically white or pale-colored; spores white, warty, amyloid, pp. 96–97.

Marasmius Fruiting body small, tough, reviving after being dried and then moistened; cap dry, margin often decurved; gills usually distant; stalk tough, cartilaginous, often hairlike; spores white, non-amyloid, pp. 98–99.

Mycena Fruiting bodies fragile, soft, tiny to small; often in troops; not reviving when moistened; caps conical, campanulate to convex; margin straight at first, at times incurved, but never inrolled; gills often with differently colored edges, adnate to decurrent; spores smooth, pp. 100–102.

Cystoderma Cap granular, mealy, dry, small to medium; gills attached to decurrent; stalk with ring (often disappearing); spores white, smooth, p. 102.

Tricholoma Caps often robust, fleshy, medium-sized to large; gills distinctly sinuate or adnexed; stalk fleshy; ring sometimes present; typically terrestrial; spores white, smooth, non-amyloid, pp. 103–108.

Catathelasma Cap robust, hard-fleshed; stalk sturdy, tapered, rootlike, with double-layered ring; gills adnate to decurrent; spores smooth, amyloid, p. 109.

Laccaria Caps typically some shade of orange-brown to brownish pink or lavender, small to medium; gills thick, waxy-looking, distant to subdistant; veil absent; spores white, with small spines, non-amyloid, p. 110.

Clitocybe gibba, a common member of the Tricholomataceae family

ORDER
Agaricales
FAMILY
Tricholomataceae
COMMON NAME
Honey Mushroom
EDIBILITY
Edible if cooked well

Brown caps with darker fibrils in center; tough, clustered stalks with whitish, cottony brown-rimmed rings; white to pinkish brown gills; clustered on wood or buried wood.

FRUITING BODIES **Cap** 4–10 cm broad, convex to convex-knobbed; light to medium brown to reddish brown without yellow tones, center with tiny, dark brown, hairy tufts; margin pinkish brown, incurved, often with traces of whitish partial veil; surface viscid or dry. **Gills** attached or slightly decurrent; nearly distant; narrow; white, becoming pinkish brown, staining brownish with age. **Stalk** 6–15 cm long x 1–1.5 cm wide; cylindrical to tapering, tough, often joined with others at base; whitish, becoming reddish brown, often yellow downy near base; thick, whitish to yellowish, cottony to membranous ring with brown pigmented margin near top of stalk, occasionally nearly disappearing. **Flesh** white when young, soon dingy pinkish to tan; thin; odor mild to musty, taste mildly astringent.

SPORES White in print, 8–11 x 5.5–7 µm, elliptical, smooth, non-amyloid.

ECOLOGY/FRUITING PATTERN In small to large clusters most frequently near or on dying or dead conifers, occasionally on hardwoods such as aspen; spreading by black, underground, bootlacelike rhizomorphs; causes root rot of conifers throughout western U.S.; can be either parasite or saprophyte; late summer to fall, upper montane ecosystems.

OBSERVATIONS *ostoyae:* honoring Paul Ostoya of the French Mycological Society. Clones of honey mushrooms, highly publicized as a "humongous fungus," inhabit acres of some forests. Species are generally difficult to tell apart. *Armillaria gallica* has a smooth cap, a thin hairy veil with or without yellow pigment, and an often swollen stalk base; it occurs in small scattered clusters on soil and woody debris. *Armillaria mellea* has a distinctly yellowish, smooth cap; a thick, white ring, often with a yellow margin; and a tapered stalk base; it occurs on deciduous stumps and occasionally on conifers in eastern North America.

Collectors should be wary of the deadly *Galerina autumnalis.* It also has a ring and grows in small clusters on wood, but its fruiting bodies are more delicate, and it has brown gills and spores.

ORDER
Agaricales
FAMILY
Tricholomataceae
EDIBILITY
Edible

Bright yellow, fading to pale yellow, scaly cap; yellow attached gills; stalk with shaggy white zones below yellowish cottony ring; in soil.

FRUITING BODIES **Cap** 4-17 cm broad; convex, becoming plano-convex; ground color straw-yellow with bright lemon yellow, shaggy scales in concentric zones; scales becoming tufted with age and finally fading somewhat in the sun to whitish; surface dry; margin incurved at first, decorated with yellow veil remnants. **Gills** adnate to notched, broad; margins ragged in age; light yellow, fading to pale lemon yellow, always lighter than cap color. **Stalk** 4-10 cm long x 1.5-2.5 cm thick; equal to bulbous at base; smooth and whitish above thick, yellow, floccose veil; thick yellow scales in concentric zones below. **Flesh** thick, white with yellow zone under cuticle; odor and taste mild.

SPORES White, 6-8 x 4-5 μm, elliptical, smooth, weakly amyloid.

ECOLOGY/FRUITING PATTERN Single to small groups; on soil in aspen and mixed conifer forests between 7,000 and 9,000 feet; quite common in central and southern Colorado and northern New Mexico; July into September.

OBSERVATIONS *straminea:* Latin for straw-colored. Also known as *Floccularia straminea*. Members of the genus *Armillaria* with amyloid spores and lacking black rhizomorphs have been transferred to the genus *Floccularia.*

   This variant was first described by Alexander Smith, visiting mycologist, and D. H. Mitchel of the Denver Botanic Gardens. At first glance the robust, yellow, scaly caps might remind one of a faded, yellowish *Amanita muscaria,* but the attached yellow gills and absence of a volva distinguish *Armillaria straminea. Armillaria albolanaripes* also has similar colors and fruits in the same habitats, but its cap is less scaly with cinnamon brown at the center, the gills are white to cream-colored, and the shaggy, white stalk appears sheathed.

ORDER	**Small, buff-colored**
Agaricales	**cap; pale decurrent**
FAMILY	**gills; rootlike threads**
Tricholomataceae	**at stalk base; in arcs,**
EDIBILITY	**near melting snow-**
Unknown	**banks in mountains.**

FRUITING BODIES Cap 2-5 cm wide, convex to depressed, undulating; pale buff to dingy tan; surface downy to water-marked. **Gills** pinkish buff, narrow, slightly decurrent. **Stalk** 2-5 cm long x 0.5-1.5 cm wide; fibrous; buff to whitish; base with white, root-like threads; ring absent. **Flesh** pale buff; odor and taste disagreeable.

SPORES White, 4.5-6 x 2.5-3.5 µm, elliptical, smooth, non-amyloid.

ECOLOGY/FRUITING PATTERN A montane species characteristic of Colorado's snowbank flora; common near recently receded snowbanks near Engelmann spruce; gregarious or in rings; June and July.

OBSERVATIONS *albirhiza:* Latin for white roots. The rootlike white threads, habitat, and growth habit are distinctive.

ORDER	**Funnel-shaped, buckskin**
Agaricales	**to pinkish-tan cap with**
FAMILY	**pale decurrent gills**
Tricholomataceae	**descending dry stalk;**
COMMON NAME	**veil absent; on soil.**
Funnel Cap	
EDIBILITY	
Not recommended	

FRUITING BODIES Cap 3-8 cm broad, depressed to funnel-shaped, smooth, dry; margin even to wavy; ochre-brown to pinkish tan. **Gills** crowded, at times forked; narrow, long decurrent; white to pale buff. **Stalk** 3-7 cm long x 0.5-1.5 cm wide; white to pale buff; usually lighter in color than cap; surface with fine longitudinal fibrils; dense white mycelium over base; ring absent. **Flesh** thin, whitish, no latex; faint odor of almonds, taste mild.

SPORES White in print, 5-8 x 3.5-5 µm, elliptical, smooth, non-amyloid.

ECOLOGY/FRUITING PATTERN Common in soil in small groups under conifers, hardwoods; montane habitats; July and August.

OBSERVATIONS *gibba:* Latin for irregularly rounded. Also known as *Clitocybe infundibuliformis.* A much larger variety, *Clitocybe gibba* var. *maxima,* attains huge sizes, up to 30 cm across.

ORDER
Agaricales
FAMILY
Tricholomataceae
EDIBILITY
Poisonous

Large crowded clusters of chalky white caps, often with wavy margins; attached white gills; dull white stalks; in disturbed ground.

FRUITING BODIES Cap 2-12 cm broad, convex, becoming flat with low broad knob; margin inrolled at first, in age undulating, often irregular from mutual pressure in cluster; chalky white to pale grayish, often faintly zonate or water-marked near margin; surface smooth, moist but not viscid. **Gills** whitish to buff, adnate to short decurrent, close, moderately broad. **Stalk** 4-14 cm long x 1-2 cm wide; central, often curved, equal; base often slightly enlarged; solid becoming hollow; surface slightly roughened; white with dingy gray-ochre stains; grown together at base at times; ring absent. **Flesh** thick, white, not staining; odor mild, taste slightly sour.

SPORES White in print, 4.5-6 x 3-3.5 μm, elliptical, smooth, non-amyloid.

ECOLOGY/FRUITING PATTERN Gregarious or in clusters of dozens of fruiting bodies in disturbed soil in the open, often along old roads; after rains in August and September; fairly common in the Rocky Mountains, the Pacific Northwest, and Alaska.

OBSERVATIONS *dilatata:* from *dilatus,* Latin for spread out. The densely clustered growth habit, the irregular spreading margins of the white caps, and the common locations along roadsides are all good field characters. *Clitocybe dilatata* is reported to contain the toxin muscarine. There are several smaller, pale-colored members of the genus *Clitocybe,* commonly occurring in groups in soil and grassy places, that have whitish stalks and close, fairly narrow, usually decurrent, whitish gills; they should not be eaten. An infamous one is *Clitocybe dealbata,* which contains the toxin muscarine. Because these small poisoners often grow near the edible *Marasmius oreades,* foragers should examine their finds carefully.

87

ORDER
Agaricales
FAMILY
Tricholomataceae
COMMON NAMES
The Blewit, Blue Hat
EDIBILITY
Edible

Large violet cap, fading
to pinkish brown with
age, with inrolled mar-
gins; violet attached gills;
sturdy violet stalk with
no ring; on ground.

FRUITING BODIES Cap medium-sized to large, 3–11 cm across, convex, flattening, edges inrolled until old age, then flaring somewhat; surface smooth, faintly viscid, finally dull and dry; lovely shades of violet-lavender when fresh, soon fading to pinkish cinnamon brown from center outward. **Gills** pale lavender, turning buff to brownish with age; narrow, crowded, attached, notched to rounded at stalk, slightly decurrent at times. **Stalk** relatively short and stocky, 3–6 cm long x 2–4 cm wide; equal or bulbous; ground color pale violet, bruising dull lavender, at maturity cinnamon brown from base upward; surface roughened, striated, with white mycelium at base; ring absent. **Flesh** dull lilac, fading to pallid; thick; soft and pliant; odor faintly fragrant, taste mild.

SPORES Pale pinkish buff in print, 5.5–8 x 3.5–5 μm, elliptical, slightly roughened, non-amyloid.

ECOLOGY/FRUITING PATTERN This beautiful mushroom is not common in any season in Colorado. Solitary to gregarious; sometimes clustered in humus and soil in rich composted areas, under trees on decaying vegetation, in yards, orchards; late summer and autumn. The specimens in the photo were found in Denver.

OBSERVATIONS *nuda:* meaning "nude" in Latin. *Clitocybe nuda* is also called *Lepista nuda*. The lavender colors, the absence of a partial veil, and the bulky shape of this popular mushroom are good field characters. Similarly shaped species of the genus *Cortinarius* have distinctly rusty spore prints and a partial veil present as a cobweblike cortina, and are usually found fruiting in mountain ecosystems.

ORDER
Agaricales
FAMILY
Tricholomataceae
EDIBILITY
Inedible

Tiny white cap; long,
slender, yellowish stalk
attached to round, nutlike
yellowish sclerotium;
in troops in rich humus,
wood, or old mush-
room remains.

FRUITING BODIES **Cap** 2-8 mm broad, convex with incurved margin when young, with very small umbo at times, becoming plano-convex; surface slightly fibrillose to hoary with age, margin striated; whitish to pinkish buff, fading to dirty white with age, disc remaining pale buff. **Gills** close to nearly distant, white to pinkish buff, narrow, adnate. **Stalk** 1-3.5 cm long x 1-1.5 mm wide; cylindrical, flexuous; thinly covered with branlike particles above, hairy near base with white rhizoids; pale tawny, whiter toward base; arising from ochre-yellow, finely hairy, nutlike sclerotium, roughly 0.5-1 cm in diameter; ring absent. **Flesh** very thin, pallid; no odor or taste.

SPORES White in print, 4.5-6 x 3-3.5 μm, short elliptical, smooth, non-amyloid.

ECOLOGY/FRUITING PATTERN Fruiting in small troops in rich humus, decayed wood, or blackened mushroom remains; in mixed aspen-conifer forests in montane and subalpine ecosystems; late July through September.

OBSERVATIONS *cookei:* named for mycologist M. C. Cooke. The presence of the little sclerotium is diagnostic but often missed unless the mushrooms are carefully extricated from the moss and debris in which the stalks are embedded. *Collybia tuberosa* is very similar in appearance and growth substrate, but its sclerotium resembles a red-brown apple seed. *Collybia cirrhata* is another look-alike growing on similar substrates, but it has no sclerotium.

ORDER
Agaricales
FAMILY
Tricholomataceae
EDIBILITY
Edible

Small, slippery, reddish brown cap; whitish attached gills; lined brown stalk with enlarged base; in needle duff under conifers.

FRUITING BODIES Cap 2-6 cm broad, broadly convex with margins incurved when young, becoming plane with low knob, margins at times eroded and flaring with age, often translucent-striated; surface smooth and buttery-feeling when young; dark reddish brown, fading to cinnamon brown. **Gills** adnexed to nearly free, close, moderately broad, edges wavy or becoming eroded at maturity; white, turning pale pinkish with age. **Stalk** equal to clavate, fibrous to brittle, soon hollow; 3-6 cm long x 0.5-1 cm wide; striated lengthwise; pinkish buff at first, honey-colored to cinnamon brown in age; downy white mycelium at base. **Flesh** pallid, soft; odor and taste mild.

SPORES Pale pinkish buff in print, 7-9 x 3.5-4.5 μm, smooth, elliptical, dextrinoid (red-brown) in Melzer's solution.

ECOLOGY/FRUITING PATTERN Gregarious or in small clusters in conifer litter in montane and subalpine ecosystems, typically near pine and spruce; widely distributed during moist weather in late summer and autumn, but not often common in Colorado.

OBSERVATIONS *butyracea:* buttery (Latin). The combination of its growth in conifer duff; the buttery feel of the young caps; the striated, club-shaped stalks; and the ragged gill edges are good field characters for recognizing *Collybia butyracea. Collybia dryophila* often looks similar, but it usually does not have striated, club-shaped stalks; its white to pale yellow spore prints lack pinkish tones; and the spores are non-amyloid in Melzer's solution.

ORDER
Agaricales
FAMILY
Tricholomataceae
EDIBILITY
Not recommended

Small to medium-sized, orange-brown cap fading to buff, with inrolled edge; pale stalk with white threads at base; on humus and wood, usually with pines.

FRUITING BODIES Cap 1–5 cm across; convex with inrolled margins in young, finally broadly convex to plane; smooth; surface moist; at times translucent-striated at margin; dark reddish brown when fresh, hygrophanous, fading to pale orangish brown. **Gills** adnexed to nearly free, close to crowded, moderately broad; creamy white to slightly yellow; edges straight, at times eroded with age. **Stalk** 3–8 cm long x 2–8 mm wide, base up to 10 mm wide; equal, at times enlarging to an abrupt basal bulb, often with white mycelial cords; surface smooth, faintly striated with age; stalk cream-colored above, soon darkening to color of cap; soon hollow; ring absent. **Flesh** whitish, thin; odor and taste mild.

SPORES Creamy white in print, 5.5–6.5 x 3–3.5 μm, elliptical, smooth, non-amyloid.

ECOLOGY/FRUITING PATTERN Widely distributed throughout the Rocky Mountain region. As the name implies, it occurs with oaks, but in Colorado, look for it mainly under pine and other conifers. Gregarious; occasionally clustered on humus or decayed wood; July through September.

OBSERVATIONS *dryophila:* means "oak-loving" in Greek. There are reports in the literature of poisonings from this mushroom; caution should be observed because some people are sensitive to it. *Collybia acervata* also occurs in Colorado and is similar, but its reddish brown fruiting bodies grow in compact bundles on rotting conifer wood and its flesh is bitter.

ORDER
Agaricales
FAMILY
Tricholomataceae
COMMON NAMES
Velvet Foot,
Winter Mushroom
EDIBILITY
Edible, a mushroom
of commerce

Orange-brown to yellowish sticky cap; whitish gills and white spores; stalk with dark brown, velvety surface; ring absent; growing in clusters on wood.

FRUITING BODIES Cap orange-brown to golden, paler yellowish near margin; 1.5–4 cm across; convex to nearly flat with age, margin incurved at first and often irregular with age; sticky smooth surface. **Gills** cream-colored to yellowish, adnate to adnexed, at times subdistant, broad. **Stalk** 2–6 cm long x 4–8 mm wide; distinctively colored yellow to tawny above, densely velvety brownish below; fibrous consistency, becoming hollow with age; ring absent; equal to slightly tapered toward base, often extended below into long blackish rhizomorph. **Flesh** white to yellowish, fairly firm; odor and taste mild.

SPORES White in print, 7–9 x 3–4 μm, elliptical, smooth, non-amyloid.

ECOLOGY/FRUITING PATTERN Saprophytic on dead aspen in the mountains and dead elms and other hardwoods in the cities; usually clustered, at times on buried wood; often abundant in Colorado and throughout the Rocky Mountain region; common during cool periods of spring, summer, and late fall, and even fruiting in winter in southern areas.

OBSERVATIONS *velutipes:* Latin for velvet foot. The gluten-covered caps and the stalks wrapped in velvet make this mushroom well equipped for chilly weather. The Velvet Foot is also known as Enokitake in Japan, where it is cultivated under light-free conditions so the dark velvety character of the stalk does not develop. This popular edible mushroom should not be mistaken in the wild for the deadly poisonous, wood-inhabiting *Galerina autumnalis,* which also has orange-brown caps but can be distinguished by its tawny gills, brown spores, and thin ring.

ORDER
Agaricales
FAMILY
Tricholomataceae
COMMON NAME
Plums and Custard
EDIBILITY
Edible

Cap and stalk yellow, covered by purplish red hairs; yellow gills and flesh; ring absent; on wood.

FRUITING BODIES **Cap** 2–12 cm across; broadly convex, becoming plane; margin initially incurved; surface dry, covered with purple-red fibrils above a yellow base color, fibrils denser over center, margins yellow. **Gills** pale yellow with roughened edges, notched at stem, crowded, broad. **Stalk** 3–8 cm long x 0.5–2 cm wide, equal, yellow with purple-red fibrils over surface, ring absent, base without mycelial threads. **Flesh** pale yellowish ochre, watery, thin; odor mild, taste mild to woody.

SPORES White in print, 5–8 x 4–5.5 µm, elliptical, smooth, non-amyloid.

ECOLOGY/FRUITING PATTERN Found in cool, moist weather growing on rotting conifer wood (especially spruce) in montane and subalpine regions; clustered or gregarious; August and September.

OBSERVATIONS *rutilans:* from *rutilus,* Latin for red or reddening. The wine-red coating of the cap contrasted with the yellow gills, and its growth on or near conifer logs and stumps, are good field characters for this attractive mushroom. *Tricholomopsis decora* is a similar conifer-wood lover, but the small scales and hairs covering the yellow-orange ground color of the cap and stalk are gray-brown, not purple-red.

ORDER
Agaricales

FAMILY
Tricholomataceae

EDIBILITY
Unknown

Medium-sized, smooth, flat, ochre to brownish cap; crowded, pale peach-colored gills; stalk pale brownish, tall and slim, enlarging toward base; ring absent; in soil.

FRUITING BODIES Cap 8–12 cm across; broadly convex to plane, often with broad knob, at times depressed; smooth; variably colored ochre-brown or darker; fading to buff or tan, but center darkening. **Gills** pale peach-colored to creamy ochre; crowded, finally broad, barely attached. **Stalk** 6–12 cm long x 1–1.5 cm wide; fibrous, enlarged at base with white mycelium; longitudinally striated from parallel lines, at times twisted; loose and stringy inside; colored about same as cap or paler, soon brown on base, staining ochre-brown upon injury; ring absent. **Flesh** white to buff; odor slightly rancid, taste bitter-astringent.

SPORES Cream-colored in print, 7–9 x 4.5–6 μm, elliptical, warts strongly amyloid.

ECOLOGY/FRUITING PATTERN Not common, but fruiting every season in subalpine ecosystems in moist locations near spruce, subalpine fir; July through August; on soil; scattered, at times gregarious.

OBSERVATIONS *cognata:* from *cognatus,* meaning "related" in Latin. This stately *Melanoleuca* is best recognized by the contrast between the brown fading cap and the lighter peach-colored, crowded, barely attached gills coupled with the often twisted-lined, straight stalk. Members of the genus have smooth, generally dark, usually knobbed caps that often fade in color; pale gills; stalks that are noticeably straight and narrow compared to the width of the caps; no veils; and amyloid spores. *Melanoleuca melaleuca* has a thin, flat, brown to dark brown, smooth cap; dingy white, wide gills; and a skinny, tan stalk.

Xeromphalina cauticinalis (Fries) Kühner and Maire

ORDER Agaricales	Tiny, bell-shaped, orange-brown
FAMILY Tricholomataceae	cap; yellow, decurrent, veined
EDIBILITY Inedible	gills; yellow-orange stalk with tawny hairs at base; among conifer debris.

FRUITING BODIES Cap 1–2 cm broad; convex, flattening, with center indentation; orange-brown, fading to ochraceous tawny, center darker. **Gills** pale yellow, narrow, decurrent, subdistant, veined. **Stalk** 2–5 cm long x 1–3 mm wide; pliant, cartilaginous, equal to small basal bulb; ochre above, red-brown below; orange-brown hairs at base. **Flesh** ochre; odor and taste mild.

SPORES White in print, 5.5–7 x 3–4 μm, elliptical, smooth, amyloid.

ECOLOGY/FRUITING PATTERN Gregarious; on ground among mosses and decayed conifer litter; summer and fall in montane and subalpine ecosystems.

OBSERVATIONS *cauticinalis:* from Latin *caulis,* pertaining to a stem. The similar-looking *Xeromphalina campanella* is sometimes common in the same habitats. It is distinguished by its caespitose growth, often by the hundreds, on rotten, usually moss-covered conifer stumps.

Lyophyllum montanum Smith

ORDER Agaricales	Silvery gray to dingy ochre cap;
FAMILY Tricholomataceae	drab gills; hoary stalk with thick
EDIBILITY Not recommended	basal mat; near conifers close to melting snow-banks.

FRUITING BODIES Cap 2–7 cm broad; convex, incurved margin, flattening, often knobbed; gray-ochre with silvery-hoary coating, smooth. **Gills** pale, drab to gray-brown, staining ashy gray; narrowly adnate, close, broad. **Stalk** 3–7 cm long x 1–1.5 cm wide, equal, deep brown with light gray-buff streaks, gray-white mycelial pad at base at maturity. **Flesh** dingy pallid; odor and taste mild.

SPORES White, 6.5–8 x 3.5–4 μm, smooth, elliptical, non-amyloid.

ECOLOGY/FRUITING PATTERN Single or grouped in soil near snowbanks and in subalpine forests after snow recedes; common in spring and early summer; near Engelmann spruce, subalpine fir.

OBSERVATIONS *montanum:* Latin for of the mountains. The hoary surfaces of *Lyophyllum montanum* adapt it to withstand the cold and intense sunlight of very high elevations. The fruiting bodies deteriorate gradually and change in appearance with age, so freshness is hard to judge. Eating *L. montanum* is not recommended.

ORDER
Agaricales
FAMILY
Tricholomataceae
EDIBILITY
Inedible

Fleshy, chalky-white, dry cap; crowded white gills; white, tough, fleshy stalk with white mycelial mat; ring absent; in soil near conifers.

FRUITING BODIES Cap 4-12 cm broad, convex, flattening somewhat, margin inrolled in young; smooth, dry and unpolished; pure white, creamy to pale tan over center. **Gills** white, drying pale buff; close, narrow, edges even; short decurrent, at maturity usually extending down stalk as lines or ridges forming a thin network; easily separable from flesh. **Stalk** 4-9 cm long x 1.5-3 cm thick; dry, chalky white; lower part covered with dense white mycelium that penetrates substrate; solid, equal, at times with basal bulb or spindle-shaped, tapering toward base; ring absent. **Flesh** thick in cap center; white, firm; odor mild to aromatic, taste disagreeable to bitter.

SPORES Pure white in print, 5-8 x 4.5-5 µm, elliptical, amyloid warts.

ECOLOGY/FRUITING PATTERN Common; fruiting in conifer litter that is often colored white from the spores; in montane areas with conifers; single to gregarious in arcs or fairy rings; July through August.

OBSERVATIONS *albissimus:* very white (*-issimus* means "superlative" in Latin). There are several varieties of this robust "whitest of white" mushroom, distinguished by slight differences in taste, color, and stalk shape. The variety pictured here is *Leucopaxillus albissimus* var. *piceinus,* distinguished by the fine network pattern of the gills as they descend down the stalk, the white to pale buff colors, and the enlarged to tapering stalk with white fibrils and mycelium at its base. *Leucopaxillus laterarius* has white caps often tinted pink, very bitter flesh, an odor of meal, and small round spores. Some species of *Clitocybe* may appear similar, but their spores are non-amyloid and their stalks do not exhibit the dense mycelium that spreads into the substrate.

ORDER
Agaricales
FAMILY
Tricholomataceae
EDIBILITY
Inedible

Medium-sized, dry, red-brown cap; white gills; thick white stalk with copious mycelium clinging to base; very bitter taste.

FRUITING BODIES **Cap** 4–10 cm broad; convex to plano-convex, margins inrolled; dark reddish cinnamon, usually paler on margins; surface dry, suedelike, cracking at times. **Gills** white to creamy; close, narrow; notched, at times with faint decurrent line; easily separable from flesh. **Stalk** 4–8 cm long x 1–3 cm wide; equal to bulbous; dry; solid, becoming hollow; white to dingy brown over base; embedded in thick, white, cottony mat of mycelial threads, often in tufts at base; ring absent. **Flesh** very white, thick, firm; odor pungent, taste exceedingly bitter.

SPORES Pure white in print, 4.5–6 x 4–5 μm, almost round, amyloid warts.

ECOLOGY/FRUITING PATTERN Fairly common; fruiting singly to numerous on soil, under a variety of conifers in montane ecosystems; July through early September; widely distributed in the Rocky Mountains.

OBSERVATIONS *amarus:* Latin for bitter. *Leucopaxillus amarus* is also known as *Leucopaxillus gentianeus*. A number of variants have been described, separated by cap colors and size. Fruiting bodies of the white-spored genus *Leucopaxillus* often superficially resemble those of the brown-spored genus *Paxillus*. In both, the narrow gills easily separate from the flesh, providing a good field test for these two unrelated genera.

ORDER
Agaricales
FAMILY
Tricholomataceae
COMMON NAMES
Fairy Ring Mushroom,
Scotch Bonnet,
Tough Shanks
EDIBILITY
Edible, but not in large
quantities

**Pale tan cap, often with
hump; widely spaced,
pale gills; straight tough
stalk; ring absent; com-
mon in grass in rings.**

FRUITING BODIES Cap 1–5 cm broad; bell-shaped
to broadly convex, often with low knob; margin
uplifted with age; smooth; varying from tawny to
reddish tan, fading to pale buff in strong light;
reviving when remoistened. **Gills** broad, adnate to
almost free, widely spaced, unequal in length, pale
yellowish tan. **Stalk** tough, not easily broken when
pulled lengthwise; 3–8 cm long x 3–5 mm across;
wider at base; minutely hairy, especially near base;
pinkish tan; ring absent. **Flesh** off-white, firm; odor
faintly almond, taste mild.

SPORES Creamy white in print, 7–10 x 3.5–6 μm,
elliptical, smooth, non-amyloid.

ECOLOGY/FRUITING PATTERN A very common
saprophyte; gregarious to clustered in grassy places
in cities, foothills, and prairies; from May to
September; fruiting bodies revive after moisture; usually in the form of
fairy rings, much to the annoyance of the caretaker of the perfect lawn.

OBSERVATIONS *oreades*: Greek, pertaining to mountain fairies or
nymphs. Fairy rings are manifestations of the outward growth of
mycelium in ever-increasing circles, fruitings of mushrooms appearing
on the periphery. The mycelial growth dries out the soil and kills the
grass. When the grass regrows, it often comes in greener than before.
Although many other mushrooms produce fairy rings, the fruitings of
grass lovers like *Marasmius oreades* are more obvious because little
obstructs the visibility of their rings. Before the fungal connection was
understood, the rings were believed to be magical places where fairies
danced or dragons breathed their fire.

The caps of *Marasmius oreades* are edible, even though they contain tiny amounts of hydrocyanic acid, as do almonds and some other
mushrooms. However, they should always be cooked and should not be
eaten frequently.

ORDER
Agaricales
FAMILY
Tricholomataceae
EDIBILITY
Inedible

Very tiny, dull white, flat cap; pale gills very widely spaced; very slender, long, flexible stalk; in troops on conifer needles; garlic odor in mass when fresh.

FRUITING BODIES
Cap very small, 1–3 mm across; convex often with tiny depression or dimple at maturity, faintly striated; dry; dull white, often brownish pink at center. **Gills** adnate to adnexed, moderately broad, distinctly widely spaced, white. **Stalk** long and threadlike, fairly firm; 1–2.5 cm long x less than 1 mm wide; light yellowish to pale red-brown; smooth to downy; attached directly to substrate (usually a spruce needle); basal mycelium lacking; ring absent. **Flesh** extremely thin, pallid; crushed flesh smells of garlic, taste faintly garlic.

SPORES White in print, 8–11.5 x 2.5–4 µm, narrowly elliptical, smooth, non-amyloid.

ECOLOGY/FRUITING PATTERN Often fruiting by the hundreds, each tiny mushroom attached to a conifer needle; late summer and fall, subalpine ecosystems. Even though the fruiting bodies are small, the mycelia are likely to be every bit as large and as important to the recycling process in forests as those fungi with larger, more noticeable fruiting bodies.

OBSERVATIONS *thujinus:* pertaining to *Thuja*, a type of coniferous tree. Mycologist C. H. Kauffman, who collected in this region in the early 1900s, named it *Marasmius piceina* because he found it growing on *Picea* (spruce) needles in the Rocky Mountains, but it was later determined to be the same as *Marasmius thujinus*, an older name. The garlic odor coming from hundreds of tiny wheels of these delicate fungi can best be detected after a spruce forest has received a good soaking from a late summer rain. Species of *Marasmius* characteristically revive when rehydrated; in this species, the garlic odor revives somewhat too.

ORDER
Agaricales
FAMILY
Tricholomataceae
EDIBILITY
Inedible

Small, sharply conical, dull red-brown, scalloped cap; pale pinkish gills; stalk pinkish, hairy base bleeds drop of red juice when cut; on wood, usually clustered.

FRUITING BODIES **Cap** 1–3 cm across, conical with distinctive sharp, pointed top; margin very thin and finely scalloped; brownish pink to rose-buff, center red-brown; surface at first frosted-looking, soon polished and appearing moist, translucent-striated. **Gills** whitish to very pale pinkish, edges same color as faces; staining bloodred near cuticle; narrowly adnate, close to subdistant, many do not reach stalk. **Stalk** 3–6 cm long x 1.5–2.5 mm thick; equal; pale pinkish above, vinaceous brown below; surface powdery above, densely hairy where base attaches to substrate; whitish hairs becoming red-brown; base exudes drop of bloodred juice when cut; ring absent. **Flesh** extremely thin and fragile; pinkish brown, staining bloodred when cut; odor mild, taste slightly bitter.

SPORES White in print, 8–11 x 5–7 μm, elliptical, smooth, amyloid.

ECOLOGY/FRUITING PATTERN Single to clustered on decaying aspen wood; July through August; montane to subalpine ecosystems; can be common in its limited habitat.

OBSERVATIONS *haematopus:* means "bloody stalk" in Latin. This beautiful little variant with its "cuspid," or very sharply pointed, caps is found quite commonly in the vicinity of the Snowmass Creek and the Frying Pan River drainages in Pitkin County, and perhaps elsewhere in the Rocky Mountain region. *Mycena haematopus* and its variants are some of the most easily recognized in the genus, characterized by their dull red colors, habitat on wood, scalloped cap margins, and the bloodred juice exuded when they are injured.

ORDER
Agaricales
FAMILY
Tricholomataceae
EDIBILITY
Not recommended

Small, grayish brown cap, at times bell-shaped; grayish gills; hairy lower stalk; clustered on rotting conifer logs, often under snow in late spring or summer at high elevations.

FRUITING BODIES Cap 1.5–4 cm broad, conical to obtusely knobbed, at times remaining bell-shaped; viscid, smooth surface with obvious striations at margins; color variable, dark to pale brownish gray to almost bluish gray. **Gills** white, staining grayish when bruised; adnate to slightly decurrent, broad, subdistant. **Stalk** 3–9 cm long x 2–4 mm wide; hollow; often curved; pallid to gray above, pale red-brown toward thickened base; dry; basal area with distinctive covering of dense white hairs; stalks often grown together, more or less rooted in woody substrate. **Flesh** very thin, watery, pallid gray; odor and taste mild.

SPORES Whitish to slightly creamy in print, 5.5–7.5 x 3.5–4 µm, smooth, elliptical, amyloid.

ECOLOGY/FRUITING PATTERN Fruiting in large clusters on rotting conifer logs and stumps in spring and early summer in montane and subalpine regions of Colorado, where it is known locally as a prominent member of the snowbank flora; fairly common.

OBSERVATIONS *overholtsii:* honoring American mycologist L. O. Overholts. Overholts, an expert in polypores from Pennsylvania, came to Colorado to collect in the 1920s. No doubt he found this interesting *Mycena* as he collected near Tolland west of Boulder and in the mountainous areas west of Denver. Later, A. H. Smith, Michigan mycologist and specialist in western mushrooms, and W. G. Solheim, University of Wyoming mycologist, named this mushroom in honor of their colleague.

ORDER
Agaricales
FAMILY
Tricholomataceae
EDIBILITY
Poisonous

Small, purple to pink-ish gray, striated cap; colors variable, fading; gills pale lilac; stalk pale grayish lavender, veil absent; on ground; radishlike odor.

FRUITING BODIES **Cap** 2–4 cm across, broadly conical or flattened, often knobbed; moist, smooth, striated; colors variable and fading: purple, lilac-gray, rosy gray, to pallid. **Gills** broad, subdistant; color variable as in caps, usually pinkish to lilac-gray, edges whitish. **Stalk** equal or enlarged below; 3–6 cm long x 2–5 mm wide; color pallid or same as cap; dry, smooth, without hairs, sometimes with twisted, longitudinal lines; ring absent. **Flesh** moderately thin, pale lilac to gray; odor and taste distinctly radishlike.

SPORES White in print, 6–9 x 3–3.5 μm, elliptical, smooth, amyloid.

ECOLOGY/FRUITING PATTERN Scattered on the ground in conifer and hardwood litter; quite common and widely distributed in montane and subalpine regions; summer and early fall in cool, moist conditions.

OBSERVATIONS *pura:* Latin for clean or pure. The distinctive characters of *Mycena pura* are its variable lilac colors, whitish to pinkish gills, radish smell, and amyloid spores. There is a complex of color variants of *M. pura,* those found in Colorado usually showing dark purple colors before fading to lilac-gray. Because this common *Mycena* may contain the toxin muscarine, it should not be eaten.

ORDER
Agaricales
FAMILY
Tricholomataceae
EDIBILITY
Unknown

Small, rusty orange-brown, granular/warty cap; white attached gills; orange-brown, scaly stalk; thin, flaky ring; in soil.

FRUITING BODIES **Cap** 1–4 cm, convex to plane; surface granular/warty; rusty orange-brown to red-brown, often bleached; margin whitish from veil. **Gills** white, broad, notched, close. **Stalk** enlarged slightly toward base, 2–5 cm long x 3–6 mm wide; smooth; white above ring, orange-brown and granular below; granular coating sheathlike, white floccose ring soon vanishing. **Flesh** white; odor and taste mild.

SPORES White, 3.5–5 x 2.5–3 μm, short elliptical, non-amyloid.

ECOLOGY/FRUITING PATTERN Small groups in soil, conifer litter; subalpine to montane habitats; summer, fall; fairly common.

OBSERVATIONS *granulosum:* granular, referring to cap surface. *Cystoderma fallax,* with a well-defined membranous ring, a granular cap typical of the genus, and amyloid spores, is common under conifers. *Cystoderma amianthinum* and its varieties have large, tawny to ochre, granular caps; floccose rings; and amyloid spores.

ORDER
Agaricales

FAMILY
Tricholomataceae

COMMON NAME
Sand Mushroom

EDIBILITY
Edible

Dingy pinkish brown caps with whitish, wavy margins; white stalks and gills, staining red-brown; densely clustered in loose, sandy soil under cottonwood trees; late fall.

FRUITING BODIES Cap 3–12 cm broad; broadly conical, some with low knob, at maturity margins flaring and irregular; surface slightly sticky-moist, allowing debris and sand to cling; dingy reddish brown, marginal areas whitish, colors streaky. **Gills** white, staining red-brown; close, moderately narrow, notched, edges even. **Stalk** solid and stocky, equal to clavate; 5–7 cm long x 1.5–3 cm wide; white, staining rusty; smooth; ring absent. **Flesh** solid, thick, very white; odor and taste of fresh meal.

SPORES Pure white in print, 5–6.5 x 3.5–4 μm, elliptical, smooth, non-amyloid.

ECOLOGY/FRUITING PATTERN Fruiting in large clusters and rings; mycorrhizal with poplars; in the Rockies found under cottonwood or rarely aspen; October and November. In Colorado's prairies where cottonwoods are the dominant tree, these mushrooms are often abundant in the fall, usually half-buried under fallen leaves in loose, sandy soil in dried-up creekbeds.

OBSERVATIONS *populinum:* of poplars (Latin). This mushroom is reported to have been a favorite food of some Native Americans, who probably had to compete with foraging mule deer for it. The deer paw through the dense cottonwood litter for this mushroom treat and pay no attention to the difficult-to-remove sand. Identification of this fairly large *Tricholoma* is not difficult if you remember the habitat requirement. All red-brown *Tricholoma* species with sticky caps not growing under poplars (aspens or cottonwoods in the West) should be avoided, particularly a poisonous look-alike, *Tricholoma pessundatum,* which grows under conifers.

ORDER
Agaricales
FAMILY
Tricholomataceae
EDIBILITY
Edible

Medium-sized, lemon yellow, sticky cap with reddish brown center at maturity; notched, sulfur-yellow gills; pale yellow to whitish stalk; in soil under pines.

FRUITING BODIES Cap 4–10 cm broad, broadly conical in young, flattening at maturity, often with low, broad center hump; bright yellow, especially in young still protected under needle debris, finally with tawny reddish brown streaking over center (but not as radiating dark fibrils); marginal area remains yellow; surface sticky, soon dry and slightly scaly at center; cuticle peelable. **Gills** bright medium yellow, evenly colored, not staining; notched to nearly free; broad, close. **Stalk** 3–6 cm long x 1–2 cm wide; pale to light yellow; solid, equal; surface dry, without ring or cortina. **Flesh** white to yellowish under skin; thick, solid, not staining; odor and taste mild, of fresh meal.

SPORES White in print, 6–7.5 x 4–5 μm, elliptical, smooth, non-amyloid.

ECOLOGY/FRUITING PATTERN Gregarious, mycorrhizal with lodgepole pine in Colorado, also found with aspen; montane and lower subalpine ecosystems; quite common in mid-August through September.

OBSERVATIONS *flavovirens:* Latin *flavus* means "yellow"; *virens* means "becoming green." *Tricholoma flavovirens* is distinguished by its yellow, sticky, young caps, which finally develop tawny to brownish centers, and its yellow notched gills. Other *Tricholoma*s fruiting in Colorado in late summer and fall have similar statures, some yellowish colors, and also lack veils. *Tricholoma sejunctum* has blackish fibrils on a more conical cap center and whitish gills with yellow only near the cap margins. *Tricholoma leucophyllum* has distinctive white gills and brownish cap centers with pale yellow elsewhere. *Tricholoma sulphureum* has an offensive odor; dry, duller yellow caps; and yellow flesh. *Tricholoma flavovirens* looks somewhat like certain species of *Cortinarius,* which may also have bright yellow and orangish sticky caps and grow out of the duff under conifers, but the latter have cortinas and rusty-colored spores.

ORDER
Agaricales
FAMILY
Tricholomataceae
EDIBILITY
Poisonous

**Medium-sized to large,
olive-gray cap with olive-
yellow margins; center
humped and darker;
whitish to pale yellow,
adnexed gills; sturdy
white stalk without ring;
soapy odor.**

FRUITING BODIES **Cap** 3–8 cm across, convex, often with broad hump, edges expanding and often wavy; color variable, olive: yellowish gray, deep olive-brown, or bronze, usually lighter and yellowish toward margin; surface not viscid. **Gills** attached, notched; pallid to creamy yellowish; broad, close, sometimes with ragged edges. **Stalk** 4–9 cm long x 2–3 cm wide; usually wider in middle, tapering toward base, often deeply rooting; minutely scaly or smooth; chalky white or flushed with olive-gray streaks, distinctively dull pinkish orange near base when injured; ring absent. **Flesh** thick; white, staining pinkish, particularly at larvae tunnels; odor variable, from pungent to reminiscent of laundry soap; taste unpleasant to bitter-mealy.

SPORES White in print, 5–6 x 3.5–4 µm, short elliptical, smooth, non-amyloid.

ECOLOGY/FRUITING PATTERN June to September; quite commonly gregarious under spruce and fir in subalpine ecosystems in well-drained soil; a mycorrhiza-former, most often associated with Engelmann spruce in Colorado.

OBSERVATIONS *saponaceum:* soapy in Latin. This common *Tricholoma* has varying appearances and odors depending probably on environment and age; however, the yellowish olive cap colors, pinkish orange staining of the stalk base, and the peculiar odor are good field characters. The collections of *Tricholoma saponaceum* I find in Colorado usually have very pale yellowish gill colors, another variable feature according to the literature. *Tricholoma sejunctum* is similar, but it usually has a more slender stalk and lacks the pinkish staining. It also has blackish to brown fibrils on the cap center, a sticky cap surface, and whitish gills with yellow colors near the margin of the cap.

ORDER
Agaricales
FAMILY
Tricholomataceae
EDIBILITY
Not recommended

**Reddish brown cap
streaked with radiating,
flattened hairs; margins
whitish and cottony in
young; hairy, red-brown
stalk; notched, whitish
gills staining red-
brown; in soil.**

FRUITING BODIES Cap 3–7 cm across, conical to convex, becoming nearly flat with low hump with age; radially arranged tufts of bright red-brown to brownish orange fibrils above buff-colored flesh create distinctive cap pattern; surface dry, scaly; margins inrolled, whitish; cottony partial veil remnants in young leave whitish hairs hanging over margin. **Gills** attached (sinuate); whitish, flecked red-brown at injury or with age; often powdered white from spores; close, broad. **Stalk** cylindrical, tapered at base; 5–10 cm long x 1–1.5 cm wide; often becoming hollow; dry, finally shaggy-fibrillose; at first pale buff but soon colored like cap, apex lighter, remaining pinkish buff; ring absent. **Flesh** soft, white to pinkish buff, slowly staining reddish brown where injured or with age; odor distinct but hard to describe, often like fresh meal but pungent; taste like fresh meal to bitter.

SPORES White in print, 6–7.5 x 4–5 μm, rounded oval, smooth, non-amyloid.

ECOLOGY/FRUITING PATTERN In sometimes large clumps or scattered to gregarious in soil; mycorrhizal with spruce and/or pine; widely distributed; one of the most common *Tricholoma*s, occurring in July to September in mixed conifer forests of upper montane and subalpine ecosystems.

OBSERVATIONS *vaccinum:* pertaining to cows (Latin). The very similar *Tricholoma imbricatum* shares the conifer habitat, but can be differentiated by its coarser, more robust appearance; a similarly colored but much less scaly cap; a solid, not hollow stalk; and the absence of the cottony veil visible in young caps of *Tricholoma vaccinum.*

ORDER
Agaricales
FAMILY
Tricholomataceae
EDIBILITY
Reported edible,
not recommended

Medium-sized, orange-brown, sticky cap; white notched gills; membranous, white partial veil on orange-brown, tapering stalk; usually under pines.

FRUITING BODIES Cap 4–12 cm broad; convex, nearly plane at maturity, with broad knob; colors varying and streaked from bright orange-brown to yellowish orange with olive tones, margins lighter; sticky-slimy when wet, finally varnished; scaly with age. **Gills** attached to notched, at times slightly decurrent; pallid whitish, staining rusty; close, finally broad. **Stalk** solid, 4–11 cm long x 1–3 cm wide; narrowing toward base; white, membranous partial veil first covers gills, later forms flaring or ragged ring near top of stalk; white above ring, below sheathlike, scaly-fibrillose, often in orange-brown zones. **Flesh** thick over stalk, solid; white, staining pale rusty; odor unpleasantly farinaceous (mealy), taste somewhat metallic.

SPORES White, 4.5–5 x 3.5–4 μm, smooth, elliptical, non-amyloid.

ECOLOGY/FRUITING PATTERN Common in montane and lower subalpine ecosystems under lodgepole pine and aspen; fruiting in mid-July through September; scattered to gregarious; often deeply rooted under pine needles.

OBSERVATIONS *zelleri:* in honor of S. M. Zeller, American mycologist. Although previously known as *Armillaria zelleri* and more recently called *Tricholoma focale,* the fruiting bodies themselves are quite consistent in spite of what we call them. *Tricholoma zelleri* is most commonly found in the fall by Matsutake *(Tricholoma magnivelare)* hunters, who head expectantly toward the little humps in the pine duff, only to be disappointed by the rank odor and orangish caps of *T. zelleri.* In its own right, however, it is an important member of the western mycoflora.

ORDER
Agaricales
FAMILY
Tricholomataceae
COMMON NAMES
White Matsutake,
Pine Mushroom
EDIBILITY
Edible, choice

Large, white cap streaked with cinnamon; white adnate gills; tapered white to cinnamon-streaked stalk with prominent flaring ring; odor spicy and memorable; in soil under pines; autumn.

FRUITING BODIES Cap 4–12 cm broad; convex, flattening to plane; shallow-dished with age; margin inrolled in young, at times with fine cottony veil remnants; sticky when young, soon dry; ivory white, usually streaked with cinnamon. **Gills** adnate, narrow, crowded; white, staining cinnamon with age; at first hidden by white veil. **Stalk** sturdy, 4–10 cm long x 2–3 cm wide; tapering to narrow base embedded in conifer duff; sheathed with soft cottony veil, leaving prominent, white, flaring, superior ring; white above, streaked cinnamon below ring. **Flesh** firm, white, not staining when cut; odor distinctly fresh-spicy and memorable, taste mild.

SPORES White in print, 5–7 x 4.5–5.5 μm, nearly round to broadly elliptical, smooth, non-amyloid.

ECOLOGY/FRUITING PATTERN During a short season in late August through September, these mycorrhizal associates commonly fruit singly to scattered under lodgepole pine in montane ecosystems, usually between 8,000 and 9,500 feet. Without late summer moisture, they are often scarce.

OBSERVATIONS *magnivelare:* Latin for large-veiled. Formerly known as *Armillaria ponderosa*, this very popular edible mushroom is favored by local residents of Asian ancestry who remember the adage, "The nose knows," and identify it mainly by its characteristic odor. The large veil, its pine habitat, its habit of pushing up the pine needles as it develops from the soil below, and its late fruiting season are important field characters. A close relative, *Tricholoma caligatum*, has darker cinnamon brown cap scales and brown zones of veil remnants sheathing the stalk. Its odor may be pungent, fragrant, or mild.

Matsutake gatherers should become familiar with the dangerous genus *Amanita*. The poisonous *Amanita smithiana* has been confused with *Tricholoma magnivelare*.

ORDER
Agaricales
FAMILY
Tricholomataceae
EDIBILITY
Edible but tough

Heavy, large, off-white to grayish, dry cap; decurrent white gills; thick tapered stalk with double veil; in summer and fall under conifers.

FRUITING BODIES Cap 8-18 cm broad; broadly convex to plane at maturity, margins even; dull white to pallid, becoming pale grayish ochre; not sticky when young. **Gills** narrow, broader with age, close, decurrent; dull white to buff, not staining. **Stalk** 6-14 cm long x 3-7 cm across; enlarged in middle, tapering downward; bulky, solid; distinctive double membranous veil; upper ring of veil white and striated, lower ring dingy ochre and sheathing stalk; stalk sunken in soil and dingy ochre to brownish. **Flesh** thick and hard, white, not staining; odor strongly farinaceous, taste disagreeable.

SPORES White in print, 9-12 x 4-5 µm, distinctly elongated, elliptical, smooth, amyloid.

ECOLOGY/FRUITING PATTERN Often solitary to two or three together; deep in soil under conifers; montane and subalpine ecosystems; August and September.

OBSERVATIONS *ventricosa:* Latin for swollen in the middle. An even larger look-alike is known in Colorado: *Catathelasma imperiale* can be up to 35 cm across; its caps are dark brown when young, with very hard flesh, and it has a tapering stalk and a double membranous veil. Both *Catathelasma* species can be distinguished from the White Matsutake, *Tricholoma magnivelare,* by their very hard flesh, decurrent gills, double veils, and lack of a pleasant, spicy odor.

ORDER
Agaricales
FAMILY
Tricholomataceae
EDIBILITY
Edible

Orange-brown, dry cap, fading to buff; widely spaced, attached pinkish gills; orange-brown, fibrous stalk with no ring; white spore print; in soil.

FRUITING BODIES Cap 1–4.5 cm broad; convex to plane, often depressed; orange-brown, fading to pinkish buff; center often darker brown-orange; dry, smooth, then finely scaly from breaking of cuticle; often striated; margin ragged at maturity. **Gills** pinkish flesh color, becoming powdery from spores; broad, thick, close to distant; adnate to short decurrent. **Stalk** 2–6.5 cm long x 5–8 mm wide; equal, occasionally slightly bulbous; fibrous, not fragile; same color as cap; fibrillose, at times longitudinally; dense white mycelium at base; ring absent. **Flesh** thin, pale orange-brown; odor pungent, taste mild.

SPORES White in print, 7.5–10 x 7–10 µm, globose to subglobose, spiny, non-amyloid.

ECOLOGY/FRUITING PATTERN Very common, sometimes abundant, usually associated with conifers throughout the summer and fall; single to gregarious in a variety of habitats, but always on the ground.

OBSERVATIONS *laccata:* from Persian word for lacquer or painted. *Laccaria nobilis,* first described from specimens found at high elevations in Colorado, is similarly colored, but is larger with distinctly scaly, deeply depressed, nonstriated caps and large, scaly, longitudinally striated stalks. *Laccaria bicolor* has lilac-tinged gills and copious lilac mycelium at the stalk base.

    Laccaria montana Singer (shown at left) has colors similar to *Laccaria laccata* and white mycelium at its base, but the former is a delicate alpine species with large spores (9–10.5 x 8–10.5 µm, round, spiny, on four-spored basidia). It is found at high elevations in Colorado under conifers or willows.

The Brown-Rotting Gilled Fungi

In spite of their superficial resemblance to members of the Tricholomataceae family, several genera traditionally included in that family have been placed by contemporary mycologists into the Polyporaceae family. Members of these select genera have gills and produce light-colored spores, but are distinguished by having enzyme systems that decay wood by producing a brown rot, leaving a residue beneficial to the forest soil. In recent years, strong emphasis has been placed on environmentally significant taxonomic characters, such as the nature of the rot produced.

Like polypores, the following five species grow on wood and have long-lived fruiting bodies that often dry up rather than decay. The genera featured here include *Heliocybe* and *Neolentinus* (formerly *Lentinus*, pp. 111–112), *Phyllotopsis* (p. 113), and *Pleurotus* (pp. 114–115). These brown-rot fungi play a significant role in nature by recycling deadwood in forest and riparian habitats.

Heliocybe sulcata (Berkeley) Redhead and Ginns

ORDER
Aphyllophorales
FAMILY
Polyporaceae
EDIBILITY
Unknown

Small, furrowed, orange-brown, scaly cap; white saw-toothed gills; short, whitish stalk with no ring; on old wood, usually aspen.

FRUITING BODIES Cap 1–4 cm broad; convex to plane; entire cap conspicuously furrowed; orange-brown, center darker brown; dry, with dark brown, radiating scales. **Gills** whitish, close, moderately broad, adnexed to adnate, edges saw-toothed at maturity. **Stalk** 1–3 cm long x 2–5 mm wide, solid, equal, pinkish tan, scaly near base. **Flesh** white, very firm; odor and taste mild.

SPORES White in print, 11–16 x 5–7 μm, bean-shaped, smooth, non-amyloid.

ECOLOGY/FRUITING PATTERN Solitary or a few together; fairly common growing on dry, decorticated logs, especially aspen, in dry sites in montane ecosystems; June through September; produces a brown rot in wood. Look for it in avalanche areas where many aspens are down and decaying.

OBSERVATIONS *sulcata: sulcate* means "furrowed" in Latin. The name *Heliocybe* refers to its radially symmetrical caps and scales. This species is also known as *Lentinus sulcatus,* but it has been segregated from *Lentinus* because of its brown-rotting characteristics. In recent years, greater taxonomic emphasis has been placed on the type of rot produced by wood-decaying fungi.

ORDER
Aphyllophorales

FAMILY
Polyporaceae

EDIBILITY
Edible when young

Very large, firm, scaly, tan cap; gills saw-toothed, whitish, staining rusty; ring absent; tough stalk rooting in dead conifer wood.

FRUITING BODIES Cap 10–30 cm across; convex, becoming plano-convex, often with depressed center; dry, cinnamon brown to yellowish tan cuticle breaking up into broad, flattened, often concentric scales, pinkish buff flesh in between. **Gills** whitish to pale buff, finally pale yellow-orange; adnate to slightly decurrent, close, narrow, edges serrated at maturity. **Stalk** 3–10 cm long x 3–7 cm wide; central to off-center; tough; narrowed toward base, often rooted in substrate; finely scaly; apex pale buff, below scattered with cinnamon scales; basal area dark reddish brown; no partial veil or ring. **Flesh** not decaying readily, thick, tough, white; odor fragrant to mild, taste mild.

SPORES Off-white to buff in print, 8–11 x 3.5–4.5 μm, elliptical, smooth, non-amyloid.

ECOLOGY/FRUITING PATTERN Solitary or in groups on or near dead conifer wood, especially pine; fairly common in montane ecosystems; early summer through August. Among the many recyclers of deadwood, it causes a brown rot.

OBSERVATIONS *ponderosus:* Latin for heavy. Also known as *Lentinus ponderosus,* this large, robust species has been found only in western North America. The fruiting bodies last a long time, drying rather than rotting. A somewhat smaller relative, *Neolentinus lepideus,* previously called *Lentinus lepideus,* also causes brown rot in conifer wood and has serrated gills, but its occurrence is more widespread. It has a partial veil that fringes the cap edge; recurved scales on the cap; a membranous, flaring, pallid ring at the apex of the stalk; and subdistant gills.

ORDER
Aphyllophorales

FAMILY
Polyporaceae

EDIBILITY
Inedible

Clusters of bright orange, very hairy, dry caps; attached to wood without stalks; bright orange gills; nauseous, disagreeable odor.

FRUITING BODIES Caps 2–8 cm across, fan-shaped, often connected in clusters or shelving masses; convex, with margins inrolled at first; deep orange, fading to pale orange; dry, densely hairy. **Gills** brilliant orange; fanning out from center point of attachment to wood, moderately narrow, close. **Stalks** absent, veils lacking. **Flesh** rather tough; deep orange just under cuticle, below paler; odor distinctly disagreeable to nauseous, at times like rotten eggs, sometimes milder; taste disagreeable.

SPORES Pinkish in print, fading in storage; 5.5–7 x 2–2.5 μm; cylindrical to sausage-shaped; smooth; non-amyloid.

ECOLOGY/FRUITING PATTERN Rather common in some seasons, late summer and early fall; growing as saprophytes on dead logs, forming a brown rot of conifer and deciduous (usually aspen) wood; moist montane and lower subalpine habitats.

OBSERVATIONS *nidulans:* Latin for nesting, because of the downy, nest-like caps. *Phyllotopsis nidulans* is easily identified by its strong smell, beautiful colors, and handsome gill pattern. Other genera of wood inhabiters that are usually sessile (lacking a stalk) occurring in the region are *Crepidotus,* with brown spores, and *Panellus,* with tough leathery caps and white to yellowish, amyloid spores.

ORDER
Aphyllophorales

FAMILY
Polyporaceae

COMMON NAME
Oyster Mushroom

EDIBILITY
Edible, choice when
harvested young

Large shelving groups of off-white to brownish gray, oyster shell–shaped caps; white to buff-colored, decurrent gills; short, hairy, whitish stalks (or none); on dead tree trunks or buried wood.

FRUITING BODIES **Caps** shelving; individuals 2.5–15 cm across, oval to oyster shell–shaped, nearly plane at maturity, often indented toward stalk; margin smooth, inrolled in young, later often striated or cracked; surface smooth; variable in color: off-white, creamy beige, pinkish brown, gray-brown, darker with age. **Gills** moderately broad, crowded, decurrent (unless stalk absent, then fanlike), with many short gills, often forking; white to pale creamy. **Stalk** short to practically absent, 1–3 cm long x 1–2 cm across; usually off-center, at times central, depending on angle of growth; tough, surface ridged and densely bristled; white; ring absent. **Flesh** solid, dull white, not staining; odor mild to aniselike in young, taste mild.

SPORES Whitish in light deposit, pale gray-lilac in heavier deposit; 7.5–10 x 3–4 µm; narrowly elliptical; smooth; non-amyloid.

ECOLOGY/FRUITING PATTERN A common saprophytic wood-rotter, usually on dead cottonwood or other deciduous wood; may fruit on buried or (rarely) live trees; sometimes in huge clusters at base of trees along country roads, stream and ditch banks, and in backyards and parks from the prairies into the foothills; less common in conifer plantings or forests, fruiting mainly on spruce and fir; during cool, moist weather in April through June and sometimes again in fall. The Oyster season in the Rockies is a long one. I have collected them from cottonwood in very chilly, late March weather in Wyoming. The Denver Botanic Gardens Herbarium of Fungi also has specimens that were found in Denver as late as December.

OBSERVATIONS *pulmonarius:* Latin, pertaining to lungs. Traditionally, this region's common Oyster Mushroom has been called *Pleurotus* *ostreatus,* but recent reports of mating studies indicate that *Pleurotus pulmonarius* is the name that should be used. *Pleurotus pulmonarius* occurs in the western United States in drier upland sites (much of the southern Rocky Mountain area), fruiting most commonly on deciduous trees in cool weather and occasionally conifers in early summer. The Oyster that occurs in the eastern United States and fruits in cool weather in riparian areas on deciduous trees is *P. ostreatus,* which is rare or absent in the western United States. The two species are difficult if not impossible to separate on field characters, but differences in their mating compatibility tests, seasonal fruiting, distribution, and host ranges distinguish them.

A synonym, *Pleurotus sapidus,* was formerly used for the Oyster Mushroom having lilac spores and occurring on a wide range of deciduous hosts in the Rockies; however, its distinctions did not hold up in mating studies.

Pleurotus populinus Hilber and Miller

Pleurotus populinus (above) is very similar to *Pleurotus pulmonarius,* differing mainly by the following characteristics:

COMMON NAME
Oyster Mushroom
EDIBILITY
Edible

FRUITING BODIES Caps ivory white to pinkish gray, lacking strong brown colors. **Gills** generally more separated.

SPORES Whitish to pale buff (not lilac) in print; longer, 9–12 x 3–5 μm.

ECOLOGY/FRUITING PATTERN On aspens in Colorado and both aspen and black cottonwoods in other montane and northern regions of the western United States.

OBSERVATIONS *populinus:* Latin for poplar trees. From all reports, this species is also very savory when young, often smelling of anise. This is a strictly northern species; in the Rocky Mountain region, it is the high-country aspen-loving Oyster. The whitish to pale buff spore print and aspen habitat are the best distinguishing features.

Family Entolomataceae and Family Plutaceae

The pink-spored, gilled mushrooms are grouped mainly into two families, Entolomataceae and Plutaceae, members of which have spore prints ranging from dull pink to reddish ochre to salmon-colored to pinkish brown. They are distinguished by a combination of features:

KEY TO FAMILIES

Entolomataceae Gills attached, spores angular or longitudinally striated, volva absent, growing on ground, p. 116.

Plutaceae Gills free, spores smooth, volva present or not, growing on wood, p. 117.

Entolomataceae is a large family of mostly woodland mushrooms with several genera. There are some dangerously poisonous species, particularly in the genus *Entoloma;* therefore none is recommended here as edible. Only one genus, *Entoloma,* is featured in this book.

Plutaceae is a small lignicolous family of two main genera: *Pluteus* (lacking a volva) and *Volvariella* (with a volva).

E n t o l o m a   l i v i d o a l b u m group (Kühner and Romagnesi) Kubicka

ORDER
Agaricales
FAMILY
Entolomataceae
EDIBILITY
Poisonous

Medium-sized to large, yellow-brown, smooth cap; white, then pink, attached gills; white, solid stalk; pink spore print; in soil.

FRUITING BODIES Cap 4–9 cm across; convex, broadening, often with low knob; margin undulating at maturity; smooth, faintly striated at times; yellow-brown, fading slightly. **Gills** white, becoming pink; attached, broad, subdistant. **Stalk** solid; white; 4–10 cm long x 1–2.5 cm wide, equal to slightly thicker in middle; distinctly striated longitudinally; ring absent. **Flesh** pallid, fairly thick; odor and taste strongly farinaceous.

SPORES Pink in print, 7–11.5 x 5–10.5 μm, angular, five- to six-sided.

ECOLOGY/FRUITING PATTERN Gregarious in soil under aspen, willow, rarely conifers; early July to early September; not common; subalpine, montane ecosystems.

OBSERVATIONS *lividoalbum:* lead- (or purple-) colored and white. Contrary to the Latin name, there is no purple color in this mushroom. *Entoloma hirtipes,* also known as *Nolanea hirtipes,* is a more delicate, pink-spored relative found in Colorado; it has a sharply pointed, dark yellow-brown cap; a long, fragile stalk with white basal mycelium; and a farinaceous odor. It fruits in coniferous forests in the spring and early summer.

ORDER
Agaricales

FAMILY
Plutaceae

COMMON NAME
Deer Mushroom

EDIBILITY
Edible

Gray-brown to dark brown cap with radiating dark fibers; free, white, soon dull pink gills; straight stalk readily separable; no ring or volva; on wood.

FRUITING BODIES Cap 4-12 cm broad; conical to broadly convex, often knobbed; brown, varying from dark brown to lighter gray-brown; surface smooth and satiny; radially streaked with dark brown, appressed fibrils. **Gills** close, broad, free; white when young, soon dull pink from spores. **Stalk** straight, 5-12 cm long x 0.5-1.5 cm wide, equal to slightly larger at base; pallid with brownish fibrils, white mycelium at base; no ring or volva. **Flesh** thin, white; odor radishlike or mild, taste mild.

SPORES Dull pink in print, 6-8.5 x 4.5-6 μm, elliptical, broad, smooth.

ECOLOGY/FRUITING PATTERN Single to grouped; an important wood rotter of hardwood (usually aspen and cottonwood) or occasionally conifers; fruiting on stumps, buried wood, or sawdust piles; widely distributed in the Rocky Mountain region, prairies to high country; July through September.

OBSERVATIONS *cervinus:* Latin, pertaining to deer. This variable mushroom represents a group of species differentiated by microscopic details, such as the features of uniquely horned sterile cells called cystidia, as well as field characters of cap colors and gill edge colors. Foragers should be wary of similar poisonous members of the pink-spored genus *Entoloma;* they differ from *Pluteus* species by their growth on the ground and their attached gills and angular spores. *Volvariella bombycina,* also with pink spores and free gills, is sometimes found fruiting on various hardwood trees in Denver in the summer; it has a distinctly deep, membranous volva.

Family Cortinariaceae

Cortinariaceae is the largest family of gilled mushrooms. It contains thousands of species found worldwide in a vast array of sizes, forms, and colors. Most are forest dwellers, usually forming essential mycorrhizal associations with trees.

Important features of the family are: stalk and cap firmly attached, not separating with a clean break; brown spore prints varying from orange-brown, rusty brown, cinnamon brown, to dull gray-brown (but not purple-brown); spores typically roughened, wrinkled, or warted and lacking a germ pore; and a filamentous (not cellular) cap cuticle. Cortinariaceae species are found with or without a partial veil. Most species have a cobwebby partial veil called a cortina (meaning "like a curtain," hence the family name) that covers the immature gills; some have a membranous partial veil. In addition, a universal veil often covers the developing mushroom but rarely leaves a remnant as the cap expands.

Cortinariaceae species are perhaps the most ubiquitous and important members of the Rocky Mountain mycoflora. There are few, if any, species known to be edible; most are suspect. Species of *Gymnopilus* and *Crepidotus,* both typically growing on wood, occur less commonly in Colorado and are not featured in this book. The main characters of four other genera—*Cortinarius, Galerina, Hebeloma,* and *Inocybe*—are described here.

FEATURED GENERA

Cortinarius Spores rusty brown, ochre-tawny, to rich cinnamon; roughened to warty. Typically with a cortina that covers the young gills and usually collapses onto the stalk surface, where it collects the rusty spores, often leaving a rusty ring or zone. Caps with varied colors, usually brown; lilac colors common in gills and stalk; fruiting bodies small to large. Nearly 2,000 species worldwide; none recommended, some deadly, pp. 119–123.

Galerina Spores ochraceous to rusty brown, with warted to wrinkled surface, often with a plage (a bare or depressed spot visible under a microscope). Caps typically small to minute, fragile, often striated, conical, smooth, usually some shade of brown or yellow-brown; stalks thin, with or without a ring. Many *Galerina*s are tiny moss inhabiters, difficult to identify. At least one is deadly; possibly many poisonous species, pp. 124–125.

Hebeloma Spores dull cinnamon, clay-colored, rarely reddish brown; wrinkled to warty. Caps small, medium-sized, to large; usually sticky; pinkish brown, ochraceous, to medium brown; stalk typically with tiny white flakes at top; gills sometimes beaded with droplets. Cortina commonly lacking, if present often scanty, and then usually gone by maturity; flesh often has radish odor. Gastrointestinal irritants, poisonous, none edible, pp. 126–127.

Inocybe Spores dull brown, grayish brown, or dull grayish umber; often angular or nodulose, sometimes smooth. Caps small, medium-sized, or rarely large; often conical; usually brown; typically radially fibrillose; margins splitting; always dry. Cortina lacking or poorly developed, usually not evident at maturity. Poisonous, many containing muscarine, pp. 128–129.

ORDER
Agaricales
FAMILY
Cortinariaceae
EDIBILITY
Not recommended

Dry and scaly, blackish violet cap; violet to dark purple-brown gills; violet stalk with fibrillose veil; rusty spores; under conifers.

FRUITING BODIES Cap 5-8 cm broad; hemispheric to convex, often with knob; surface dry, finely scaly to hairy; dark violet with metallic shine when young, becoming grayish black with age. **Gills** deep violet, then colored rusty from spores; narrow, adnate, subdistant. **Stalk** 4-11 cm long x 1-3 cm wide; equal to clavate; dark violet; veil hairy, grayish, leaving ring that becomes rusty from spores; basal mycelium bluish. **Flesh** thick, firm, pale to dark violet; odor weakly of cedarwood, taste mild to somewhat sweet.

SPORES Rusty brown, 12-16 x 8-10 µm, broadly elliptical, warty.

ECOLOGY/FRUITING PATTERN Single to gregarious; rather uncommon; in old-growth subalpine forests, with spruce, often near rotting logs; August, September.

OBSERVATIONS *violaceus:* purple (Latin). Few mushrooms have such intensely colored fruiting bodies; the bright rusty spores contrast beautifully with the dark violet stalk. This remarkable mushroom could be confused with other species of *Cortinarius* with violet tones in their fruiting bodies, but the intense colors and the dry, fibrillose to minutely scaly surfaces distinguish *Cortinarius violaceus.* Because of the suspect nature of the entire genus, no species of *Cortinarius* are recommended as edibles.

ORDER
Agaricales
FAMILY
Cortinariaceae
EDIBILITY
Not recommended

Cap pale bluish lilac,
with pale rust center;
violet gills turning
rusty; whitish cortina
in young; rusty annu-
lar zone at maturity;
pungent odor.

FRUITING BODIES Cap 4–9 cm broad,
convex to plano-convex; margins irregular,
fibrillose; pale bluish lilac to almost white,
becoming very pale rusty from center; dry, silky, with grayish white,
dense fibrils. **Gills** pale violet in young, soon rusty; adnate, crowded,
moderately broad. **Stalk** cylindrical to enlarged in middle; 4–7 cm long
x 1.5–2.5 cm wide; dry, fibrillose; pale bluish lilac, interior flesh violet;
sparse pale veil, rusty-colored from falling spores. **Flesh** firm, bluish
violet when young, near stalk juncture deep violet; odor disagreeably
pungent, fetid; taste not recorded.

SPORES Rusty brown, 8.5–11 x 5–6 µm, elliptical, warty.

ECOLOGY/FRUITING PATTERN Gregarious to single, mycorrhizal with
spruce and fir in Colorado's subalpine areas; rather common, August to
early September.

OBSERVATIONS *camphoratus:* odor of camphor. *Cortinarius traganus*
looks similar and fruits among conifers, but it differs by its ochre-brown
flesh; its pungent, sometimes fruitlike, odor; and the lack of violet colors
in young gills.

ORDER
Agaricales
FAMILY
Cortinariaceae
EDIBILITY
Not recommended

Pale brown cap with
gray-violet tinges;
violet flesh through-
out; stalk with gray-
ish fibrillose veil in
zones; rusty spores.

FRUITING BODIES Cap 3–5 cm across, convex; pale violet gray-brown, with shades of
cinnamon; silky, not viscid; gray-buff cortina at
inrolled margins in young. **Gills** pale lavender
when young, soon cinnamon-colored; close,
adnate, moderately broad. **Stalk** 3–7 cm long x 1–1.5 cm wide; equal to
clavate; pale lavender on grayish background; grayish veil remnants form
rusty, ragged ring; stalk interior violet. **Flesh** pallid-lavender; odor and
taste mild.

SPORES Rusty brown, 7.5–9 x 6–7.5 µm, nearly globose, roughened.

ECOLOGY/FRUITING PATTERN Gregarious, scattered; rather common in
late summer; under spruce in moist forests and mixed woods.

OBSERVATIONS *anomalus:* Latin for paradoxical. Similar-looking
Cortinarius alboviolaceus is silvery white to gray-violet when young
and has a thick, white, fibrillose veil; a bulkier stalk; and elliptical spores.

ORDER
Agaricales
FAMILY
Cortinariaceae
EDIBILITY
Not recommended

Bulky-looking; cap colors variable: ochraceous to cinnamon to olive; finely fibrillose under sticky surface; young gills lilac; stalk dry, abruptly bulbous, lilac at top.

FRUITING BODIES **Cap** 4–12 cm wide; hemispheric, then broadly convex to flat; margin curved under and often wavy; ochre gray-brown, cinnamon, orange-olive, to olive, usually reddish brown in center with brownish, appressed fibers in streaks; slimy to tacky. **Gills** light gray-violet in young, soon grayish brown; crowded, attached, moderately broad. **Stalk** 4–10 cm long x 1.5–3 cm wide; with an abrupt bulb that is rimmed when young, becoming less so with age; solid, pale blue-violet at top of stalk when young, coloration fading; streaked below with whitish cortina, soon rusty when spores mature; ragged, rusty, narrow ring at upper stalk. **Flesh** solid, pallid; violet in stalk apex when young, ochre-brown in bulb; odor and taste slightly farinaceous or nondistinctive.

SPORES Rusty brown, 7.5–9 x 4.5–6 μm, elliptical, warty.

ECOLOGY/FRUITING PATTERN One of the most common "corts" in the Rocky Mountain region, often growing in clusters and fairy rings in soil; mycorrhizal with various conifers in montane and subalpine ecosystems; August into October.

OBSERVATIONS *glaucopus:* Latin for bluish green foot (or stalk). *Cortinarius glaucopus*, as found here, represents a group of very similar variants with a confusing array of cap colors. The presence of appressed fibers under the mature cap cuticle is a reliable field character, along with the bulbous stem with bluish tints at its top. Cut the stem to see this coloration for which the specific epithet was chosen. Considering that many of this region's species are not yet described and that some *Cortinarius* species are known to be deadly poisonous, anyone eating members of this fairly recognizable genus should also be a *Cortinarius* expert.

ORDER
Agaricales
FAMILY
Cortinariaceae
EDIBILITY
Not recommended

**Small to medium-sized,
red-brown to olive-brown
cap; surface dry, fibril-
lose; young gills ochre-
yellow; stalk yellowish;
thin veil in young; in soil,
mosses, under conifers.**

FRUITING BODIES Cap 1.5–6 cm across, hemispheric to campanulate, then plano-convex; at
maturity with low knob; dark red-brown to olive
yellow–brown, paler olive-yellow toward margin;
surface dry, thinly covered with brownish fibrils.
Gills yellow to ochraceous yellow, sometimes with
reddish olive tinges; crowded, adnate to notched,
broad. **Stalk** 3–7 cm long x 3–10 mm wide; cylindrical; golden yellow, paler at top, base darkening;
basal mycelium pale yellow to reddish yellow at
times; veil yellowish, turning reddish brown; dry,
lightly scaly-floccose, at times with hairy, ragged,
rusty ring; interior dark yellow, brown at base.
Flesh pale yellow to dark greenish yellow, thick
over stalk, thin otherwise; odor slight, of raw potato
or radish; taste slightly bitter.

SPORES Rusty brown in print, 6.5–8 x 4–5 μm, elliptical, warty.

ECOLOGY/FRUITING PATTERN Widely distributed among conifers,
especially under lodgepole pine, Douglas-fir in Colorado; early July at
lower elevations to September at higher elevations.

OBSERVATIONS *croceus:* from *crocea,* meaning "saffron-colored." Also
known as *Dermocybe crocea, Cortinarius croceus* represents a complex of similar varieties or species in Colorado that vary by subtle color
differences, slight differences in the veil, and spore sizes. *Cortinarius
cinnamomeus* is very similar-looking, but it has distinctly bright orange
gills, especially in young caps. *Cortinarius semisanguineus* is distinguished in the field by its bloodred young gills and paler stalk. Because
similar-looking *Cortinarius* species, all of which could be considered
LBMs, are deadly poisonous, none should ever be eaten.
    Cortinarius species known as dermocybes contain pigments that
are easily water-soluble and can be used to dye wool, producing various
nuances of yellow, orange, and red. These dyes are as colorfast as the
best conventional plant dyes.

ORDER
Agaricales
FAMILY
Cortinariaceae
EDIBILITY
Not recommended

Glutinous, orange-brown cap on long, slimy, belted stalk; pale grayish slime with bluish tinges; rusty gills and spores; under conifers.

FRUITING BODIES Cap 3–8 cm across, narrowly convex; margin inrolled, finally flattening, often with low broad knob; tawny orange-brown to reddish brown, often darker at center in young, margin lighter; slimy bluish veil binds cap and stalk apex in young; cap surface sticky, shiny at maturity. **Gills** grayish white in young, becoming rusty brown from spores; broad, adnate to notched, close. **Stalk** 5–12 cm long x 0.5–2 cm wide; equal or tapering downward; covered with pale bluish violet, glutinous veil, often in broad bands; upper stalk with pale hairy cortina leaving thin ring, soon rusty from spores; lower stalk surface breaks into brownish belts or irregular brownish bands. **Flesh** dingy grayish, brownish at stalk base; odor and taste indistinct.

SPORES Rusty brown, 13–17 x 7.5–9.5 μm, almond-shaped, warty.

ECOLOGY/FRUITING PATTERN Scattered in moist subalpine forests, associated with spruce; late August through September; fairly common.

OBSERVATIONS *collinitus:* covered with slime (Latin). Also known as *Cortinarius muscigenus.* The bluish violet slime layer in wide belts on the stalk and the association with spruce are good field characters. *Cortinarius trivialis,* an aspen associate in the Rocky Mountain region, differs from *Cortinarius collinitus* by its white, not bluish, slime layer (thus lacking bluish colorations on the stalk); pale bluish gray gills when young; a more pronounced netlike pattern on the brownish lower stalk; and smaller spores. *Cortinarius mucosus* has a dark red-brown, sticky cap; it is a pine associate with a grayish white slime veil on a white, firm-textured stem.

ORDER
Agaricales
FAMILY
Cortinariaceae
COMMON NAME
Deadly *Galerina*
EDIBILITY
Deadly poisonous

Small, sticky to shiny, yellow-brown to orange-brown cap, fading to pale buff; orange-brown gills; thin, dark brown stalk with small, whitish ring; on decaying wood.

FRUITING BODIES Cap 1.5–4.5 cm broad; convex, then plane or with low knob; smooth, margin at times translucent-striated; viscid; orange-brown to ochraceous tawny, fading to ochraceous to warm buff, disc often remaining darker. **Gills** adnate to slightly decurrent, broad, close, yellowish to dull orange-brown. **Stalk** 3–8 cm long x 3–6 mm wide; equal to slightly enlarged at base; brown with dingy gray, streaky, fibrillose covering, darkening with age from base upward; interior brown; basal mycelium white; smooth at apex; ring thin, membranous to somewhat fibrillose, high on stalk, whitish to dingy brown, often nearly disappearing. **Flesh** watery brown; odor mild, slightly mealy, or faintly of cucumber; taste not recorded. Caution: deadly poisonous!

SPORES Rusty brown in print, 8.5–11 x 5–6.5 µm, elliptical, minutely roughened with smooth depression, lacking a germ pore.

ECOLOGY/FRUITING PATTERN Gregarious or in small clusters on well-rotted conifer and hardwood logs; rather common; August and September; montane and subalpine ecosystems of Colorado and throughout the Rocky Mountains.

OBSERVATIONS *autumnalis:* Latin, meaning "of the autumn." This dangerous mushroom has been found in other seasons besides autumn. *Galerina marginata,* also reported in Colorado, is a less viscid look-alike, fruiting mainly on decaying conifers and often lacking a ring on mature specimens, but it has the same dangerous amanitin toxins as *Galerina autumnalis.* The edible *Armillaria ostoyae* and its relatives, all known as honey mushrooms, also grow in clusters on wood and have rings and brown stalk interiors, but their fruiting bodies are larger and they have white spore prints. *Pholiota mutabilis* also grows on deadwood, but usually in more massive clusters; its stalk is covered with recurved brownish scales, and its spores are smooth.

ORDER	**FRUITING BODIES Cap** small, 3–12 mm across;
Agaricales	hemispheric to broadly conical, at times campanu-
FAMILY	late; rich tawny red-brown, paler between striations,
Cortinariaceae	entire cap fading to buff as it dries; striated to disc
EDIBILITY	when moist; surface at first pruinose (appearing to
Unknown	be covered with a very fine powder), best visible
	with hand lens. **Gills** broadly adnate, distant, broad;
Tiny, red-brown, fading,	pale ochraceous when young, soon tawny; edges
striated caps; pale yel-	whitish. **Stalk** very slender and fragile; 2–4.5 cm
low-orange, attached	long x 1–2 mm thick; at first pale tawny entire
gills; slender, red-brown,	length, then darkening over lower portion to
fragile, pruinose stalk;	distinct red-brown; surface pruinose at all ages; ring
ring lacking; in moss.	absent. **Flesh** thin, fragile, ochre; odor and taste not
	distinctive.

SPORES Tawny, rusty brown; 11–15 x 6–9 μm; on two-spored basidia; almond-shaped; warty, with a plage.

ECOLOGY/FRUITING PATTERN Common, gregarious on mosses in forests dominated by spruce; subalpine ecosystems; late July to September.

OBSERVATIONS *atkinsoniana:* named for G. F. Atkinson, American mycologist. *Galerina vittaeformis* and its variants have very similar colors and red-brown pruinose stalks, but the caps lack the pruinose surface of *Galerina atkinsoniana.* Although some *Galerina* species grow in humus and on rotting wood, mosses are the most common sub-strates for species found in Colorado's mountains. It is safe to say that most small, fragile, ochre-brown to orange-brown mushrooms with striated caps growing on moss are members of the genus *Galerina.* Because there are many very similar-looking *Galerina* species, a microscopic examination is usually needed to separate them.

ORDER
Agaricales
FAMILY
Cortinariaceae
EDIBILITY
Not recommended

**Small, gray-brown cap
with dark center; cap and
its margin with thin hairy
veil that soon disappears;
pale brown, fragile splitting stalk with veil fibrils;
odor of radish; in soil
under spruce.**

FRUITING BODIES Cap 1–3 cm across; convex, expanding to plane, at times with low knob; margin inrolled; dark cinnamon brown at center, shading to pale gray-brown toward margins, finally overall a warm, pale gray-brown; center smooth and slightly viscid, surface with thin coating of pallid to buff fibrils, fibrils remaining until maturity as faint buff patches (visible with hand lens); thin hairy veil remnants at times on cap margin. **Gills** pale brownish gray, becoming dull cinnamon; broad, subdistant, adnexed. **Stalk** 2–5 cm long x 3–4 mm wide; fragile, splitting lengthwise; never white; pallid and pruinose at top, dingy pale brown below, darkening at base to rusty brown; surface fibrillose from buff veil fibrils, at times leaving narrow thin ring; interior flesh dull brown. **Flesh** thin, brownish gray; faint odor of radish, taste somewhat bitter.

SPORES   Dull cinnamon in print, 10–12.5 x 6–7.5 μm, elliptical, slightly roughened, not dextrinoid.

ECOLOGY/FRUITING PATTERN   Gregarious to clustered on mossy, wet soil under Engelmann spruce; subalpine ecosystems; August, September; fairly common.

OBSERVATIONS   *aggregatum:* Latin, meaning "aggregated" or "clustered." Many small, veiled *Hebeloma* species fruit in Colorado's mountains, forming mycorrhizal associations with willow, spruce, and other trees. Many can be differentiated only by microscopic features. *Hebeloma aggregatum* is closely related to *Hebeloma marginatulum,* an alpine species associated with willows, which has more yellow-brown in the cap, a whitish veil, and a mild, then radish taste. *Hebeloma mesophaeum* differs from both of these species by its larger dark-centered cap, usually more distinct ring, and smaller spores. Several species of *Hebeloma* are known to be poisonous; all are suspect.

ORDER
Agaricales
FAMILY
Cortinariaceae
EDIBILITY
Not recommended

Large, sticky, brown to pinkish tan cap; brown gills with beads or tiny brown spots; stalk sturdy, scaly, bulbous; ring absent; pungent odor.

FRUITING BODIES **Cap** 5-10 cm broad; convex, becoming broadly convex, flattening somewhat; smooth, sticky, but soon drying; pinkish brown to cinnamon brown in center, margin whitish with faint, cottony patches in young and minutely striated. **Gills** at first pallid, soon pinkish cinnamon, then grayish red-brown with age; close, moderately broad, notched at juncture with stalk; small droplets or beads scattered on edges in moist weather, often drying to tiny brown spots. **Stalk** 4-7 cm long x 1-3 cm wide; equal above abruptly bulbous base; white to pallid, at times becoming powdered red-brown from falling spores; lightly scaly near top; thicker, pallid scales decorating remainder of surface, scales sometimes concentric near base; ring absent; hollow near top. **Flesh** thick, whitish; odor pungent/radishlike, taste of radish to mild.

SPORES Dull reddish brown in print, 11.5-15 x 6.5-8 µm, almond-shaped, warty, dextrinoid.

ECOLOGY/FRUITING PATTERN In some seasons common in mixed conifer and aspen forests; montane to subalpine; gregarious to single; August and September.

OBSERVATIONS *insigne:* means "badge" or "remarkable" in Latin. *Hebeloma crustuliniforme* shares the feature of not having a visible veil at any stage of development. It is differentiated from *Hebeloma insigne* and relatives by its pale cream to pale crusty brown cap; much less scaly, white stalk; and smaller, less ornamented spores. *Hebeloma crustuliniforme* and its variants, often called Poison Pie, have a radish odor and are poisonous.

Species of *Hebeloma* fruit in similar habitats and at similar times as many *Cortinarius* species and could be confused with them. *Hebeloma* species usually lack the well-developed, fibrillose cortina characteristic of the genus *Cortinarius,* and spores of the latter are more rusty brown.

ORDER
Agaricales
FAMILY
Cortinariaceae
EDIBILITY
Poisonous

Small, dry, conical to bell-shaped cap; lilac, changing to pale tan; hairy in radial pattern when expanded; stalk pale lavender, then whitish, hairy; spermatic and disagreeable odor.

FRUITING BODIES Cap 1-3 cm across; conical, expanding to bell-shaped with rather sharp knob; lilac in buttons, becoming pale tan at maturity; copious white fibrils on buttons; surface radially fibrillose, dry, silky; margin incurved, then ragged and lacerated at maturity. **Gills** close, adnate to notched, broad; at first whitish with lavender tints, then pale dull brown; edges rough. **Stalk** equal, 2-6 cm long x 3-10 mm wide; solid; pale lavender in buttons, then pinkish brown with age; top surface finely powdered; minutely hairy below; partial veil leaves either scattered fibrils or inconspicuous hairy ring, often disappearing. **Flesh** fairly firm, thin, whitish; odor and taste disagreeable, spermatic.

SPORES Dull brown in print, 6.5-9 x 4.5-5.5 μm, smooth, elliptical.

ECOLOGY/FRUITING PATTERN Gregarious to scattered; under conifers and hardwoods; July through September; widely distributed in the Rocky Mountain region, sometimes in yards with trees and along roads, more commonly in montane and subalpine ecosystems.

OBSERVATIONS *geophylla:* earth-gills (Greek). *Inocybe geophylla* var. *geophylla* lacks the initial lilac colors. Similarly colored species of *Cortinarius* differ by their rusty brown spores. *Inocybe,* a large genus with many look-alike species, is recognized by the combination of radially fibrillose caps, typically pale brown colors, dull brown gills and spore prints, and growth in soil under trees. A high percentage of *Inocybe* species contain the toxin muscarine, often in dangerous amounts. Obviously none is recommended for eating.

ORDER
Agaricales
FAMILY
Cortinariaceae
EDIBILITY
Poisonous

Medium-sized to large, radially fibrillose, straw-yellow, knobbed cap; pale yellow-brown gills at maturity; pungent odor of unripe corn.

FRUITING BODIES Cap 2-6 (up to 10) cm broad; conical to bell-shaped, becoming flatter but distinctly knobbed; straw-yellow to duller yellow-brown, disc brownish; dry, distinctly cracked at maturity with fibers radiating from center; margin ragged. **Gills** at first pallid grayish, soon pale yellow-brown; narrow, close, adnate to barely attached; edges minutely fringed and whitish. **Stalk** 3-7 (up to 10) cm long x 2-8 (up to 15) mm wide; equal with slight basal enlargement; whitish to pallid in young, then dingy pale brown; surface with fine scales and fibrils; ring lacking. **Flesh** thin, pallid or yellowish; odor pungent, of green corn; taste not recorded.

SPORES Dull brown in print, 9-13 x 5.5-6.5 μm, short, elliptical, smooth.

ECOLOGY/FRUITING PATTERN Single to gregarious in mixed hardwoods and conifers; quite common after rains in August and September; montane to lower subalpine habitats; sizes of fruiting bodies quite variable depending on weather.

OBSERVATIONS *sororia:* pertaining to sisterhood (Latin). The meaning of the specific epithet leads me to imagine groups of little, blond girls—sisters—all together in the forest, but this may not be what Dr. Kauffman intended when he named it. The pale, straw-blond, fibrillose caps and the distinct pungent odor make *Inocybe sororia* fairly easy to recognize in the field. A poisonous, related look-alike, *Inocybe fastigiata,* occurs in similar areas, but its cap color is darker yellow-brown, its odor is spermatic, and its spores are smaller (6.5–10 x 4.5–6 μm).

129

Family Coprinaceae

Often fragile and ephemeral, these saprophytes recycle dung, waste organic material, or rotting woody debris. They have cap cuticles with large, pear-shaped cells and black spores (rarely dark reddish brown) that usually have an obvious germ pore. Some species are well-known edibles, whereas others are poisonous. Genera featured here include *Coprinus, Panaeolus,* and *Psathyrella.*

Coprinus species, or inky caps, are probably the most well-known members of the family, distinguished by the autodigestion or deliquescence of their gills, which produces an inky fluid containing the smooth black spores. This black "ink" disperses the spores by sticking to plants that are eaten by animals. The spores pass unscathed through the animals' guts. *Panaeolus* species usually grow on dung or very rich soil and have grayish, blackish, or brown caps with gill faces often becoming mottled during maturation. *Psathyrella* species have very fragile caps and easily broken stalks, are commonly found in clusters on rich organic material and woody debris, and often have hygrophanous caps with black (to less commonly dark red) smooth spores.

Coprinus niveus (Fries) Fries

ORDER
Agaricales
FAMILY
Coprinaceae
EDIBILITY
Not recommended

Small to medium-sized, snow-white, powdery, conical cap; long, white stalk; gills white in young, becoming inky black; on manure.

FRUITING BODIES Cap 2-4 cm across; nearly cylindrical, becoming conical to bell-shaped; margin striated to splitting; surface with pure white, loose, mealy particles. **Gills** crowded, narrow, barely attached; white to pinkish, then inky black and dissolving. **Stalk** 4-10 cm tall x 3-6 mm wide; equal to slightly enlarged base; hollow; white, mealy, more or less smooth at maturity; fragile; ring absent. **Flesh** thin, gray; no odor or taste.

SPORES Black, 14-19 x 9-13 μm, elliptical, compressed, with pore.

ECOLOGY/FRUITING PATTERN Not common; found in old cowpies and other dung; solitary or a few together; widely distributed in farming and ranching areas and in the high country where cattle are grazed; spring, summer, and fall.

OBSERVATIONS *niveus:* means "like snow" (Latin). Other *Coprinus* species with white caps, such as *Coprinus lagopus* and its relatives, are smaller and are found in damp forests or among grasses.

ORDER
Agaricales
FAMILY
Coprinaceae
COMMON NAME
Mica Cap
EDIBILITY
Edible

Small, bell-shaped, tawny, finely grooved caps with sparkling surface particles, soon bald; gills pale, then black, turning somewhat inky; white stalk; in dense clusters on rotting or buried wood.

FRUITING BODIES
Cap 2-4 cm high x 2-3.5 cm wide; hemispheric to bell-shaped; at first sprinkled with micalike, granular veil remnants, granules soon disappearing; striated more than halfway to center, margin usually split at maturity; tawny, honey brown, cinnamon brown, or warm buff, becoming grayer with age. **Gills** pale buff, then brownish, finally black; deliquescing only partially at times; close, narrow, barely attached. **Stalk** 4-8 cm long x 3-4 mm wide, equal; very white, brittle, fraying at base; ring absent. **Flesh** thin, soft, pale brown; odor and taste mild.

SPORES Blackish in print, 7-10 x 4.5-6 μm, elliptical, often compressed, smooth, with pore.

ECOLOGY/FRUITING PATTERN Widely distributed; very common in urban settings and along roadsides, usually in rather open areas; fruiting in clusters, often hundreds of caps; on rotting wood or woody debris, at the base of old trees, or on underground wood and rotting tree roots; found sporadically in Colorado from late spring through fall.

OBSERVATIONS *micaceus:* from *mica,* meaning "crumb" in Latin, referring to the granules on the caps. The micalike granules, which are remains of the universal veil, are visible only on young, fresh caps. What is called *Coprinus micaceus* in Colorado is a complex of very similar species distinguishable mainly by microscopic characters.

Like *Coprinus micaceus, Coprinus disseminatus* (also called *Pseudocoprinus disseminatus*) grows on wood in large clusters. It has tiny, pale, gray-ochre, pleated, translucent caps (5-12 mm across) and nonliquefying gills.

ORDER
Agaricales
FAMILY
Coprinaceae
COMMON NAMES
Shaggy Mane, Lawyer's Wig
EDIBILITY
Edible

Tall, white, cylindrical to oval cap with brown scales; elongated, white gills becoming gray, soon dissolving into ink; straight, white stalk; ring near base; in soil and grass.

FRUITING BODIES Cap 4–18 cm tall x 2–5 cm wide; cylindrical to oval; edges of cap at first close to stalk, expanding and eventually curling upward; white with brown, hairy, recurved scales, giving shaggy appearance; center brown, smooth. **Gills** white at first, then grayish with dull pinkish cast, progressively becoming black from lower margins upward, finally deliquescing into ink; crowded, free or nearly so, broad, edges white, floccose. **Stalk** 5–18 cm long x 1–2 cm thick; cylindrical, base slightly larger, sometimes rooting; hollow at maturity; white, with narrow, thin ring near base; volva absent. **Flesh** white, thin, soft; odor and taste mild.

SPORES Black, 10–14 x 5.5–8 μm, elliptical, smooth, with germ pore.

ECOLOGY/FRUITING PATTERN Very common in yards, parks, at roadsides; growing saprophytically on nutrient-rich soils and compost heaps throughout the Rocky Mountain region, even at high elevations; single to clustered, often in large troops; sometimes pushing up through hard-packed soil and even asphalt; partial to cool weather; June through October.

OBSERVATIONS *comatus:* means "shaggy" in Latin. This is an easy mushroom for beginners to identify and enjoy eating, but prepare only young caps and cook them immediately or you will have ink. *Coprinus atramentarius,* the Alcohol Inky Cap, which should never be eaten with alcohol, has smoother, nonshaggy, brown-gray caps. The immature caps of the poisonous *Chlorophyllum molybdites,* also commonly found in city lawns, resemble unexpanded *Coprinus comatus,* and many poisonings result from confusing the two. The stalk interior of *Chlorophyllum molybdites* will change color to reddish brown when cut, while stalks of *Coprinus comatus* will remain chalky white inside. In addition, an expanded, mature cap of *Chlorophyllum molybdites* will produce a greenish spore print, and the initially white gills soon turn gray-green from the spores.

ORDER
Agaricales
FAMILY
Coprinaceae
COMMON NAME
Alcohol Inky Cap
EDIBILITY
Poisonous with alcohol

Grayish, nonshaggy cap with dingy brown center and furrowed surface; gills white, becoming brown, then black and inky; white stalk; usually clustered on or near wood.

FRUITING BODIES **Cap** 3-7 cm broad x up to 7 cm high; conical to bell-shaped; margin irregularly puckered at first and connected to thin veil, which sheaths stalk base; margin splits with age; bald or with a few small scales, surface furrowed; tan to grayish brown, grayer with age. **Gills** free or nearly so, broad, crowded; white, turning gray; deliquescing, finally becoming inky fluid. **Stalk** 8-15 cm long x 0.5-1.5 cm wide; equal, cylindrical, hollow; white to dingy buff; veil remnants as thin fibers over base. **Flesh** soft, white; odor pleasant, taste mild.

SPORES Black in mass, 7-11 x 4-6 μm, elliptical, smooth, with germ pore.

ECOLOGY/FRUITING PATTERN Very common; clustered on or near rotting or buried wood; a saprophyte fruiting in spring and fall during cool moist weather in many habitats, including lawns, gardens, and hardwood or mixed forests; commonly in large groups under aspen and on old chip piles where Colorado's ski runs have been cleared.

OBSERVATIONS *atramentarius:* pertaining to ink (Latin). The Alcohol Inky Cap should not be eaten with or followed by alcohol because of the severe poisoning that could result (see page 27 for additional information). The edible *Coprinus comatus* also has inky gills at maturity, but its cap is taller and shaggy with recurved scales.

ORDER
Agaricales
FAMILY
Coprinaceae
EDIBILITY
Inedible

Tall, off-white, sticky caps, shaped like half an egg; whitish gills becoming mottled deep brown to black; tall, straight, white stalk with ring in middle; on dung.

FRUITING BODIES Cap 3-9 cm broad; hemispheric to ovoid, rounded at top; pale yellowish tan, fading to pallid whitish; surface smooth, viscid when wet, satiny-shiny when dried; margin not expanding, smooth, without veil fragments. **Gills** pallid, becoming mottled with black as spores mature unevenly, finally entirely black; adnate to adnexed, broad, not close. **Stalk** tall and straight; 8-15 cm long x 0.5-1 cm wide; cylindrical, base enlarged; at times hollow; whitish to buff, lower surface increasingly ochre-brown near base; ring membranous, whitish in middle of stalk, soon blackened by falling spores, often barely evident or absent; surface above ring often striated. **Flesh** soft, pallid, thick in center of cap, thin toward margin; odor and taste faintly fungoid.

SPORES Blackish in print, 15-20 x 8-11 µm, elliptical, smooth, with germ pore.

ECOLOGY/FRUITING PATTERN Common; fruiting in groups or singly; typically on horse manure, also on cowpies or other dung; June through September; in a variety of Colorado habitats wherever manure is distributed. I have found this mushroom in the high country of Colorado all the way to treeline where people have ridden horses over the Continental Divide.

OBSERVATIONS *semiovatus:* half egg–shaped (Latin). Another dung-lover, *Panaeolus campanulatus,* is distinguished by its smaller, brown to gray-brown, bell-shaped cap with pretty teethlike veil remnants at the margin, nonviscid cap surface, and a thin, brown stalk lacking a ring. Mushrooms that are saprophytes on dung are described as being coprophilic.

ORDER
Agaricales

FAMILY
Coprinaceae

COMMON NAMES
Mower's Mushroom,
Haymaker's Mushroom

EDIBILITY
Poisonous

Fragile, conical, brown
cap; fading, often in
bands; dark brown gills;
purple-brown spores;
spindly, whitish stalk;
ring absent; in grass.

FRUITING BODIES Cap 1-3 cm broad, hemispheric to bluntly conical-campanulate when young; surface smooth, moist but not sticky; margin smooth; dark reddish brown to grayish brown, fading to creamy tan when dry, often with darker band when partially dried. **Gills** at first adnate, seceding to almost free; broad, ventricose, nearly distant; light gray-brown in young, later somewhat mottled dark brown to violet-brown. **Stalk** 4-7 cm long x 1-3 mm wide; cylindrical, hollow, fragile; dingy brownish; smooth; ring absent. **Flesh** fragile, brownish; odor mild, taste slightly acidic.

SPORES Dark purple-brown in print, 12-15 x 6.5-9 µm, elliptical with small rounded warts, with germ pore.

ECOLOGY/FRUITING PATTERN Common, widely distributed throughout the Rocky Mountain region; single to scattered in grassy soil, not on dung; in lawns, parks, and other grassy places; usually gone within a day; prim-arily spring and early summer.

OBSERVATIONS *foenisecii:* pertaining to dry hay, in reference to its occurrence with grasses. Also called *Psathyrella foenisecii,* this common mushroom has been moved around taxonomically. Because its roughened, dark purple-brown spores are not typical of either *Panaeolus* or *Psathyrella,* some authors call it *Panaeolina foenisecii.* Some collections of *Panaeolus foenisecii* contain small amounts of hallucinogenic compounds; these toxins are not yet well understood. This ubiquitous mushroom should not be eaten.

ORDER
Agaricales
FAMILY
Coprinaceae
EDIBILITY
Not recommended

Fragile, honey-colored to buff, rounded caps; white, fringed cap edges; purplish to grayish brown gills; fragile, white stalk; on dead or buried wood; common in lawns.

FRUITING BODIES Cap 3-7 cm across; broadly conical, convex to nearly flat; margins in young with hanging whitish veil remnants, finally smooth; colors variable: off-white to light ochre to buff, center often retaining brownish coloration. **Gills** at first whitish, then grayish purple, finally dark brown; close, adnate, broad. **Stalk** 3-10 cm long x 3-8 mm wide; equal; white, apex whitish floccose; ring usually absent, or surface at most thinly fibrillose. **Flesh** fragile, thin, watery gray-brown; odor and taste mild.

SPORES Purplish brown in print, 7-10 x 4-5 µm, smooth, elliptical, with germ pore.

ECOLOGY/FRUITING PATTERN Usually clustered on dead hardwood such as cottonwood or elm stumps, or near buried wood; lawns, parks, especially in urban settings; quite common; June through August.

OBSERVATIONS *candolleana*: named to honor A. P. de Candolle, French mycologist. The mushroom recognized as *Psathyrella candolleana* is actually a complex of very similar species that together present variable field characters. The cap colors vary from almost white to light honey-brown to light ochre with lilac tones. The persistence of veil remnants on the margins of the cap is also a changeable feature. Information on the microscopic characters of the spores and sterile cells on the gills is needed to differentiate varieties or species. *Psathyrella candolleana* is often listed as edible, but because of the danger of confusing it with similar-looking, poisonous mushrooms in grassy habitats, I do not recommend it.

ORDER
Agaricales
FAMILY
Coprinaceae
EDIBILITY
Unknown

Cap fragile, red-brown, fading to grayish yellow; gills attached, pallid, becoming dark brown; stalk slender with white, cottony ring; in humus under aspens.

FRUITING BODIES **Cap** 2-6 cm broad; convex, expanding to plane with slight knob; smooth, moist, fading as moisture is lost; rich red-brown, fading to grayish yellow. **Gills** adnate, close, narrow to moderately broad; pale gray-brown to deep vinaceous brown, edges pallid. **Stalk** somewhat rooting; 5-10 cm long x 3-6 mm wide; pallid; pruinose above, with cottony white patches of veil fibrils below ring and white tomentum at base; ring membranous, fairly thick, cottony, with a flaring edge, white, drying pinkish gray. **Flesh** fragile, thin, pallid; odor and taste mild.

SPORES Dark brown, 7.5-9 x 4.5-5 μm, often truncated, elliptical, smooth, with small germ pore.

ECOLOGY/FRUITING PATTERN Gregarious in rich humus and litter under aspen; montane and subalpine ecosystems; uncommon; July and August.

OBSERVATIONS *barrowsii:* honoring Chuck Barrows, New Mexican collector. There are several fairly common, aspen-loving species of *Psathyrella* in Colorado, which must be differentiated by microscopic examination. *Psathyrella kauffmanii* looks very similar, but it has a thinner, pallid, membranous ring distant from the stalk apex and much larger sterile cells on the gills than does *Psathyrella barrowsii*. *Psathyrella circellatipes* grows in dense clusters on or near aspen wood and is characteristic of aspen areas in the Rockies. It has very slender stalks with tawny mycelium at their bases, no rings, and larger spores than the above-mentioned species.

 Good field characters for species of *Psathyrella* are the dark spores (and mature gills), the fragile cap flesh with distinct color changes (hygrophanous), and the fragility of the stalk, which snaps easily and cleanly in half when broken. These mushrooms often fruit on or near rotten wood.

137

Family Strophariaceae

This is a large family of mostly saprophytic species that grow on soil, wood, or dung. They have attached gills; stalks not readily separable from the caps; and purple-brown, grayish brown, dull rusty brown, to blackish brown spore prints. The spores are smooth, typically with a germ pore, and the cap cuticle is filamentous rather than cellular.

FEATURED GENERA

Stropharia Typically colorful, sticky, yellowish caps; deep brown, purple-brown, to purple-black spores; partial veil usually forming a ring on a solid stalk; not caespitose, pp. 138–139.

Pholiota Dull, rusty, cinnamon brown, to gray-brown spores; usually scaly, sometimes smooth caps; brown gills; stalks with a membranous ring or fibrillose zones; almost all saprophytic on wood, pp. 140–141.

Psilocybe Purplish to purple-brown spores; typically small, brown, smooth, often bell-shaped caps; usually slender, ringless stalks, often turning bluish when handled; many saprophytic species, a few hallucinogenic, p. 142.

Hypholoma (Naematoloma) Without a ring (but may have fringe of veil on young caps); often caespitose in tufts on wood (or possibly on ground); purple-brown spore prints, p. 143.

Stropharia semiglobata (Batsch) Quélet

ORDER
Agaricales
FAMILY
Strophariaceae
EDIBILITY
Not recommended

Small, hemispheric, yellow, sticky cap; lilac-brown gills; off-white, viscid stalk with ring often disappearing; on dung or composted soil.

FRUITING BODIES Cap 1–5 cm broad; hemispheric to convex, smooth, viscid; slimy in wet weather; evenly pale yellow to yellow-brown. **Gills** adnate, broad, subdistant; grayish pallid, then purplish brown. **Stalk** 5–8 cm long x 2–5 mm wide; sticky-slimy if wet, varnished when dry; whitish to pale yellow; slimy veil or ring zone, at times disappearing. **Flesh** thin, pale or watery yellowish; odor and taste mild.

SPORES Purple-brown, 15–19 x 7.5–11 μm, elliptical, smooth, thick-walled with germ pore.

ECOLOGY/FRUITING PATTERN Rather common saprophyte on dung or manured soil; June to September; in watered grasslands, foothills, even Colorado's high country where horses have been stabled or ridden.

OBSERVATIONS *semiglobata:* half-spherical, referring to shape of cap. *Agrocybe pediades* is also yellowish brown and slender, but it has brown gills and no purplish tint to its spore print and grows in grasses.

ORDER
Agaricales
FAMILY
Strophariaceae
EDIBILITY
Inedible

Medium-sized to large, densely scaled, yellow-brown caps; drab brown to purple-brown, attached gills; stalk scaly below membranous ring.

FRUITING BODIES Cap 6-16 cm across; convex, becoming plane; cap margin incurved in youth, finally with irregular flaring margins at maturity; tawny to yellow-brown with brown, conspicuous scales densely scattered over surface; dry, cracked-looking near disc; margin often with attached partial veil remnants. **Gills** adnate or notched, narrow, close; pallid at first, drab brown to violaceous gray at maturity; fragile. **Stalk** 5-10 cm long x 1.5-2.5 cm wide; more or less equal, base somewhat enlarged; whitish with dingy yellow-brown, conspicuous, erect or recurved scales above and below veil line; ring membranous, whitish, often collapsing and leaving zone of veil material. **Flesh** white, quite thick, not staining; odor and taste nauseous to slightly putrid.

SPORES Dark purple-brown in print, 6-8.5 x 3.5-4.5 µm, elliptical, smooth, pore absent or minuscule.

ECOLOGY/FRUITING PATTERN Uncommon, single to gregarious, in rich organic soil, often near rotting aspen logs; montane and subalpine ecosystems; July to September.

OBSERVATIONS *kauffmanii:* named for C. H. Kauffman, American mycologist (1869-1931). This rather large *Stropharia* has the general aspect of a species of *Agaricus* until you turn it over and examine the gill attachment. Species of *Agaricus* typically have free gills, whereas the gills of *Stropharia* species are attached, especially in young specimens. C. H. Kauffman collected in Colorado and Wyoming in the early 1900s and later inspired his student, Alexander Smith, to study the western fungi. Smith, a longtime professor at the University of Michigan, spent many seasons collecting fungi in Colorado. Together these two great scientists made enormous contributions to the understanding of the fungi of the Rocky Mountains.

Pholiota vernalis   (Peck) Smith and Hesler

ORDER
Agaricales
FAMILY
Strophariaceae
EDIBILITY
Not recommended

Clustered, smooth, yellow-brown caps, fading to pale ochre-brown; dingy brown stalks with fibrils but no scales; on rotting logs.

FRUITING BODIES **Cap** 1-4 cm broad; convex to broadly conical, flattening, often with low knob; honey brown when moist, distinctly fading from center outward to pale ochre; smooth, slightly sticky; translucent-striated, with appressed veil remnants along margins when young. **Gills** light ochre, becoming dark cinnamon brown; adnate, moderately broad, close. **Stalk** 3-6 cm long x 1-3 mm wide; equal, hollow; honey brownish, and finally rusty brown from base upward; surface covered with gray fibrils but not scaly; ring at times mere fibrous zone. **Flesh** dull buff, thin; odor and taste mild.

SPORES Cinnamon brown in print, 5.5-7.5 x 3-4.5 µm, elliptical, smooth, with germ pore.

ECOLOGY/FRUITING PATTERN Common; caespitose to gregarious, on rotten conifer wood and occasionally hardwood; widely distributed in the Rockies at high elevations in subalpine ecosystems; June through mid-August.

OBSERVATIONS *vernalis:* vernal or spring. Often called *Kuehneromyces vernalis.* A close relative, *Pholiota mutabilis* (also called *Kuehneromyces mutabilis*), has similar fading caps, but the stalks are conspicuously scaly and it fruits in dense masses on confier wood. *Pholiota vernalis* is confined to high elevations and fruits in the spring on rotten conifer wood as a typical member of the snowbank flora.

The Deadly *Galerina, Galerina autumnalis,* resembles *Pholiota vernalis,* but fruits in small clusters on conifer logs, has a viscid brown cap, and has a ring on the stalk. Its spores differ from those of the *Pholiota* species by being rough to wrinkled and lacking a germ pore. Because collectors could confuse them with the Deadly *Galerina,* neither *P. vernalis* nor *P. mutabilis* is recommended for the table.

ORDER
Agaricales
FAMILY
Strophariaceae
EDIBILITY
Poisonous

Large, dry, densely scaly, brownish yellow caps; brownish gills; very scaly stalk with ring; clustered at base of trees.

FRUITING BODIES Cap 3-10 cm broad; hemispheric, becoming broadly convex; margin with veil remnants appendiculate at first; dry, covered with dense, downcurled, tawny brown scales; surface brownish yellow between scales. **Gills** crowded, narrow, adnate; pale yellow, becoming slightly greenish, finally dull brown from spores. **Stalk** 4-10 cm long x 1-2 cm wide; equal, often tapering and grown together at base with others; densely scaly and colored as on cap; partial veil yellowish, leaving ring at top of stalk. **Flesh** pliant, yellowish; odor and taste mild, or more commonly of garlic.

SPORES Dull rusty brown in print, 6.5-8 x 3.5-4.5 µm, elliptical, smooth, with germ pore.

ECOLOGY/FRUITING PATTERN Common; often in large clusters on wood of conifers and hardwoods, particularly spruce, fir, and aspen; at the base of both dead and living trees; late July to September in montane and lower subalpine ecosystems.

OBSERVATIONS *squarrosa:* Latin for scurfy, scaly. An easily identified mushroom, *Pholiota squarrosa* has long been considered edible, but unless you are already an experienced mycophagist of this species, I would not recommend it. Some people become very sick with severe gastrointestinal problems soon after eating it. *Pholiota squarrosa* has been confused with the Honey Mushroom, the *Armillaria ostoyae* group, which also grows in large clusters often at the base of trees. However, the Honey Mushroom lacks the dense, recurved scales on the caps and stalks and its spores are white. *Pholiota destruens* has a buff to beige cap with soft, cottony scales; a copious veil; and a thick, hard, scaly stalk. It grows in clusters on wood, particularly in cracks and on cut surfaces of cottonwood stumps in Colorado.

ORDER
Agaricales
FAMILY
Strophariaceae
EDIBILITY
Inedible

Small, sticky, dark red-dish brown to yellowish brown cap with white margin in young; brown gills; roughened brown stalk with no ring; on dung.

FRUITING BODIES Cap 0.5–3 cm broad; hemispheric to convex, flattening somewhat with age, sharp knob lacking; margin not flaring, at times striated, distinctly decorated with tiny, white particles or patches when young; dark reddish brown, fading irregularly upon drying to pale ochre-brown or tan; surface smooth, sticky when young and moist. **Gills** pallid, becoming brownish to purplish brown, margins light; broad, adnate to slightly decurrent, subdistant. **Stalk** 2–4 cm long x 2–3 mm wide, cylindrical, surface white floccose on reddish brown background, no bluish staining; ring absent. **Flesh** thin; odor and taste mild.

SPORES Purplish brown in print; 12–16 x 8–10 μm; smooth; elliptical in some views, some faintly angular; germ pore at tip.

ECOLOGY/FRUITING PATTERN Widely distributed but reported only rarely in Colorado, fruiting on horse and cow dung (but reported on moose dung in Alaska); May to September, depending apparently on moist conditions; sometimes reaching subalpine elevations.

OBSERVATIONS *coprophila:* means "dung-loving" in Latin. *Stropharia semiglobata* could be confused with *Psilocybe coprophila* because of its small size and dung-loving habit, but the former has always rounded, much yellower caps and the slender stalks possess a thin ring. Other dung lovers, species of *Coprinus,* have very black spores and often have liquefying gills. There are other LBMs that also fruit on dung that are hard to distinguish except on microscopic characters; none should be eaten because of the possibility of unknown poisons. *Psilocybe coprophila* is sometimes considered to be mildly hallucinogenic; it is not recommended as an edible.

ORDER
Agaricales
FAMILY
Strophariaceae
COMMON NAME
Sulfur Tuft
EDIBILITY
Poisonous

Orange-yellow caps with olive-yellow margins; gills greenish yellow, finally becoming purple-brown; bitter flesh; stalks clustered on decaying or buried wood.

FRUITING BODIES **Cap** 1–5 cm across; convex when young, later plane; margin remaining incurved for long time, fraying slightly; veil remnants yellowish, often persistent on margins; disc area smooth; orange-yellow to orange-brown in center, shading to yellow to olive-yellow near margins. **Gills** narrow, crowded, adnate; sulfur yellow at first, then greenish to gray-green, finally purple-brown from spores. **Stalk** 4–9 cm long x 5–10 mm wide; solid when young, hollow when old; equal to slightly enlarged base; often grown together; yellow-brown, darker at base; surface fibrillose, at times with a light yellow zone of veil fibrils. **Flesh** yellow to greenish yellow, firm; odor mild, taste very bitter.

SPORES Purple-brown in print, 6–8 x 4–4.5 μm, elliptical, smooth, with distinct germ pore.

ECOLOGY/FRUITING PATTERN Clustered on dead deciduous and conifer wood, often appearing on the ground but growing on buried wood or wood chips; July through September; not frequently reported in Colorado; montane to subalpine ecosystems.

OBSERVATIONS *fasciculare:* Latin for tufted. Also called *Naematoloma fasciculare.* This bitter mushroom has a reputation for being poisonous. The taste keeps most from trying it. A nonpoisonous look-alike, *Hypholoma capnoides* (also called *Naematoloma capnoides*), has mild flesh and smoky gray (not greenish) gills and grows in clusters only on conifer wood.

Family Bolbitiaceae

Some of the most common suburban mushrooms in the Rocky Mountain region, members of this small family of saprophytes usually have little, fragile fruiting bodies and are frequently found in lawns, gardens, manured soil, and old fields. The family is known for its brown spore colors ranging from rusty yellow-brown to yellow-brown to rusty red to cinnamon brown or dark grayish brown; cap cuticles made of a layer of inflated cells; and smooth spores with a germ pore at the apex. In the field they often resemble members of the Coprinaceae family; the latter, however, have black spore prints.

Representatives of three genera are featured here. Species of *Bolbitius* have soft fruiting bodies with bright tawny to rusty red spores, viscid, striated caps, and free gills. True to their name, species of *Conocybe* (which means "cone head") typically have conical to convex caps, very slender fragile stalks, and bright rusty brown spores; they usually grow in grassy areas. *Agrocybe* species have more pliant stalks, often with a fibrous partial veil, attached gills, and duller yellow-brown to dark brown spore deposits; they tend to fruit gregariously in cultivated soil.

Bolbitius vitellinus (Persoon) Fries

ORDER Agaricales
FAMILY Bolbitiaceae
EDIBILITY Inedible

Yellow to greenish yellow, fading, sticky cap; yellowish to yellow-cinnamon gills; pale yellow, slender, fragile stalk; veil absent; on manure or rich compost.

FRUITING BODIES Cap 2–6 cm across; conical to bell-shaped, flattening somewhat; bright yellow to greenish yellow, fading at times; disc pale cinnamon-tawny; sticky, especially in young; finely striated. **Gills** close, moderately narrow; finely adnexed, then nearly free; pallid, becoming yellow-cinnamon, finally medium reddish brown; edges minutely roughened. **Stalk** cylindrical, with gradual basal enlargement; hollow, fragile; 5–11 cm long x 3–6 mm wide; yellow most of length, paler yellow at base; veil absent; surface scurfy from pale yellow, soft particles. **Flesh** thin, watery, pale yellow; odor and taste not distinctive.

SPORES Reddish ochre-brown in print, 11–14 x 7–8 μm, elliptical, smooth, with germ pore.

ECOLOGY/FRUITING PATTERN A short-lived saprophyte, fruiting gregariously on manure, compost, manured straw, highly organic soil; quite common in many habitats where domestic animals are pastured or where soil is composted, such as urban parks. Moist, warm weather from late spring to early fall can bring out frequent crops.

OBSERVATIONS *vitellinus:* pertaining to egg yolk (Latin). This species is highly variable in the colors of the fruiting body, dependent apparently on the substrate, age, and weather. Usually only the very young caps exhibit the bright egg-yolk yellow, which soon fades. Some species of *Coprinus* share the same habitats and times of fruiting, but they will soon show liquefying gills and black spores.

Conocybe lactea (Lange) Métrod

ORDER
Agaricales
FAMILY
Bolbitiaceae
EDIBILITY
Inedible

Delicate, coni-
cal, dull white
cap; cinnamon
gills; long,
fragile, white
stalk; in grass.

FRUITING BODIES Cap 1–3 cm broad, conical; dry, often wrinkled; dull white; disc buff. **Gills** pale ochre to brownish orange, close, narrow, nearly free. **Stalk** spindly, fragile, hollow, 4–9 cm long x 1–3 mm wide, cylindrical, whitish, few fibrils, veil absent. **Flesh** whitish; odor and taste mild.

SPORES Reddish brown in print, 12–16 x 7–9 µm, smooth, elliptical, thick-walled, with germ pore.

ECOLOGY/FRUITING PATTERN A saprophyte, scattered in grass and turf; common in lawns and city parks; June through September.

OBSERVATIONS *lactea:* means "milky" in Latin. Visible as tiny cones peeking out of the grass early in the morning, they are often wilted within hours.

Agrocybe praecox (Persoon) Fayod

ORDER
Agaricales
FAMILY
Bolbitiaceae
COMMON NAME
Spring *Agrocybe*
EDIBILITY
Not
recommended

Medium-sized,
light brown
cap; brown,
attached gills;
thin ring on
whitish stalk;
strings at
base; on soil
in spring.

FRUITING BODIES Cap 2–8 cm, convex to plane, often knobbed; smooth; cream-colored to yellow-brown; margins often with veil remnants. **Gills** adnate, broad, close; pallid, then brownish gray, finally brown. **Stalk** 3–10 cm long x 3–15 mm wide; slender, slightly bulbous; hollow; white; ring thin, whitish, superior, soon broken; white threads at base. **Flesh** soft, whitish; odor and taste farinaceous.

SPORES Dull brown, 8–11 x 5–6 µm, elliptical, smooth, with pore.

ECOLOGY/FRUITING PATTERN A saprophyte; usually gregarious, on soil, often mulched with wood chips, fairly common; varied habitats; spring.

OBSERVATIONS *praecox:* precocious, early (Latin). *Agrocybe dura* fruits later, has a cracked-looking cap and somewhat larger spores. *Agrocybe pediades,* a yellowish, viscid-capped grass inhabiter, has a slender ring-less stalk. Because there are several poorly understood variants related to *Agrocybe praecox,* it is not recommended as an edible.

Family Agaricaceae

An important family economically, Agaricaceae has one main genus, *Agaricus,* some species of which have been cultivated commercially all over the world. For example, *Agaricus bisporus* is mass-produced and is commonly known as the Button Mushroom. Colorado has a large wild *Agaricus* population made up of many species found in all its ecosystems. Collections may be recognized as *Agaricus,* but some species are difficult to tell apart and remain unnamed. *Agaricus* species have chocolate brown spore prints; free gills that are usually pinkish, then brown; an easily separating cap and stalk; and typically a ring but no basal cup. Important field characters are the general stature and size, characters of the ring, the staining reactions of the cap cuticle and the base of the stalk when injured, and the odor. There are several popular edible *Agaricus* species in the Rocky Mountains as well as a few poisonous species, the latter with yellow staining reactions and faint or strong odors of phenol, carbolic acid, or ink.

Agaricus campestris Fries

ORDER
Agaricales
FAMILY
Agaricaceae
COMMON NAMES
Meadow
Mushroom,
Pink Bottom
EDIBILITY
Edible

Small to medium-sized, white cap; gills free, pink in young, then dark brown; short, white stalk; thin bandlike ring; cup absent; in grassy areas.

FRUITING BODIES Cap 3–8 cm broad, convex, becoming flattened; margin inrolled in young, at times with cottony veil remnants; smooth or with pale brown scales in center; white to pale gray-brown. **Gills** free, crowded, broad; at first bright pink, then gray-pink, finally dark blackish brown. **Stalk** 2–5 cm long x 1–2 cm wide; tapering, slim, not bulbous; white; smooth to thinly floccose; ring thin, white, bandlike, often obliterated; cup absent. **Flesh** white, slowly becoming vinaceous brown with age, firm; odor and taste mild.

SPORES Dark brown in print, 6.5–8 x 4–5.5 μm, elliptical, smooth.

ECOLOGY/FRUITING PATTERN Very common, especially at lower elevations in Colorado; single to gregarious, often in arcs or rings in grass or meadows; saprophytic in soil and compost; spring, summer, and fall, especially after rains.

OBSERVATIONS *campestris:* of the fields (Latin). *Agaricus campestris,* one of the most popular wild mushrooms in the world, is not the commercially produced *Agaricus bisporus;* in fact it is far superior in flavor. *Agaricus bitorquis,* also a popular edible, fruits in hard-packed soil along sidewalks and grassy areas. It has a stout stature, firm flesh that barely stains pale pink, a strongly inrolled cap margin, a mild odor, and a very solid stalk with a sheathing, collarlike (not skirtlike) veil. It often develops underground and surfaces when sporulating.

ORDER
Agaricales

FAMILY
Agaricaceae

EDIBILITY
Unknown

Moderately large, buff
to brown cap; thick,
whitish stalk with thin,
skirtlike ring, brown-
tipped rings at base;
flesh immediately turning
reddish orange when
bruised; in conifer litter
at high elevations.

FRUITING BODIES Cap 5–13 cm across, hemi-spheric to broadly convex, disc depressed at times; dry; appressed fibrous scales deep brown over pale buff ground color; bruising reddish brown. **Gills** free, close, quite narrow; pinkish in young, finally dark blackish brown. **Stalk** 4–10 cm long x 1.5–2 cm wide, with enlarged or slightly bulbous base up to 4 cm across; surface white, smooth above, bruising bright reddish orange or yellow-orange; thin, skirtlike, white ring with thick, brownish margin; base with brownish veil tissue as two or three brown-tipped rings more or less concentrically arranged. **Flesh** white, firm; immediate color change to reddish brown when exposed; odor mild and fruity; taste mild.

SPORES Dark brown in print, 6–6.7 x 4.8–5.3 μm, elliptical, smooth.

ECOLOGY/FRUITING PATTERN Gregarious or in arcs in deep conifer litter; under spruce and subalpine fir at high elevations; August and early September; probably more common than has been reported.

OBSERVATIONS *amicosus: amicus* means "friend" in Latin; *-osus* signifies abundance. According to its original description, this attractive, rather large *Agaricus* is quite common in the southern Rocky Mountains, but it is usually not recognized. I have found it in Colorado as far south as Conejos County and as far north as Rocky Mountain National Park, always at high elevations. Distinguishing field characters of *Agaricus amicosus* are the immediate red staining of the flesh when it is exposed, its high-elevation habitat, and the overall warm brown colors of the cap.

ORDER
Agaricales
FAMILY
Agaricaceae
COMMON NAME
Woodland *Agaricus*
EDIBILITY
Not recommended

White cap, staining faintly yellow; free gray gills, turning blackish brown; white stalk with thin, flaring ring; no basal cup; in forests.

FRUITING BODIES Cap 5-18 cm across; convex to nearly plane; smooth to finely scaly; ivory white, becoming yellowish over center, staining pale lemon yellow where bruised. **Gills** free, broad, close; pallid, then gray, finally dark brown. **Stalk** 6-18 cm long x 1-2.5 cm wide; equal or slightly enlarged toward base, sometimes abruptly bulbous; surface white and smooth above thin, flaring, white ring; ring at times with yellowish floccose patches on lower side, sometimes with cogwheel pattern; white below ring, faintly floccose; interior white and not chrome yellow at base. **Flesh** white, at times faintly yellow under cuticle when cut; odor of crushed flesh faintly of almonds, taste mild.

SPORES Dark purple-brown in print, 5-6.5 x 4-4.5 μm, elliptical, smooth.

ECOLOGY/FRUITING PATTERN Scattered to gregarious in forests, in litter, usually of conifers in montane regions; August through September; widely distributed in the Rocky Mountains; quite common in most seasons.

OBSERVATIONS *silvicola:* means "forest dweller" in Latin. *Agaricus silvicola* is a variable species or perhaps represents a group of closely related species recognized by its field characters of white caps, yellow staining, almond odor, and forest habitat. Reports on edibility vary. *Agaricus arvensis* is a similar-looking mushroom with yellow staining and an almond odor, but it fruits in grasslands, not in forests, and has larger spores. Another yellow-staining *Agaricus* that has a bad reputation for causing poisonings is *Agaricus xanthodermus*. This good-sized, white mushroom turns chrome yellow, especially in the cut stalk base, and has an unpleasant chemical odor of phenol. Collectors should examine their finds carefully to avoid picking deadly *Amanita* species that have statures, colors, and rings similar to those of *Agaricus silvicola* and its relatives, but have a volva or cup at the base, white gills when young and at maturity, and white spore prints.

ORDER	**White cap, bruis-**
Agaricales	**ing bright orange-**
FAMILY	**yellow; gills free,**
Agaricaceae	**grayish pink,**
EDIBILITY	**then dark brown;**
Not	**bulbous stalk with**
recommended	**thin skirtlike veil;**
	almond odor.

FRUITING BODIES Cap 6-14 cm across, convex to plane; lightly scaly, dry; white, bruising bright orange-yellow. **Gills** free, close, broad; at first grayish pink, then dark blackish brown. **Stalk** 5-10 cm long x 1.5-2.5 cm wide, up to 4.5 cm wide at bulb; white; nearly smooth; interior white to yellowish; ring pendant, thin, white, staining yellow, with soft patches on underside. **Flesh** firm; white, becoming yellow when exposed; odor of almonds, taste mild.

SPORES Dark brown in print, 6-7.5 x 4.5-5 µm, elliptical, smooth.

ECOLOGY/FRUITING PATTERN Fairly common; montane and subalpine ecosystems; single to gregarious; under conifers; August and September.

OBSERVATIONS *albolutescens: albo* means "white" and *lutescens* means "becoming yellow" in Latin. A relative, *Agaricus silvicola,* is also a forest dweller with an almond scent, but it stains pale yellowish, not orange-yellow, and its stalks are generally taller than those of *Agaricus albolutescens. Agaricus albolutescens* is reported to cause rather severe gastrointestinal upset in some people.

ORDER	**Medium-sized to**
Agaricales	**large, whitish cap**
FAMILY	**with dull brown**
Agaricaceae	**center, bruising**
COMMON	**yellow; stalk with**
NAME	**whitish ring, base**
Yellow Stainer	**bright yellow at**
EDIBILITY	**cut; chemical**
Poisonous	**odor; in grass.**

FRUITING BODIES Cap 4-15 cm broad; convex to plane; buttons with straight sides resemble marshmallows; chalky white, bruising yellow; center pale dull brown, browner with age, slightly scaly. **Gills** free; white to gray-pink, finally blackish brown. **Stalk** 5-12 cm long x 1.5-2 cm wide; equal to bulbous; smooth; white, browner with age; ring thick, white, underside floccose. **Flesh** white, then yellow; odor of phenol, library paste, or ink; taste unpleasant.

SPORES Chocolate brown, 4.5-6 x 3.5-4.5 µm, elliptical, smooth.

ECOLOGY/FRUITING PATTERN Cosmopolitan, common, scattered in city lawns, paths; sometimes in large groups; June through September.

OBSERVATIONS *xanthodermus:* Latin for yellow skin. Many people become ill from this mushroom. The odor and yellow staining are enhanced by a drop of KOH (see photo).

ORDER
Agaricales
FAMILY
Agaricaceae
COMMON NAME
Horse Mushroom
EDIBILITY
Edible

Medium-sized to large, white to buff caps, bruising yellow; gills pale gray, then dark brown; nonbulbous stalk; ring with patches on underside; almond odor; in grasslands.

FRUITING BODIES **Cap** 7–15 cm broad; ovoid, soon convex to plane; pale yellow-brown scales on disc; margin at times with adhering white veil remnants; white to creamy, staining yellow when bruised or desiccated. **Gills** free, close, broad; white to gray (not pink), finally blackish brown. **Stalk** 5–12 cm x 1.5–2.5 cm; equal to slightly clavate at base; white; smooth above and below the white to yellowish ring; underside of ring with cottony patches, often in cogwheel-like pattern before veil breaks; interior white, faintly yellow at times, but not chrome yellow at base; few white patches around base, but no cup or volva. **Flesh** firm, thick when young, white; odor of almonds when young, taste mild.

SPORES Dark purple-brown in print, 7–8 x 5–6 µm, elliptical, smooth.

ECOLOGY/FRUITING PATTERN Widely distributed and common in grasslands, pastures, lawns, parks at lower elevations of Colorado; gregarious, at times in rings or arcs; early summer and fall.

OBSERVATIONS *arvensis:* growing in fields (Latin). Known for its occurrence in grasslands and fields, *Agaricus arvensis* is among a group of species of yellow-staining *Agaricus* that includes *Agaricus silvicola*, differentiated by its occurrence in woodlands and its larger spores; *Agaricus augustus,* a popular edible with its large size, brown cap, floccose stalk, and strong almond odor; and the poisonous *Agaricus xanthodermus,* which grows in lawns and grassy places and has an offensive phenol or inklike odor. *Agaricus arvensis* is a popular edible, recognized by its combination of medium size, yellow-staining cap, pleasant almond odor, and habitat.

Family Gomphidiaceae

The Gomphidiaceae is a small family of fungi important to the Rocky Mountains because its members all form mycorrhizal relationships with conifers. The name is derived from *gomphos*, meaning "peg" in Greek. Indeed, most species do have a peglike shape to their fruiting bodies. They are distinguished by their long, narrow, smoky gray to black spores and thick, decurrent gills. Members of this family are closely related to the Boletaceae family; their spores are similar in shape and the layer of gills can be easily peeled from the cap like the tube layer of a bolete. Two genera are featured here.

FEATURED GENERA

Chroogomphus Flesh not white (beige, orange-buff), turning blue in Melzer's solution, cap surface sticky or dry, p. 151.

Gomphidius Flesh white, not turning blue in Melzer's solution, cap surface sticky-gelatinous, p. 152.

Chroogomphus vinicolor (Peck) O. K. Miller

ORDER
Agaricales
FAMILY
Gomphidiaceae
EDIBILITY
Edible

Sticky, dark red-brown, often pointed, conical cap; pinkish to orange flesh; grayish, wide-spaced gills, extending down stalk; on ground under conifers.

FRUITING BODIES Cap 2–6 cm broad; conical to turban-shaped, often sharply pointed; margin incurved; slimy to tacky, drying shiny; ochraceous brown to dark burgundy. **Gills** ochre in young, smoky black at maturity; decurrent, broad, subdistant, thick. **Stalk** long, slender; 5–10 cm long x 0.5–2 cm thick; equal to tapered; orange-buff to pale wine-colored; partial veil as thin, hairy, superior ring. **Flesh** ochraceous to orangish, turning deep violet-blue when spotted with Melzer's solution; odor and taste mild.

SPORES Smoky gray to black in print, 17–22 x 4.5–7 μm, narrowly elliptical to spindle-shaped, smooth.

ECOLOGY/FRUITING PATTERN Common; mycorrhizal with conifers (lodgepole and ponderosa pine) in montane ecosystems or even in yards and parks where conifers grow; late summer and fall.

OBSERVATIONS *vinicolor*: the color of wine (Latin). A related look-alike, *Chroogomphus rutilus*, fruits in similar habitats and seasons, but its caps are broader, less conical, and more brownish than those of *Chroogomphus vinicolor*.

ORDER
Agaricales
FAMILY
Gomphidiaceae
EDIBILITY
Edible

Glutinous purple-brown caps; decurrent, pale drab, distant gills; thick, white stalk with bright yellow base; under conifers.

FRUITING BODIES Cap 3-10 cm across; convex, flattening, margins often upturned; smooth, without hairs; slimy-glutinous when fresh, shiny at maturity, skin peeling easily; purple drab to dull lilac-brown, often spotted with black stains. **Gills** whitish in young, turning smoky gray with age; distinctly decurrent, thick, narrow, close, becoming subdistant; at first covered with thick slime veil. **Stalk** sturdy, 4-10 cm tall x 1-3 cm thick; tapered toward base; white above glutinous ring, chrome yellow below; partial veil colorless and slimy with white fibrillose veil beneath it, forming bandlike superior ring that darkens from trapped spores. **Flesh** thick; soft; whitish above, bright yellow in stalk base; odor and taste not distinctive.

SPORES Smoky gray to blackish, 16-20 x 5-7 μm, elliptical to spindle-shaped, smooth.

ECOLOGY/FRUITING PATTERN Fairly common; typically a high-elevation species that fruits under conifers, especially spruce and subalpine fir; solitary to gregarious on the ground; August to October.

OBSERVATIONS *glutinosus:* with gluten, slimy (Latin; *-osus* indicates abundance). *Gomphidius oregonensis* looks similar and is also found in comparable habitats in the West, but it has slimy, pinkish orange to red-brown caps, grows in clusters usually from deep within the soil, and has smaller spores. *Gomphidius subroseus* looks similar, but its glutinous caps are dull pink to reddish. It grows with Douglas-fir in Colorado, often accompanied by a bolete, *Suillus lakei,* growing nearby.

Family Paxillaceae

A family of relatively few species, Paxillaceae is represented in this book by one genus: *Paxillus*. These are fleshy, medium-sized mushrooms growing on soil or wood. The decurrent, often forked or veined gills can easily be separated from the cap flesh; the fruiting bodies of at least one species are stalkless; and the spores are dull yellow-brown to nearly chocolate brown in mass, are smooth, and lack a germ pore. Although they have gills, members of the Paxillaceae family are often considered to be closely allied to the Boletaceae family. Like the boletes, *Paxillus* species are forest fungi. At least one, *Paxillus involutus*, can be deadly poisonous.

Paxillus vernalis (Batch) Fries

ORDER
Agaricales
FAMILY
Paxillaceae
EDIBILITY
Not recommended

Medium-sized to large, yellow-brown, flattened caps with distinctly inrolled margins; narrow, decurrent, yellow-brown gills, bruising brown and separating easily from cap; sturdy, ringless stalk; under aspens.

FRUITING BODIES Cap 6-20 cm broad, occasionally wider; convex to flattened, often depressed; margin distinctly inrolled, cottony in young, finally smooth or obscurely ribbed; sticky at first, soon dry; pale brownish yellow when young, medium rusty brown at maturity with matted brownish hairs stuck to surface. **Gills** crowded, narrow; yellowish olive, bruising quickly to brown to red-brown; decurrent, often forking near stalk, fusing at times to form a few angular pores; entire gill layer easily separated from cap. **Stalk** solid and stumpy, equal to slightly tapered; short in relation to cap; 3-9 cm long x 3-5 cm wide; central or off-center; dry, fibrillose; dingy yellowish brown, staining rusty reddish brown where handled and with age; ring absent. **Flesh** firm, solid; yellow, soon staining red-brown when cut; odor mild to aromatic, taste acidic.

SPORES Deep brown to nearly chocolate brown in thick print, 7.5-10 x 5-5.5 μm, elliptical, smooth.

ECOLOGY/FRUITING PATTERN Scattered under aspen in montane to subalpine ecosystems; July and August; common in some seasons.

OBSERVATIONS *vernalis:* means "of spring" in Latin. The slightly smaller *Paxillus involutus*, with more slender stalks, has a yellow-brown spore print and slightly different microscopic characters. There are reports from Europe of acute hemolytic anemia and deaths from consuming *P. involutus*, apparently caused by hypersensitization, which can occur suddenly. Both species should be considered poisonous.

153

Family Boletaceae

These mushrooms have fleshy, easily rotting fruiting bodies consisting of a cap, a central stalk, and many tiny tubes arranged vertically on the underside of the cap. Basidiospores form inside these tubes and eventually drop out of tiny openings or pores.

Commonly called boletes, Boletaceae species are typically terrestrial, mycorrhizal forest dwellers. The group contains some delicious edibles—and a few very poisonous ones. (Watch out for boletes with orange to red pores, especially those that bruise blue.) In Colorado the most frequently encountered boletes belong to three genera:

FEATURED GENERA

Boletus Typically dry fruiting body; bulky stalk often ornamented with surface veins or reticulations near top; spores olive to olive-brown, rarely cinnamon brown; lacking veil, pp. 154-157.

Suillus Cap yellow, yellow-orange, or brownish, sticky to fibrillose; spores pale to dark yellow-brown or olive; often radially oriented pores; stalk frequently dotted with colored spots or having veil that leaves ring; always with conifers, pp. 158-159.

Leccinum Cap reddish, orange, or brownish, usually large; stalk dry, lacking a ring, with conspicuous scabers that usually turn blackish with age; pores very small; spores yellow-brown to cinnamon brown, pp. 160-161.

Boletus chrysenteron Fries

ORDER Agaricales
FAMILY Boletaceae
EDIBILITY Edible

Olive-brown, dry caps with cracked surface showing reddish stains and yellow flesh; tubes yellow, staining greenish; stalk yellow, but reddish near base.

FRUITING BODIES Cap 3-7 cm across; hemispheric to convex; velvety, dry; dull olive-brown with cracks in surface showing yellow flesh; pink stains common in cracks. **Tubes** yellow to olive, bruising bluish green; tube mouths (pores) irregularly angular, dull yellow; depressed at stalk. **Stalk** 3-8 cm long x 1-2 cm wide, typically rather slender; cylindrical to clavate; solid; dull yellow, but reddish below or streaked reddish, interior bruising blue; dry to scurfy and at times with longitudinal ridges, but not reticulate; ring absent. **Flesh** soft; white, soon yellowish, sometimes with pinkish stains, especially near cuticle, usually blueing slowly; odor and taste mild.

SPORES Olive-brown in print, 10-14 x 4-5.5 µm, long, elliptical, not truncated.

ECOLOGY/FRUITING PATTERN Found near scrub oak and aspen in southern Colorado; widely distributed throughout the region but not common; late summer into fall.

OBSERVATIONS *chrysenteron:* Greek *krysos* means "gold" and *enteron* means "inner." Some consider this bolete edible, but its mushy texture does not particularly recommend it. The specimen pictured here was collected near Wolf Creek Pass in September. *Boletus truncatus* is similar but has truncated spores (appearing cut-off) and a more robust stalk.

ORDER
Agaricales
FAMILY
Boletaceae
EDIBILITY
Inedible

Small to medium-sized, tawny red cap with cinnamon tubes and reddish pores; yellowish stalk base; peppery taste.

FRUITING BODIES Cap 1.5–5 cm, at times up to 7 cm across; hemispheric to convex, flattening; yellow-brown to orange-brown; smooth, dry to sticky in wet weather. **Tubes** ochre, becoming red-brown; broadly attached to stalk, at times as veins at juncture; tube mouths (pores) large and angular, yellowish, becoming deep rusty red, slightly darker at bruises, but not blueing. **Stalk** 2–8 cm long x 0.5–1.5 cm wide, equal to tapered toward base; yellow to reddish cinnamon, more red toward top; yellowish at base; surface dry, without glandular dots, lines extending with age from tubes down upper portion of stalk; veil absent. **Flesh** yellow throughout cap and stalk, reddish above tube layer; odor mild, taste peppery, burning.

SPORES Reddish brown in print, 8–10 x 3.5–4.5 μm, elongated, elliptical, smooth.

ECOLOGY/FRUITING PATTERN Fairly common; scattered to gregarious in soil under spruce, fir, and pine in montane regions; July through September.

OBSERVATIONS *piperatus:* Latin for peppery. Also called *Chalciporus piperatus*. This small *Boletus* species is often inconspicuous but memorable if you nibble one and feel the slowly increasing burning sensation on your tongue! Although it is not reported to be poisonous if cooked well, *Boletus piperatus*'s peppery nature does not recommend it as an edible and could cause stomach upset. To differentiate *Suillus* species, compare colors and test for the peppery taste (and immediately spit out the raw piece). *Suillus* species also differ in having either remnants of a veil or glandular dots on the stalk.

ORDER
Agaricales
FAMILY
Boletaceae
COMMON NAMES
King Bolete,
Porcini, Steinpilz
EDIBILITY
Edible, choice

Large, solid, dry, reddish brown cap; whitish to olive-colored tubes and pores; robust stalk with whitish veins at top; flesh white and not staining.

FRUITING BODIES Cap large, 6–20 cm, rarely up to 30 cm across; convex to plane; margins undulating with age; red-brown, deep yellow-brown, to cinnamon brown, buttons lighter; dry to sticky in wet weather. **Tubes** 1–4 cm long; first white, maturing to greenish yellow; depressed at stalk; tube mouths (pores) white, small, round, covered by white hyphae when young, at times bruising tawny, never blue; at maturity olive-brown from spores. **Stalk** bulky; 10–20 cm long x 2–6 cm thick; rarely equal, usually clavate or bulbous; white to pale yellow-brown, surface with white to pinkish, raised, veined network most prominent on upper stalk; veil absent. **Flesh** white and firm in young specimens, long remaining white; at maturity or beyond, becoming softer, often by then riddled by larvae; odor pleasantly mild, taste mild.

SPORES Olive-brown in print, 12–20 x 4–6 μm, elongated, elliptical, smooth.

ECOLOGY/FRUITING PATTERN Widely distributed, in some seasons abundant; scattered in well-drained forested sites from upper foothills to within a few hundred feet of timberline; mycorrhizal with Engelmann spruce and other conifers, also hardwoods; often fruiting around its host just where the newest roots are growing; mid-July to September.

OBSERVATIONS *edulis:* Latin meaning "edible." Many collectors know that *Boletus edulis* and the Fly Agaric, *Amanita muscaria*, often fruit in the same vicinity at about the same time, the one being a signal to look for the other. Because the King Bolete is a prized edible, much attention has been paid to the many color variations of the western collections, some achieving species or variety status. A yellow-brown variant fruiting under pine is sometimes called *Boletus edulis* var. *pinicola. Boletus barrowsii* is similar to *B. edulis* in shape, flesh colors, and stalk surface pattern, but its cap colors are almost white and it fruits early under pines in Colorado's montane regions and southward into New Mexico.

Agaricales
FAMILY
Boletaceae
COMMON NAME
White King Bolete
EDIBILITY
Edible, choice

Large, off-white to gray-ish, dry cap; olive-colored tubes and mature pore mouths; solid robust stalk with whitish veined pattern; under pines.

FRUITING BODIES Cap large, 6–25 cm across, convex to plane; dull white to grayish buff; dry and smooth, not viscid. **Tubes** white when young; yellow, becoming olive-yellow with age; depressed at stipe at maturity; tube mouths (pores) very small and round, stuffed with white hyphae when very young, soon olive-yellow from spores. **Stalk** robust, usually thicker below; 6–14 cm long x 3–8 cm at widest part; solid in young; colored like cap; upper surfaces covered with dingy white to pale brownish, netlike veining; ring absent. **Flesh** solid, white, not blueing where exposed; odor mild and pleasant, taste nutty.

SPORES Dark olive-brown in print, 11–14 x 4–5 μm, elongated, elliptical, smooth.

ECOLOGY/FRUITING PATTERN Mycorrhizal with conifers; fruiting in warm sites after summer rainfall from late June through August; scattered to single; common in New Mexico, southern Colorado, and warm, exposed sites along the Front Range. It has been my experience that this large bolete will fruit year after year under the same tree.

OBSERVATIONS *barrowsii:* named to honor Chuck Barrows, New Mexican collector. *Boletus barrowsii* is an excellent edible mushroom equal (or some say better) in flavor to its more highly colored cousin, *Boletus edulis.* A collector could confuse the buttons with those of *B. edulis* if the latter were very young and protected from the sun, with very little of characteristic cap color yet developed. *Boletus barrowsii* differs from *B. edulis* by very different cap colors, its nonsticky dry caps, and slightly smaller spores.

ORDER
Agaricales
FAMILY
Boletaceae
EDIBILITY
Edible

Sticky yellow to cinnamon cap; pale yellow pores; yellowish stalk with red-brown dots; under pines.

FRUITING BODIES Cap 3–10 cm across; convex to plane; pinkish yellow, soon brownish yellow to cinnamon brown, often streaked; sticky, then shiny; margin smooth. **Tubes** whitish in young, soon yellow, yellow-brown at maturity, notched; pores pale yellow to brownish yellow, staining brown, angular, two to three per mm. **Stalk** 3–7 cm long x 1–2 cm wide, equal; whitish, bright yellow at apex; red-brown dots and smears scattered over lower two-thirds of surface; veil absent. **Flesh** white, soon yellowish, not staining; soft; odor mild to slightly fragrant, taste mild.

SPORES Cinnamon, 7–9 x 3–3.5 µm, elongated, elliptical, smooth.

ECOLOGY/FRUITING PATTERN Common; mycorrhizal with pines; gregarious in foothills, montane ecosystems; occasionally in Denver area where pines have been planted; June to September.

OBSERVATIONS *granulatus:* means "with granules." The similar-looking *Suillus brevipes* has a short, white, nondotted stem. *Suillus umbonatus* has a knobbed cap and a slime veil on a slender stalk. *Suillus albivelatus* has white veil remnants near the cap margin, sometimes an annular zone, and lacks dots on the stalk.

ORDER
Agaricales
FAMILY
Boletaceae
EDIBILITY
Edible

Sticky, yellow to red-brown, smooth cap; yellow tube layer; short, whitish, smooth stalk; no ring; with conifers.

FRUITING BODIES Cap convex to flat; 4–9 cm across; brownish, becoming ochre-brown with age; glutinous, smooth, shiny when dry; cuticle peels easily; margin smooth. **Tubes** pale yellow, dingy olivaceous at maturity; attached; pores small (two to three per mm), pale yellow, not staining. **Stalk** white, becoming yellowish; smooth, dry, equal, stubby; 2–5 cm long x 1–2 cm wide; ring absent. **Flesh** firm, white to yellow; odor mild, taste mild to acidic.

SPORES Cinnamon, 7–9.5 x 2.5–3.5 µm, narrow, elliptical, smooth.

ECOLOGY/FRUITING PATTERN Very common; mountains and valleys; mycorrhizal with conifers, especially lodgepole pine; July through September; single to gregarious.

OBSERVATIONS *brevipes:* short-footed (Latin). *Suillus granulatus* grows in similar habitats, but it has red-brown dots on its stalk and an irregularly colored cap. Removing the skin makes *Suillus brevipes* a nice edible when cooked.

Suillus lakei (Murrill) Smith and Thiers

ORDER Agaricales
FAMILY Boletaceae
EDIBILITY Edible

Sticky yellow cap with reddish brown scales; yellow pores; stalk apex yellow; white ring; under Douglas-fir.

FRUITING BODIES Cap 3–7 cm across, convex; margins inrolled, fibrillose from white veil; viscid; scales of reddish brown fibrils cover yellow flesh, fibrils finally grayish to dingy yellow. **Tubes** adnate to decurrent; lemon yellow; pores yellow, bruising pinkish brown, angular, large, about 1 mm across. **Stalk** 3–8 cm long x 1–2 cm wide; yellow at apex; ring thin, white, may disappear; reddish brown, streaked below ring, no glandular dots; lower interior yellow; base bruising greenish, basal mycelium white. **Flesh** yellow, bruising pinkish red; odor and taste mild.

SPORES Dull cinnamon, 8–10.5 x 3.5–4 µm, elliptical, smooth.

ECOLOGY/FRUITING PATTERN Common; under Douglas-fir, montane ecosystems; summer to fall; often near *Gomphidius subroseus.*

OBSERVATIONS *lakei:* named for E. R. Lake, mycologist. *Suillus lakei* var. *pseudopictus* differs by its nonviscid cap and smaller spores. Both varieties are edible when young, but rather coarse and tasteless.

Suillus tomentosus (Kauffman) Singer, Snell, and Dick

ORDER Agaricales
FAMILY Boletaceae
EDIBILITY Edible

Yellow-brown, sticky, fibrillose cap; pores cinnamon, staining brown; flesh bruising bluish; yellow stalk with brown dots; under pines.

FRUITING BODIES Cap 5–12 cm broad; convex, flatter with age, edges inrolled; yellow-brown, with gray-brown hairs on surface, becoming nearly smooth with age; sticky when humid, then dry; margins naked. **Tubes** short, adnate, or descending stalk; brownish yellow; pores small (two to three per mm); cinnamon brown, darker in young, bruising bluish brown. **Stalk** 3–10 cm long x 2–3 cm wide; equal or clavate, dry; orangish yellow; brownish glandular dots on upper surface, white tomentum below; base stains bluish; no ring. **Flesh** yellowish, bruising blue; odor and taste mild to acidic.

SPORES Olive-brown, 7–11 x 3–4 µm, elongated, elliptical, smooth.

ECOLOGY/FRUITING PATTERN Very common; single to gregarious under pines; montane, subalpine ecosystems; July through September.

OBSERVATIONS *tomentosus:* hairy (Latin). *Suillus tomentosus* has a reputation for being a second-class edible and is best when very young.

ORDER
Agaricales
FAMILY
Boletaceae
COMMON NAME
Aspen Orange Cap
EDIBILITY
Edible (but see caution)

Orangish cap; marginal skin flap; red-brown to dark brown tufts on stalk; flesh staining purplish gray without first turning burgundy wine–colored; under aspens.

FRUITING BODIES Cap 5-18 cm across; reddish orange to tawny orange-brown, somewhat browner with age (but not deep brick-red); suedelike but not hairy, often becoming sticky with age; convex to broadly convex; margin with skin flaps hanging over edge. **Tubes** depressed around stalk; dull yellowish buff, bruising yellow-gray to brownish; pores yellowish, tiny, round. **Stalk** clavate at maturity, 7-12 cm long x 1-2.5 cm thick, up to 4 cm thick at base; surface with short rigid tufts (scabers) that are pallid, then red-brown to dark brown, finally nearly black; stalk surface at times bruising blue-green; interior pallid, changing to purplish gray without first staining burgundy. **Flesh** solid, white, bruising purplish gray to finally blackish gray without first showing burgundy colors; odor mild, taste pleasant.

SPORES Yellow-brown, 13-16 x 4.5-5 µm, elongated, elliptical, smooth.

ECOLOGY/FRUITING PATTERN Common; associated with aspens in Colorado; late June through September; single to gregarious; often at edges of aspen groves.

OBSERVATIONS *insigne:* badge, distinguished (Latin). *Leccinum aurantiacum* is a similar, often more robust look-alike fruiting under conifers and aspen in Colorado. It has rusty orange-red caps with marginal skin flaps, off-white young pores, and white flesh staining burgundy wine–colored before turning purplish to blackish gray. *Leccinum insigne* has an oranger cap (with a less stable pigment, thus the dried specimens are not as rusty reddish), more yellow in the pores, and a long clavate stalk with flesh that stains purple-gray without a preliminary vinaceous red stage.

Caution: The Rocky Mountain Poison Center receives occasional reports of serious gastric problems, some requiring hospitalization, from eating moderate amounts of so-called orange caps, usually well cooked, found under aspen in various parts of Colorado. Mycophagists are urged to report to the Rocky Mountain Poison Center any problems associated with eating the Aspen Orange Cap or similar *Leccinum*s. It is becoming obvious that Colorado has a poisonous species or variety of *L. insigne* or *L. auranticum,* but so far it has not been identified.

ORDER
Agaricales
FAMILY
Boletaceae
EDIBILITY
Edible

Large, deep red-brown, fibrillose caps, marginal flaps; stalk with blackish brown tufts; flesh stains vinaceous, then purple-gray when exposed; under conifers.

FRUITING BODIES Cap 7–25 cm across; convex, becoming broadly convex; margin appendiculate with sterile extension of cap cuticle; surface dry to sticky when moist; red-brown surface densely covered by matted, dull, deep red-brown fibrils. **Tubes** pallid grayish, staining brown where bruised or with age; tube layer depressed at stalk; pores dingy buff, staining brownish. **Stalk** 4–12 cm long x 2–5 cm wide; equal or narrowed above; solid; surface white, densely covered with scales that soon blacken with age; interior flesh staining red-wine colors when cut or bruised, then turning gray to gray-black; blue to greenish stains common in or around base. **Flesh** solid; white; exposed flesh in cap and top of stalk immediately flushing pinkish, then changing to muddy purple and nearly black after several minutes; odor and taste mild.

SPORES Olive-brown, 14–18 x 3.7–5 µm, elongated, elliptical, smooth.

ECOLOGY/FRUITING PATTERN Scattered to gregarious at high elevations under lodgepole pine and occasionally spruce; montane to subalpine ecosystems; common after rains in August and September.

OBSERVATIONS *fibrillosum:* fibrillose means "with fibers." Members of the *Leccinum aurantiacum* complex are very similar to *Leccinum fibrillosum,* but their caps lack the dense fibrillose surface and the colors are usually more red-orange. *Leccinum fibrillosum* has dark reddish brown caps and always fruits under conifers.

Fat-stalked *Leccinum subalpinum* also has a fibrillose cap with colors similar to those of *Leccinum fibrillosum* and fruits under conifers at high elevations of the southwestern United States. Its cut flesh is unchanging or does not have a reddish intermediate phase before it turns very slowly to deep gray.

Collectors are warned about a potentially poisonous, aspen-associated *Leccinum* in Colorado (see preceding page).

Order Aphyllophorales

A very diverse order of fungi, this large group of basidiomycetes features mushrooms with spore-bearing surfaces not on gills but on clubs, folds and veins, teeth and spines, and inside nondetachable tubes. Aphyllophorales means "without a bearer of gills."

KEY TO FAMILIES

Spores borne inside nondetachable tubes on leathery, woody, rarely fleshy fruiting bodies, with or without stalks:

Polyporaceae and related families, p. 171

Spores on outside of teeth, spines, folds, veins, clubs, or tips of coral-like fruiting bodies:

Hydnaceae	Fertile surface on teeth or spines, pp. 167–170.
Clavariaceae	Fertile surface on clubs or coral-shaped fruiting bodies, pp. 164–166.
Cantharellaceae	Fertile surface on veins or folds, usually running down sides of tapered stalk, pp. 162–163.

(Certain polypores have ragged, teethlike pore edges; see Polyporaceae and related families, p. 171.)

Gomphus floccosus (Schweinitz) Singer

ORDER	Large, vase-shaped
Aphyllophorales	fruiting body; yellow
FAMILY	to orange-red,
Cantharellaceae	coarsely scaly cap;
COMMON NAME	whitish ridges
Scaly Vase	descending sturdy
Chanterelle	stalk; in soil under
EDIBILITY	conifers.
Not recommended	

FRUITING BODIES 6–20 cm high. **Cap** 5–15 cm broad; cylindrical, becoming dish- to vase-shaped; margin wavy; moist to sticky, smooth, developing coarse surface scales near center, flattened scales near margin; deep orange-yellow to orange-red. **Spore-producing surface** descending over almost entire outer surface of stalk; veins blunt-edged, forking, often pore-like. **Stalk** 8–15 cm long x 1–3 cm thick; not distinctly separated from cap; whitish; tapering downward, fibrous, hollow. **Flesh** fairly thick, whitish; odor mild, taste mild to sour.

SPORES Ochre in print, 10–16 x 5–8 µm, elliptical, slightly wrinkled.

ECOLOGY/FRUITING PATTERN Scattered to clustered, on soil under conifers; montane, subalpine habitats; uncommon; August, September.

OBSERVATIONS *floccosus:* Latin meaning "wooly." Conifer-loving *Gomphus kauffmanii* has tan to ochre-tawny caps, thick brittle scales, and very large (up to 35 cm broad) fruiting bodies. Also fruiting under conifers, often in clusters, *Gomphus clavatus* has purple to tan, club- to funnel-shaped caps; shallow, purplish buff veins; and short, often fused stalks. All of these species have variable reputations regarding their edibility; some produce gastrointestinal upset in some people.

ORDER
Aphyllophorales
FAMILY
Cantharellaceae
COMMON NAMES
Chanterelle,
Pfifferling, Girolle
EDIBILITY
Edible, choice

Bright golden yellow caps with scalloped edges, depressed centers when mature; yellow, thick, forked, gill-like ridges running down tapered stalk; in soil near conifers.

FRUITING BODIES Cap 3–12 cm broad, bright golden yellow, fading in sunlight, edges often bleached whitish; convex with inrolled margins, finally sunken in center; margins scalloped and wavy at maturity; surface fibrous to smooth, occasionally cracked, not sticky. **Spore-producing surface** gill-like, with blunt ridges; thick, shallow, descending stalk, finally becoming mere raised lines; cross-veins and forking common; bright orange to pale yellow (often more intensely colored than faded cap). **Stalk** 2–6 cm long x 0.5–2.5 cm wide; solid; central to off-center at times; equal to tapering toward base; bases often clustered; colored like cap; surface usually smooth. **Flesh** firm, thick, pale yellowish to buff; odor pleasantly fruity, taste mild and rather sweet.

SPORES Pale yellow in print, on surfaces of gill-like folds and ridges; 8–10 x 4.5–5.5 μm; elliptical; smooth; non-amyloid.

ECOLOGY/FRUITING PATTERN Scattered to gregarious, at times in caespitose clusters; in soil in lodgepole pine and mixed conifer stands or so-called scrub aspen groves, usually above elevations of 8,000 feet in Colorado; July and August; sometimes common, other years hard to find.

OBSERVATIONS *cibarius:* Latin for edible. Successful collectors look for the popular Chanterelles at the edges of clearings and along old roads in conifer woods in well-drained or rocky soil, often among huckleberry plants with aspen nearby. Similarly colored *Gomphus floccosus* has thick, erect scales on large, trumpet-shaped caps and a whitish, veined fertile surface descending the entire stalk. It is poisonous to some people. *Hygrophoropsis aurantiaca,* often called a false chanterelle, has distinctly sharp-edged, truly forking gills; has tough, cartilaginous, brownish orange stalks; and grows on or near decaying wood. This questionable edible also lacks the fruity odor so characteristic of the Chanterelle.

ORDER
Aphyllophorales
FAMILY
Clavariaceae
EDIBILITY
Edible

Small to medium-sized, pale yellowish, multi-branched coral fungus; tips with tiny "crowns"; on dead hardwoods, especially aspen; peppery taste.

FRUITING BODIES 4-10 cm high; multibranched coral-like clusters arising from common base; overall creamy pale yellow to pinkish buff, becoming dull ochre at maturity; basal branches browner with age; outer surfaces smooth. **Branches** rising in tiers from ends of branches below; ends of uppermost branches distinctively cupped into minute crownlike shapes, each having three to seven tiny erect side branches. **Flesh** whitish, rather tough; odor mild, taste peppery.

SPORES White in print, formed on outer surfaces, 3.5-4.5 x 2-3 μm, elliptical, smooth, amyloid.

ECOLOGY/FRUITING PATTERN In small clusters of several branching stalks; growing from cracks of dead hardwood logs (usually aspen in Colorado); early summer at lower elevations to early September in higher subalpine regions; not common.

OBSERVATIONS *pyxidata:* from Greek *pyxis,* meaning "box," referring to the shape of the ends of the branches. These pretty corals are easy to recognize because of their habit of growing directly on wood, combined with their pale colors and unusual crownlike tips. If you are lucky enough to find these miniature candelabras, get out your hand lens for a good look at some of the intricacies of nature. *Ramaria stricta,* a look-alike that also grows on wood, has compact clusters of distinctively upright branches with yellowish tips that are not crownlike.

ORDER
Aphyllophorales
FAMILY
Clavariaceae
COMMON NAMES
Fairy Fingers
EDIBILITY
Edible

Clusters of unbranched, tapered, pale purple clubs; in moist soil under conifers.

FRUITING BODIES Club 2-10 cm long x 2-7 mm thick; erect; unbranched, spindle-shaped with tapered tips; hollow, often compressed laterally. **Spore-producing surface** deep purple, reddish purple, to grayish purple; smooth; dry, minutely frosted. **Base** usually clustered with others, whitish, slightly hairy. **Flesh** white to purplish, fragile, brittle; odor and taste mild.

SPORES White in mass, 6-9 x 3-5 µm, elliptical, smooth.

ECOLOGY/FRUITING PATTERN Clustered by the dozens under conifers, often spruce; mid-July into September; upper montane and subalpine ecosystems; widespread and quite common after heavy rains.

OBSERVATIONS *purpurea:* purple (Latin). These "tiny purple flames leap up from the litter of the forest floor," according to the poetic description by D. H. Mitchel in *Colorado Mushrooms* (1966).

Clavariadelphus truncatus var. lovejoyae (Wells and Kempton) Corner

ORDER
Aphyllophorales
FAMILY
Clavariaceae
EDIBILITY
Unknown

Small, reddish orange, clublike coral fungus; in soil under conifers

FRUITING BODIES Cap continuous with stalk, 0.5-3 cm across at apex; club-shaped; top convex, plane, to slightly concave; dull red to red-orange. **Spore-producing surface**

on sides, shading to dull orange-red, smooth. **Stalk** 3-8 cm long x 10-12 mm wide, at times with long grooves near base, buff to ochraceous. **Flesh** cream-colored, spongy; odor mild, taste sweet.

SPORES White in print, produced on sides of fruiting body, 9.5-12.5 x 4.5-6.5 µm, broadly elliptical, smooth.

ECOLOGY/FRUITING PATTERN Gregarious to clustered; not common; on soil under conifers in subalpine ecosystems; summer, fall.

OBSERVATIONS *truncatus:* cut off (Latin). The type specimen of this variety is from Wyoming. This is a high-elevation *Clavariadelphus* recognized for its reddish colors and white spore print. *Clavariadelphus truncatus* var. *truncatus* is common in Colorado in coniferous forests; it has pale yellow spores, a generally more robust body, oranger colors, and a distinctly flattened (truncated) cap.

ORDER
Aphyllophorales
FAMILY
Clavariaceae
EDIBILITY
Not recommended

Large clumps of profusely branched, bright to pale orange-yellow, coral-like mushrooms; thick, white to yellow stalk; not staining at injury; on soil in conifer forests.

FRUITING BODIES Up to 16 cm high and about the same in width. **Branches** densely clustered; arising from fused stalk, pointed upward; lower branches 1–2 cm wide; divided several times, ultimately ending in two or three rounded tips; bright orange to orange-yellow, tips at times slightly darker orange. **Stalk** thick; single or fused; 3–4 cm across, branching several times; white, blending to yellow upward; interior white to yellowish; firm, neither cartilaginous, gelatinous, nor marbled; white basal tomentum. **Flesh** fleshy-fibrous, white, not staining at injury; odor slightly sweet, taste mild.

SPORES Golden yellow in print, 11–15 x 3.5–5 µm, elliptical, with irregular coarse warts.

ECOLOGY/FRUITING PATTERN Gregarious; sometimes in arcs and rings; moist high-elevation forests under conifers, especially spruce; after summer rains, August and September.

OBSERVATIONS *largentii:* named for American mycologist David Largent. Yellow to orange coral mushrooms, notoriously difficult to name, are common in the high country among conifers. Many have been called *Ramaria aurea* locally; however, specialists claim that *R. aurea* is a rather rare fungus growing under beech trees in Europe. The *Ramaria largentii* pictured here is deep orange, and the spores are large and ornamented. Other orange to yellow, high-elevation *Ramaria*s in this region are likely to be one of several species distinguishable mainly on microscopic characters. Reports of edibility vary. Some yellow *Ramaria*s may have a laxative effect on some people. *Ramaria* collections with gelatinous tissue should not be eaten.

ORDER
Aphyllophorales
FAMILY
Hydnaceae
EDIBILITY
Incdible

Wedge-shaped, hairy, dull white to brown caps with bluish margins; short spines; tough, zoned flesh; stalks rusty orange at base; often clustered in soil.

FRUITING BODIES Caps irregularly rounded and continuous with stalks; 3–12 cm across, variable in size and often grown together; convex to depressed; velvety, soon hairy to shaggy, or pitted; margin rounded and hairy; dull white, soon brown at center, margin finally deep indigo blue. **Fertile surfaces** on short, sharp spines; spines white with blue tints, becoming medium brown; up to 3–4 mm long, descending stalks. **Stalks** stubby, tough, corky; 2–7 cm long x 1–3 cm wide; embedded in soil, usually attached to substrate debris; dull orange-brown, interior of base rusty orange. **Flesh** fibrous, with distinct dark zones; deep bluish gray and brownish layers; odor and taste farinaceous, not aromatic.

SPORES Medium brown in print, 4.5–6.5 x 4.5–5 μm, nearly round, warted.

ECOLOGY/FRUITING PATTERN At times single, but usually clustered; spreading, indeterminate growth often encompassing grasses and sticks; in soil, deeply attached to substrate litter, under spruce and pine; upper montane to subalpine ecosystems; late summer, fall; fairly common.

OBSERVATIONS *caeruleum:* from Latin, meaning "blue." *Hydnellum suaveolens* is similar, but it has a blue stalk inside and outside, an overpowering aromatic odor, and differently shaped spores. *Hydnellum aurantiacum* has orange to rusty cinnamon colors, two-layered flesh, and a bright cinnamon stalk without blue tones. Members of the genus *Sarcodon* have pale-colored teeth and brown spore prints, but their flesh is soft and homogeneous. Members of another genus with teeth, *Hydnum,* can be differentiated by their white spores combined with soft, homogeneous flesh. Many authors now place *Hydnellum* in the family Thelephoraceae.

167

ORDER
Aphyllophorales
FAMILY
Hydnaceae
COMMON NAME
Strawberries and Cream
EDIBILITY
Inedible

Tough, creamy white cap exuding drops of reddish juice; undersurface with brownish spines descending short stalk; on soil under conifers.

FRUITING BODIES Cap continuous with stalk; 3–15 cm across; irregularly rounded, more or less indeterminate in shape, encompassing vegetation; broadly convex to depressed; surface at first feltlike, becoming scaly, jagged, often ridged with age; white at first, then reddish brown, darkening to blackish brown in old age; dotted with clear red drops of acrid-tasting liquid when young, liquid becoming brownish with age. **Fertile surface** on underside of cap, composed of short teeth or spines, 2–5 mm long, crowded, decurrent, white, aging to gray-brown. **Stalk** 3–5 cm long x 1–3 cm thick, tapering; often embedded in soil; outer surface whitish, finally brownish, covered with spines on upper part, below very hairy and fused with substrate; interior tough, zoned, dingy brown. **Flesh** very solid to tough and woody, faintly zoned, dingy reddish brown; odor mild to disagreeable, taste acrid.

SPORES Medium brown in print, 4.5–5.5 x 4–4.5 μm, subglobose, warty.

ECOLOGY/FRUITING PATTERN Solitary, or several fruiting bodies fused together on ground; under conifers; not common; during summer months; montane to subalpine ecosystems.

OBSERVATIONS *peckii:* named for American mycologist C. H. Peck. If you are lucky enough to find this interesting fungus when it is young and fresh, the red liquid drops make it fairly easy to identify. As the picture shows, it really does look like a bowl of strawberries and cream when fresh, but if you go back and look at it another day, those lovely colors will have turned unattractive and dull. There are several *Hydnellum* species in the Rocky Mountain region, but none are as distinctive as this one.

ORDER
Aphyllophorales
FAMILY
Hydnaceae
COMMON NAMES
Hedgehog Mushroom,
Sweet Tooth
EDIBILITY
Edible

Medium-sized, orange-tawny, fleshy cap with wavy margin; long, pointed, cream-colored spines; whitish, brittle flesh; pale orange stalk; in soil under trees.

FRUITING BODIES Cap 3-9 cm across; at first convex with inrolled margins, becoming flattened with wavy, lobed margins; color variable, from pale orange-brown to reddish tawny; surface smooth, hairless, cracking into scales with age. **Fertile surface** in form of cream-colored spines; lengths varying, giving surface a shaggy look; 4-8 mm long; often extending down stalk; crowded; sharply tipped; rusty brown when dried. **Stalk** central or somewhat off-center; solid; equal to slightly enlarged at base; 3-8 cm long x 1.5-2 cm wide; light buff, discoloring or aging to orangish buff; fairly smooth, hairless, dry. **Flesh** brittle, white to creamy buff, discoloring ochre at bruises; odor and taste mild.

SPORES White in print, 6.5-9 x 6-8 μm, nearly globose, smooth.

ECOLOGY/FRUITING PATTERN Solitary to gregarious; fruiting in Colorado in late August and September; on the ground in mixed conifer forests; usually appearing in the same area year after year; upper montane to subalpine ecosystems.

OBSERVATIONS *repandum:* means "turned back" in Latin. Has also been called *Dentinum repandum*. These attractive mushrooms are easy to recognize by their turned-back, or repand, cap edges, their orangish colors, and their pointed cream-colored teeth or spines.

Members of the genus *Hericium,* another group of popular edible teeth fungi, have masses of long, white, iciclelike, downward-pointing spines growing in beautiful clusters from wood. They are rarely reported in Colorado but are always a memorable find, both for the mycophagist and the photographer.

ORDER
Aphyllophorales
FAMILY
Hydnaceae
COMMON NAME
Hawk's Wing
EDIBILITY
Edible

Brown, irregular cap
with distinctive coarse,
raised, brownish scales;
brown spines; thick
hollow stalk; on ground.

FRUITING BODIES Cap 5–20 cm across; convex with edges turned under, soon flattening with center sunken; at maturity sometimes having a center hole connecting to hollow stalk; surface dry, with large, erect, dark brown, thick, concentrically arranged scales; overall color light brown when fresh, becoming darker with age. **Fertile surface** spine-covered; spines at first grayish white, then darkening to brown, pointed, usually descending stalk, 0.5–1.5 cm long. **Stalk** central to off-center; bulky, becoming hollow with age; 4–10 cm long x 1–3 cm wide, enlarging toward base; surface smooth, pale dull brown; interior light brown, but not blackish olive. **Flesh** thick, white to light brownish; odor mild, taste mild to distinctly bitter.

SPORES Medium brown in print, on surfaces of teeth, 6–8 x 5–7 µm, subglobose, strongly warty.

ECOLOGY/FRUITING PATTERN Very common after rains in montane and subalpine habitats; usually gregarious; on the ground under conifers and in mixed forests; July through September, depending on rainfall.

OBSERVATIONS *imbricatus:* Latin for overlapping, shingled. Formerly known as *Hydnum imbricatum, Sarcodon imbricatus* is one of Colorado's most common fungi in the montane to subalpine forests. It fruits from July until the weather gets too cold in September. One late September, I saw hundreds of these fruiting bodies frozen into black statues under spruce on Tin Cup Pass. Only mild, young fruiting bodies should be eaten, as this fungus makes some people slightly ill.

Among similar *Sarcodon* species are members of the *Sarcodon scabrosus* group, which have chestnut brown, less scaly caps; distinctive olive-black to dark bluish green coloration in the stalk bases; and a bitter taste. The genus *Sarcodon* is placed in the family Thelephoraceae by some authors.

Family Polyporaceae

Included in this huge, multifaceted family are fungi of great contrast. They may be woody to leathery, crustlike to fleshy, stalked to sessile, large to small, but they all typically form basidiospores on the inside of tubes that are not separable from the flesh. In recent decades, groups with natural affinities to each other have been segregated from Polyporaceae and placed into many other families.

The commonly used term *polypore* (meaning "many pored" in Latin) describes the spore-producing layer that is usually easily visible as tubes, with pore mouths on the underside of the often woody cap. However, sometimes the openings of the tubes are only recognizable as gill-like, mazelike, or teethlike structures. Some members of the family are resupinate, lying flat against the substrate with the fertile layer exposed. Some species are perennials; others are annuals.

Members of the unrelated Boletaceae family also bear their spores inside tubes and release them from pores on the underside of the caps. However, the boletes differ markedly from the polypores by virtue of their rapidly decaying flesh, soft-fleshed caps with tubes that separate easily from the flesh, central stalks, and terrestrial habit.

Polyporus arcularius Batsch

ORDER
Aphyllophorales
FAMILY
Polyporaceae
EDIBILITY
Inedible

Small, tough-fleshed, yellow-brown cap; hairy edges; large, hexagonal pores; central stalk attached to wood.

FRUITING BODIES Cap 1–3 cm across; roughly circular; convex with dimple in center; surface lightly scaly; edge with distinct, sharp hairs; tough; golden to dark yellow-brown. **Tubes** white to yellowish; slightly decurrent; pores large, hexagonal, one to two per mm. **Stalk** 2–4 cm long x 3–5 mm thick; central; equal; pale yellowish brown; lightly scaly, white tomentum at attachment to wood. **Flesh** tough, whitish; odor and taste mild.

SPORES White, 7–9 x 2.5–3 µm, cylindrical, smooth, non-amyloid.

ECOLOGY/FRUITING PATTERN Producing a white rot of dead hardwood, such as cottonwood, Gambel oak, and conifers; commonly found in early spring, summer; widely distributed; foothills to montane shrublands to montane forests.

OBSERVATIONS *arcularius:* like a paintbox (Latin), referring to the partitioned tube layer. Members of the formerly huge genus *Polyporus* are now limited to those with stalked fruiting bodies, growing on wood, with light or white, non-amyloid, smooth, cylindrical spores. *Polyporus elegans* has tan caps with smaller, often circular pores and a distinctive black stalk base. *Polyporus varius* also has a black stalk base, but its pale buff caps have radially aligned, darker striations.

ORDER
Aphyllophorales
FAMILY
Polyporaceae
EDIBILITY
Edible

Fleshy, pinkish tan caps; tubes with tiny, white, rounded pores descending thick stalks; in confluent masses; in soil near conifers.

FRUITING BODIES Annual. **Cap** 4-20 cm across; often in confluent masses; convex; margins irregular; pinkish tan to apricot-colored; dry, cracked. **Tube layer** shallow, white, decurrent; pores round, white, staining tan. **Stalk** 3-6 cm long x 1-3 cm wide, tapered, white, clustered. **Flesh** thick; white, staining tan; odor aromatic, taste latently bitter.

SPORES White, 4-5 x 3-4 μm, elliptical, smooth, weakly amyloid.

ECOLOGY/FRUITING PATTERN In arcs or fairy rings of dozens of fruiting bodies; widely distributed, montane to subalpine ecosystems; with conifers; at times very common; late July to late September.

OBSERVATIONS *confluens:* confluent, running together. The weathered caps are often tinged with a green, algal surface growth. Species of *Albatrellus* are sometimes confused with boletes because they grow on the ground, but *Albatrellus* tube layers are thin, tough, and not detachable.

ORDER
Aphyllophorales
FAMILY
Polyporaceae
COMMON NAME
Sheep Polypore
EDIBILITY
Edible

Fleshy, whitish cap with yellowish cracks; thin layer of white tubes descending sturdy stalk; terrestrial near conifers.

FRUITING BODIES Annual. **Cap** convex, roughly circular, at times fused, irregularly shaped; 4-15 cm across; whitish buff to cream-colored; dry, cracked; yellowish coloration showing through cracks. **Tubes** shallow, white to yellowish, decurrent; pores tiny, circular near margin, angular near stalk, white to pale yellow. **Stalk** white; 3-8 cm long x 1-3 cm wide near base, often confluent near bases to form cluster. **Flesh** cream-colored, firm; odor aromatic, taste mild.

SPORES White, 4-5 x 3-3.5 μm, subglobose, smooth, non-amyloid.

ECOLOGY/FRUITING PATTERN Common at high elevations in the Rocky Mountain region under conifers; late July through September; montane and subalpine ecosystems.

OBSERVATIONS *ovinus:* pertaining to sheep (Latin). *Albatrellus ovinus* often fruits near *Albatrellus confluens,* which has more intensely colored, pinkish tan caps and typically fruits in large, confluent masses.

ORDER	**Small, round,**
Aphyllophorales	**hard, yellow-**
FAMILY	**brown fruiting**
Polyporaceae	**bodies; tubes and**
COMMON	**light brown pore**
NAME	**surface covered**
Veiled Polypore	**by leathery mem-**
EDIBILITY	**brane; stalkless;**
Inedible	**on dead conifers.**

FRUITING BODIES Annual. **Cap** 2–7
cm broad; globose, compressed, hooflike, hollow; tough or corky; pale
yellow-brown, darkening; dry, lacquerlike surface; margin rounded, continuous, forming leathery membrane covering pore surface, membrane
perforated by worm holes. **Tubes** pale yellow; pores minute, circular,
light brown. **Stalk** absent. **Flesh** white, corky; odor fragrant when fresh,
taste mild to bitter.

SPORES Pale pinkish tan in mass, 12–16.5 x 4–4.5 μm, smooth,
cylindrical, non-amyloid.

ECOLOGY/FRUITING PATTERN Quite common; scattered to gregarious;
attached to trunks of recently killed or dying conifer trees, often pine;
producing a soft, grayish white rot of the sapwood; July, August.

OBSERVATIONS *volvatus:* Latin, meaning "with a volva" (that which is
rolled or turned around anything). The leathery membrane over the
pores helps preserve moisture for sporulation during dry periods.

ORDER	**Semicircular,**
Aphyllophorales	**hairy brackets;**
FAMILY	**rusty brown with**
Polyporaceae	**yellow to orange**
COMMON	**outer zones;**
NAME	**brown, gill-like**
Gilled Polypore	**under surface; in**
EDIBILITY	**cracks in dead**
Inedible	**conifers, fences.**

FRUITING BODIES Annual to
perennial. **Cap** 3–10 cm across; fan-shaped to broadly funnel-shaped;
concentric dark to rusty brown zones; when fresh, growing edge bright
yellow-orange; hairy. **Spore-producing area** gill-like, mazelike plates or
elongated pores, golden brown to dull brown. **Stalk** absent. **Flesh** dark
brown, fibrous, blackening in KOH; no odor, taste bitter.

SPORES White in mass, 9–13 x 3–5 μm, cylindrical, smooth.

ECOLOGY/FRUITING PATTERN Usually gregarious, often in rows;
causing brown rot of various dead conifer wood; occasionally on aspen
wood; common throughout growing season.

OBSERVATIONS *sepiarium:* Latin, meaning "sepia-colored" or dark.
Formerly known as *Lenzites sepiaria,* this saprophyte forms brown-
rot residues that are valuable to forest soils. Look for it in cracks or cut
ends of dead logs, stumps, lumber, and wooden fences and buildings.

ORDER Aphyllophorales
FAMILY Polyporaceae
COMMON NAME Artist's Conk
EDIBILITY Inedible

Large, shelflike, woody conk attached to wood; dull cinnamon to gray-brown upper surface; white margin and under-surface; pores minute, white, but immediately dark brown when bruised.

FRUITING BODIES Perennial. **Cap** 5–35 cm wide; broadly fan-shaped; upper surface with concentric undulations or furrows, smooth, dull, often covered with its own rust brown spore deposit; light brown when young, then pale gray-brown to cinnamon brown; margin thin, white in actively growing fruiting bodies. **Tubes** medium brown; stratified, each layer separated by thin, brown hyphal tissue, 4–12 mm long per season; pores minute, five to six per mm; circular, white; when bruised, pore layer undergoes immediate oxidation to brown. **Stalk** absent. **Flesh** corky, hard, red-brown to dark brown with whitish streaks; odor and taste not distinctive.

SPORES Rusty brown in mass, 9–12 x 6.5–8 μm, broadly oval, truncated, indistinctly warty with thick double walls.

ECOLOGY/FRUITING PATTERN Common in aspen forests throughout the Rockies, all seasons; causing white, soft rot of roots and butts of living aspens; also found on dead, standing, or fallen hardwoods of other species, rarely on conifers; riparian, montane, and subalpine habitats.

OBSERVATIONS *applanatum:* Latin, meaning "all on one plane" or flat. Formerly known as *Fomes applanatum,* this polypore is called the Artist's Conk because a mark on the fresh pore surface turns brown immediately and permanently. This feature can be used to differentiate *Ganoderma applanatum* from other large conks such as *Fomitopsis pinicola,* which has a nonbrowning pore layer, white flesh, and pale smooth spores.

The Artist's Conk is renowned for its prolific spore production. Some estimates go as high as twenty million spores released per minute every day of the entire five or so months of the spore-fall period. This spore production can be a good field character because litter all around an actively sporulating fruiting body is often colored red-brown.

Fomitopsis pinicola (Swartz) Karsten

ORDER
Aphyllophorales
FAMILY
Polyporaceae
COMMON NAME
Red-Belted Polypore
EDIBILITY
Inedible

Large, woody, dull gray, bracketlike cap with resinous crust and reddish brown, marginal belt; pore surface buff, bruising pale yellow; stalkless; broadly attached to tree trunks.

FRUITING BODIES
Perennial. **Cap** 6–30 cm broad; woody; bracketlike, often semicircular in outline; seasonal growth zones evidenced on surface as concentric waves and grooves; upper surface at first with sticky, red-brown, resinous layer (which often persists over marginal area), finally hard and dull gray to dull red-brown; outer margin rounded with distinctly bright red-brown zone, often with narrow ochraceous band. **Tubes** stratified; buff; pore surface cream-colored, yellow where bruised; pores minute, four to five per mm, circular. **Stalk** absent. **Flesh** very tough, corky; cream-colored to buff, bruising pinkish; odor pungent-fungal when fresh, taste often bitter.

SPORES White to pale yellowish in mass, 6–9 x 3.5–4.5 μm, cylindrical-elliptical, smooth.

ECOLOGY/FRUITING PATTERN One of the most common polypores in conifer areas throughout the Rocky Mountain region; perennial and visible during all seasons; attached to dead conifers, rarely hardwoods, occasionally on living trees; producing a brown, cubical rot.

OBSERVATIONS *pinicola:* Latin for pine dweller. This species is quite variable in color and form. The cap is usually red-brown somewhere, often as a brighter outer belt; the flesh is cream-colored (compared with the brown flesh of members of the genus *Phellinus*); the spores are white; and the pore layer is pallid, but does not bruise brown like the pore layer of the brown-spored *Ganoderma applanatum.* It is a major producer of the brown-rot residues so beneficial to the soils of coniferous forests.

175

ORDER
Aphyllophorales
FAMILY
Polyporaceae
COMMON NAME
Dye Polypore
EDIBILITY
Inedible

Brown, hairy, fused caps arising stalkless or from common, very short base; margins yellow-orange, aging to brown; pore layer mustard yellow to greenish yellow, bruising dark brown; on base of living trees or stumps.

FRUITING BODIES   Annual; usually compound, series of fused caps in rosettelike clusters, often with enclosed plants or twigs. **Cap** 5–25 cm across; densely hairy-fibrous; faintly zonate; ochre-orange when actively growing, finally dark brown; margins often bright rusty yellow. **Tubes** decurrent if stipe is evident; dull mustard to greenish yellow, becoming brown; short, often less than 1 cm long; pores mustard yellow to green-yellow, turning brown when bruised; irregular, angular to circular, one to three per mm. **Stalk** absent, or if present, 1–6 cm long, tapered or rooting, brown. **Flesh** spongy, watery, brittle when dry, dark brown at maturity; odor not distinctive, taste sour.

SPORES   Whitish in mass, 6–9 x 2.5–5 μm, elliptical, smooth.

ECOLOGY/FRUITING PATTERN   Single to gregarious on the ground attached to roots, typically at base of dead or dying conifers, especially pine and Douglas-fir; widely distributed and common. An aggressive parasite, the mycelium attacks roots and heartwood, producing a brown rot of the butt and roots of the host.

OBSERVATIONS   *schweinitzii:* honoring American mycologist L. D. von Schweinitz. Because of the color changes as it ages, *Phaeolus schweinitzii* can be difficult for beginners to identify, but its presence at the base of conifers, its yellowish to dull yellow-green pore layer, and its orange-yellow tones in young caps should be diagnostic. Dye makers use this fungus to produce natural pigments for dyeing fabric and wool.

ORDER
Aphyllophorales
FAMILY
Polyporaceae
EDIBILITY
Inedible

Large, straw-yellow, fan-shaped, hairy, stalkless caps; often overlapping or in rosettes; tiny, irregular, white pores; attached to bases and trunks of conifers.

FRUITING BODIES Annual. **Caps** 4–15 cm long x 8 cm wide; fan-shaped to semicircular, flat; caps usually overlapping or in rosettes up to 40 cm across; surface very hairy or tufted with short, stiff hairs; creamy white to straw-yellow when fresh, deep straw-colored when dry. **Tubes** light straw-colored, up to 5 mm deep; pores angular and slightly toothed, about one to two per mm, cream- to straw-colored. **Stalk** absent or stubby. **Flesh** in fresh state flexible only when young and then juicy inside, becoming firm and fibrous; two-layered; odor and taste mild.

SPORES White in mass, 4.5–6.5 x 3–4.5 μm, broadly elliptical, smooth.

ECOLOGY/FRUITING PATTERN An unusual find in Colorado; producing a white rot of living conifers and continuing to decay dead stumps; a northern and high-elevation species in subalpine ecosystems; developing in summer, remaining through fall.

OBSERVATIONS *borealis:* means "northern" in Latin. This distinctive wood lover is noticeable because of its large size, juicy flesh when young, and attractive colors. After a very large cluster dries out, it is remarkably light in weight.

A large specimen in September

Oligoporus leucospongia (Cooke and Harkness) Gilbertson and Ryvarden

ORDER
Aphyllophorales
FAMILY
Polyporaceae
EDIBILITY
Inedible

White to pinkish, spongy, rounded, stalkless cap; on conifer wood; at high elevations in early spring and summer.

FRUITING BODIES Annual, broadly attached to wood. **Cap** elongated, rounded, 3–9 cm long x 1–4 cm wide, 1–3 cm thick; margin turned down and partially covering pore surface; soft, finely wrinkled; off-white to pinkish cinnamon, margin pale reddish brown. **Tubes** up to 5 mm thick; firm; pores circular to angular, two to four per mm, edges rough, white to creamy. **Stalk** absent. **Flesh** cottony soft above, hard near tubes; buff; odor and taste mild.

SPORES White, 4.5–6 x 1–1.5 μm, sausage-shaped, smooth.

ECOLOGY/FRUITING PATTERN Single to a few together; attached to old, low-lying conifer logs and stumps that have been under deep snow; quite common in spring at high elevations of subalpine ecosystems; a brown rotter.

OBSERVATIONS *leucospongia:* Latin, meaning "white and spongy." This member of the snowbank fungi in the western mountains develops under the snow and eventually deteriorates after the snow melts.

Phellinus tremulae (Bondarzew) Bondarzew and Borisov

ORDER
Aphyllophorales
FAMILY
Hymenochaetaceae
EDIBILITY
Inedible

Woody, perennial, hoof-shaped conk; rough, gray to black top; yellow-brown pore layer; on aspens.

FRUITING BODIES Perennial. **Cap** hard and woody, broadly attached to tree trunk, triangular in longitudinal section; upper surface crustlike, gray, becoming blackened. **Tubes** indistinctly stratified, very short, stuffed with white mycelium; pore surface deep purple-brown, yellow-brown; pores circular, five to seven per mm. **Stalk** absent. **Flesh** woody, dark brown; odor not distinctive.

SPORES White, 4.5–5 x 4–4.5 μm, nearly round, smooth.

ECOLOGY/FRUITING PATTERN A major decay fungus of aspen, and restricted to it; common; perennial; visible on live aspen in all seasons; wherever aspens grow throughout the Rocky Mountains.

OBSERVATIONS *tremulae:* pertaining to quaking aspen. It is unusual to find a grove of aspen trees without this fungus, its fruiting bodies developing at branch scars, sometimes high on the trunks.

Phellinus pini is a similar-looking conk growing on conifers and is responsible for the major loss of those trees in the West.

ORDER
Aphyllophorales
FAMILY
Polyporaceae
COMMON NAME
Orange Sponge Polypore
EDIBILITY
Inedible

Soft, spongy, bright orange, spreading fungus; undersurface orange, shaggy, with long, teeth-like tube mouths; on dead-wood; at high elevations.

FRUITING BODIES Annual. **Cap** 5–15 cm long, at times spreading along a log for 50 or more cm; spongelike, soft; bright orange, eventually fading to pale orange or whitish. **Tube layer** up to 3 cm thick; same color as cap, fading to pale orange with age; pores mostly larger than 1 mm in diameter, angular, shaggy-appearing, splitting to resemble sharp irregular teeth. **Stalk** absent. **Flesh** soft, felty, pale orange; odor mild.

SPORES White, 9–14 x 3–3.5 μm, cylindrical, smooth.

ECOLOGY/FRUITING PATTERN
Producing a brown rot of conifer and occasionally aspen logs that have lain under deep, winter snows; fruiting bodies develop in spring and persist until they deteriorate in midsummer; fairly common in subalpine ecosystems of the Rocky Mountain region.

OBSERVATIONS *alboluteus:* Latin, meaning "a combination of white and yellow." *Pycnoporellus alboluteus,* formerly called *Polyporus alboluteus,* is a conspicuous fungus in high-elevation subalpine regions, where it can be found in large masses on the lower surfaces of downed fir and spruce logs. It is one of the important decomposers and producers of brown-rot residues. These residues are extremely stable, vital, organic components of forest soils.

Another orange polypore found at high elevations in Colorado is *Pycnoporus cinnabarinus,* distinguished by its shelflike, tough, rounded cap; bright cinnabar to orange-red colors; and small pores. It produces a white rot of dead hardwoods and occasionally conifers.

ORDER
Aphyllophorales
FAMILY
Polyporaceae
COMMON NAME
Turkey Tail
EDIBILITY
Inedible

Thin, dry, overlapping clusters of caps with multi-colored zones; very small, whitish to yellow pores on underside; stalkless; common on deadwood.

FRUITING BODIES Annual. **Caps** 2.5–9 cm across; semicircular to spoon-shaped, often in large overlapping clusters or rosettes, frequently fused laterally; surface dry, smooth to hairy, with sharply contrasted concentric zones varying in color from brown, red-brown, olive-green, to bluish gray, gray, buff, to whitish; outermost growing zone lighter, usually pale ochre-yellow. **Tube layer** shallow, continuous with very thin flesh. **Stalk** absent. **Flesh** cream-colored, tough-fibrous; odor mild.

SPORES White, 5–6 x 1.5–2 µm, cylindrical, slightly curved, smooth.

ECOLOGY/FRUITING PATTERN Common on stumps and deadwood, producing a white rot of hardwoods; summer through fall, sometimes persisting for months; often encompassing grasses and other vegetation in riparian areas of plains and foothills; frequently collected from cultivated yards and back lots of Denver's urban areas.

OBSERVATIONS *versicolor:* Latin for multicolored. Also known as *Coriolus versicolor.* The common name Turkey Tail brings to mind the feathered pattern of a strutting turkey tom. Pieces of these easily dried, beautiful little fungi are often fashioned into jewelry and other craft objects.

Some species of the genus *Stereum* may superficially resemble polypores such as the Turkey Tail. However, close examination of the underside of their thin, leathery fruiting bodies will show that they have smooth to slightly roughened, unspecialized spore-producing surfaces, not the tubes and pores characteristic of the polypores.

Trichaptum biforme (Fries) Ryvarden

ORDER Aphyllophorales
FAMILY Polyporaceae
COMMON NAME Violet-Pored Bracket
EDIBILITY Inedible

Tough, white to grayish caps; underside purplish, fading to brown; pores becoming irregular, teethlike; broadly attached to dead hardwood.

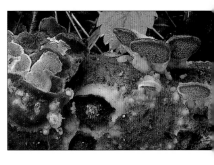

FRUITING BODIES Annual. **Caps** fan-shaped to semicircular, thin; up to 7 cm wide x 2-5 mm thick; surface grayish white, with soft velvety hairs, finally nearly smooth; marginal zone purplish. **Tube layer** thin; pores angular, often splitting, resembling teeth, three to four per mm; deep purple in young, becoming purplish brown, pale buff with age. **Stalk** absent. **Flesh** very thin, tough; odor mild.

SPORES Whitish, 6-8 x 2-2.5 µm, cylindrical, slightly curved, smooth.

ECOLOGY/FRUITING PATTERN Common; usually visible in all seasons; solitary or shelving; often on dead aspen in Colorado's mountain regions, causing a white rot.

OBSERVATIONS *biforme:* Latin, meaning "two forms." *Trichaptum abietinum* is very similar, but it rots conifer wood and its caps are narrower and tend to lie flat against the substrate with the hymenium exposed.

Peniophora rufa (Fries) Boudier

ORDER Aphyllophorales
FAMILY Corticiaceae
EDIBILITY Inedible

Small, red to purplish, wartlike, stalkless incrustations on aspen wood.

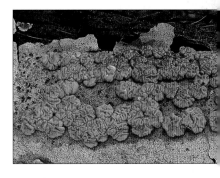

FRUITING BODIES Single or fused; wartlike; stalkless, broadly and centrally attached to substrate; 0.5-1 cm wide x about 1 mm high; convex, becoming coarsely wrinkled over entire surface; red to red-orange, at times with deep purplish tones, becoming duller upon drying; sides of warts whitish in some. **Flesh** firm, waxy, becoming hard.

SPORES White, 6-8.5 x 1.5-2 µm, cylindrical, smooth.

ECOLOGY/FRUITING PATTERN Common; scattered or massed on fallen aspen twigs and logs, usually with bark; montane to subalpine habitats; visible throughout the season, often as dried-up warts; an important wood rotter.

OBSERVATIONS *rufa:* reddish (Latin). *Peniophora rufa* is one of the more colorful members of a myriad of wood-loving fungi that do not have tubes but are resupinate (lying flat on the substrate with the spore-producing surface fully exposed).

The Gasteromycetes

The prefix *gaster,* meaning "stomach" in Latin, is most appropriate for this large diverse group of basidia-producing fungi. Its species are characterized by the development of the spore mass, or gleba, inside one or more layers of protective tissue called the peridium (Fig. 7). A sterile base may or may not be present. There is no forcible discharge of spores as in many other fungi. Commonly fruiting in dry or harsh environments—the region's grasslands and alpine tundra—gasteromycetes have evolved ways to protect the spore mass until external forces, such as wind, rain, insects, and mammals, spread the spores.

The gasteromycetes featured here include species in the following orders: Lycoperdales, the true puffballs; Nidulariales, the bird's nest fungi; Sclerodermatales, the earthballs; Phallales, the stinkhorns; Tulostomatales, the stalked puffballs; and Hymenogastrales, the hypogeous fungi. Because of their unique shapes, most genera are easily recognized as belonging to one of the groups; elucidating the species sometimes requires microscopic determination. Spore prints are not obtainable. Instead, observe the color of the mature gleba.

peridium

gleba

sterile base

Figure 7 Cross-section of a puffball

B o v i s t a p l u m b e a Persoon

ORDER
Lycoperdales
FAMILY
Lycoperdaceae
COMMON NAME
Tumbling Puffball
EDIBILITY
Edible

Small, very round puffballs without sterile bases; white, smooth outer surface peeling to reveal blue-gray inner skin.

FRUITING BODIES Spore case 1–3 cm across, nearly spherical; whitish, outer skin paper-thin, cracking, peeling away to reveal blue-gray, smooth inner skin; opening slitlike. **Sterile base** absent; hairs at base trap soil. **Flesh** (gleba) white, soon yellow and mushy; finally deep brown, powdery; odor and taste mild when young.

SPORES Deep brown, 5.5–7 x 4.5–6 μm, oval, minutely spiny to nearly smooth, long pointed appendage on each.

ECOLOGY/FRUITING PATTERN Solitary to gregarious, in soil among leaf litter, grasses; widely distributed, foothills to subalpine ecosystems; midsummer to fall; puffballs persist, finally weathering away and dispersing their spores as they are tumbled by air currents.

OBSERVATIONS *plumbea:* Latin, meaning "lead-colored." *Bovista pila* is similar but is slightly larger than *Bovista plumbea,* attaches to the ground with a single rootlike cord, is more bronze-colored at maturity, and has spores with no appendages.

Calbovista subsculpta Morse

ORDER Lycoperdales **FAMILY** Lycoperdaceae **EDIBILITY** Edible	Softball-sized, white to brown puffball; feltlike, warty surface, becoming scaly; yellow-brown gleba; large sterile base.

FRUITING BODIES Spore case
nearly round to flattened, 8–20 cm across; white, turning brownish
ochre; surface with deciduous, felty, angular, but not pyramid-shaped
patches, each with brownish, hairy center; patches separate from inner
skin; inner skin cracks to expose spores. **Base** outer surface nearly
smooth; sterile base whitish, one-fourth to one-third of volume of spore
case. **Flesh** white, homogeneous in young, finally powdered; spore mass
yellow-brown to umber; odor and taste mild when young.

SPORES Dark yellow-brown to umber, 3–5 μm in diameter, globose,
nearly smooth.

ECOLOGY/FRUITING PATTERN Single to scattered; at high elevations in
the Rockies; open slopes and meadows; June through September.

OBSERVATIONS *subsculpta:* Latin for somewhat sculptured. The sterile
bases shaped like little brown saucers often remain for months.
Calvatia booniana is much larger, does not have brownish centers in
the surface patches, and differs in microscopic characters of the gleba.

Calvatia fumosa Zeller

ORDER Lycoperdales **FAMILY** Lycoperdaceae **EDIBILITY** Unknown	Medium-sized, oval, hard, smoke-gray puff- balls; thick, persistent skin; on ground under spruce and fir in mountains.

FRUITING BODIES Spore case
round to oval; 3–8 cm in diameter; firm to hard; outer skin very thick,
up to 4 mm wide, whitish, smoke gray on top; smooth to cracked. **Base**
stalkless or with short, rootlike point of attachment; sterile base absent.
Flesh (gleba) chalky white, maturing to olive, then deep olive-brown,
becoming powdery; odor mild, finally very unpleasant; taste bitter.

SPORES Dark olive-brown, 5–7.5 μm in diameter, globose, spiny.

ECOLOGY/FRUITING PATTERN Common in high-elevation spruce/fir
regions; late spring to summer; gregarious to single; often half-buried.

OBSERVATIONS *fumosa:* Latin for smoky. Collectors may think at first
they have found a species of *Scleroderma* because of the thick and hard
skin, but the young white gleba that becomes deep olive at maturity
distinguishes *Calvatia fumosa.*

183

ORDER
Lycoperdales
FAMILY
Lycoperdaceae
COMMON NAME
Giant Western Puffball
EDIBILITY
Edible

Basketball-sized or larger white puffball, often lobed; surface with flattened warts; base absent or rudimentary; interior white, becoming olive-brown; in exposed areas or semiarid soils.

FRUITING BODIES Spore case spherical to flattened on top, sometimes with lobes; 20–60 cm across, up to 30 cm high; dull white, with large, flat, tan, medallionlike scales; scales crack away, leaving persistent underskin that eventually disintegrates to release spores. **Base** simply sits on soil or at best has rudimentary basal attachment; sterile base absent. **Flesh** spore mass white in youth, becoming yellow-brown, then olive-brown and powdery; odor mild, currylike when old; taste mild.

SPORES Olive-brown, 4–6 x 3.5–5 µm, spherical or nearly so, smooth to minutely ornamented.

ECOLOGY/FRUITING PATTERN Fruiting sporadically, July until fall; semiarid or exposed areas of western states, from semidesert shrublands and lower foothills to montane ecosystems; usually gregarious, sometimes in fairy rings in grassy pastures, among sagebrush, and even on ski slopes.

OBSERVATIONS *booniana:* honoring W. J. Boone, former president of the College of Idaho. The Goliath of its tribe, this puffball is a joy to find, even if you discover it too late for dinner. There are probably more pictures of these giant long-lived puffballs, with their proud finders, published in local newspapers than of any other mushroom. A similar giant puffball, *Calvatia gigantea,* grows in eastern North America but has a much smoother outer surface and remains more spherical. *Calbovista subsculpta* is considerably smaller and has fine brown hairs at the center of the warts on its surface.

There are stories of western puffballs being used by Native Americans and settlers as food and, in emergencies, to fill holes in sod houses to keep the wind out. Cheyenne Indians put puffball spores to many uses, including as baby powder and as styptics to stop bleeding.

ORDER
Lycoperdales
FAMILY
Lycoperdaceae
EDIBILITY
Edible

**Large, pear-shaped, white
to pinkish tan puffball;
surface cracked, check-
ered; interior white to
purple-brown at maturity;
sterile base persistent,
dull purplish, vase-
like remains.**

FRUITING BODIES Spore case large, pear-shaped, rounded on top, narrower toward base; 5–19 cm across, up to 15 cm high; outer surface pinkish tan at first, finally wood brown with age, soon cracked, checkered, flaking away; underlayer brownish, finally breaking up irregularly to release purple-brown spore mass. **Base** large; sterile base white, chambered, occupying large volume of lower part of fruiting body, persistent, remaining on ground after spores are dispersed as vaselike shell. **Flesh** at first homogeneous; white, soon yellowing, finally brown to purple-brown as spores mature; odor and taste mild when young and white.

SPORES Purple-brown, 3.5–7 µm in diameter, globose, with spines.

ECOLOGY/FRUITING PATTERN Solitary to scattered on ground in grasslands, pastures, golf courses; widely distributed in the Rocky Mountain region from plains to foothills; midsummer to late fall. There are reports of huge fairy rings of these large puffballs in the grasslands of eastern Colorado; the same mycelia may have been fruiting there for more than five hundred years.

OBSERVATIONS *cyathiformis:* Latin for cuplike. The purplish color of the gleba is a good field character for this species if you find it in the mature state. *Calvatia fragilis* also has a purplish brown spore mass and is fairly common in Colorado, but its spore cases are smaller, the sterile base is inconspicuous, and the spores are smooth. *Calvatia craniformis* is similar in size to *Calvatia cyathiformis* but can be distinguished by its smoother surface and yellow-greenish mature gleba. All these puffballs are commonly eaten when young if the inside is pure white and firm. Note the warning to puffball eaters on page 22 about checking for dangerous *Amanita* buttons by cutting all puffballs from top to bottom and examining them carefully.

ORDER
Lycoperdales
FAMILY
Lycoperdaceae
COMMON NAME
Gem-Studded Puffball
EDIBILITY
Edible

Small to medium-sized, white puffballs; conical spines that leave pock-marks; nipplelike opening on top at maturity; olive-brown spores; on soil.

FRUITING BODIES Spore case 2–5 cm broad x 2–7 cm tall; broader above and abruptly narrowed at base, sometimes almost spherical with tapered base; white to pale gray-brown; variably sized, white to brownish, conelike spines cover top, eventually flaking off, leaving small scars; tops of caps eventually open into a pore where spores are released. **Base** sterile, well developed, chambered. **Flesh** white in young, soon yellow-olive to olive-brown and powdery; odor and taste mild.

SPORES Olive-brown, 3–4 μm, spherical, minutely warty.

ECOLOGY/FRUITING PATTERN Solitary or in groups, at times dozens clustered on humus or moist soil; common from foothills to subalpine ecosystems throughout late summer and fall. As with other members of the order Lycoperdales, their lifestyle is saprophytic; they decompose and recycle organic materials.

OBSERVATIONS *perlatum:* Latin, meaning "widespread." This puffball is called the Gem-Studded Puffball because of the distinctive pattern left by the loose spines on the surface when they drop off. *Lycoperdon pyriforme* grows clustered on rotting wood in similar habitats; it has white, rootlike strings at the base and lacks deciduous spines. To prevent mistaking dangerous *Amanita* buttons for edible puffballs, slice puffballs from top to bottom and examine for immature gills and stalk. Puffballs at the edible stage should be homogeneous and white throughout.

ORDER
Lycoperdales
FAMILY
Lycoperdaceae
COMMON NAME
Pear-Shaped Puffball
EDIBILITY
Edible

Small, whitish to brown, pear-shaped puffballs with distinct white, root-like strings at base; clustered on rotting wood.

FRUITING BODIES Spore case 2–4 cm across x 2–5 cm tall; pear-shaped; tops rounded with abrupt transition into conical stalk; whitish when young, aging to ochre-brown; surface smooth at first, developing coarse granules, appearing rough; outer skin rupturing to form slitlike, apical pore at maturity. **Base** whitish, tapering; white, stringlike rhizoids projecting into substrate; sterile base white, homogeneous, one-third to one-half of total height of fruiting body. **Flesh** white, homogeneous in young, becoming yellow-brown to olive-brown and powdery; odor and taste mild.

SPORES Olive-brown, 3–3.5 µm across, globose, smooth.

ECOLOGY/FRUITING PATTERN Clustered, sometimes by the dozens; on dead logs and bases of stumps in conifer and deciduous forests; common in late summer and fall. Sometimes in the spring after the snow melts, you can find clusters of old, weathered, flattened fruiting bodies, often with sterile bases still intact and showing the characteristic ruptured pore at the top.

OBSERVATIONS *pyriforme:* Latin, meaning "pear-shaped." The lignicolous habit is characteristic of *Lycoperdon pyriforme.* Equally common in similar habitats is a close relative, *Lycoperdon perlatum,* which grows instead on soil and humus. The latter is further distinguished by its tiny, conical, deciduous spines, which leave smooth, little scars on the top, and its lack of white basal rhizoids. Both are commonly eaten by foragers, but one should heed the warning about always checking puffballs by cutting them lengthwise (see page 22). Both species are sometimes called Devil's Snuffbox because of their powdery spores.

ORDER
Sclerodermatales
FAMILY
Astraeaceae
COMMON NAME
Water-Measuring Earthstar
EDIBILITY
Inedible

Hairy, gray, ball-like spore case, encircled by starlike, cracked rays that open when wet and close inward over spore case when dry; in loose or arid soil.

FRUITING BODIES Roughly spherical; 2–5 cm broad; grayish; two-layered; outer layer splits into seven to fifteen pointed rays that extend outward when moist and close inward when dry; exposed inner surface of rays conspicuously cracked or checkered, light in color, becoming dark with age. **Spore case** surrounded by rays; puffball-shaped; gray; finely hairy; opening at maturity irregular, not a pore. **Base** absent. **Flesh** white to cocoa brown at maturity; odor mild, taste not recorded.

SPORES Cocoa brown, 7–10.5 μm in diameter, globose, spiny.

ECOLOGY/FRUITING PATTERN Widely distributed in Colorado and the southern Rocky Mountain region; fruiting in groups of two or three in loose, sandy soil, developing just under soil surface and becoming exposed when mature; usually fruiting in late summer and fall; in arid lands, meadows, along roads; reported in lower montane regions of Colorado under ponderosa pines.

OBSERVATIONS *hygrometricus:* moisture-measuring (Latin). The hard outer skin places *Astraeus hygrometricus* with the sclerodermas, or earthballs, which are poisonous. However, it differs from the sclerodermas by having a unique mechanism to increase the exposure of the spore sac and its spores to the air currents during a moist period. The outer skin splits into rays that open and curve backward, effectively raising the spore sac upward. Species of *Geastrum* in the order Lycoperdales have similar splitting rays, but the ray surfaces are not as cracked and checkered, and usually they do not open and close in response to moisture changes.

ORDER Lycoperdales

FAMILY Geastraceae

COMMON NAME Earthstar

EDIBILITY Inedible

Oval brown spore case on short stalk; rays arched, standing on tips, attached to mycelial, cuplike structure; on ground.

FRUITING BODIES Spherical or flattened when young and not yet open; 2–2.5 cm broad; multilayered skin splits, forming rays and central spore case. **Spore case** 1–2 cm in diameter; oval, on short stalk; chocolate brown; smooth to velvety; with a distinct, well-defined, conical mouth, set apart by a lighter color and a small pore. **Rays** numbering four to five; ochre-brown to pinkish tan; 2–4 cm long; arching, bending out and downward, elevating spore case above litter; exposed rays covered with dark brown patches of tissue; rays attached at tips to a base of mycelium and debris; mycelial "cup" remains partially buried. **Flesh** (gleba) white in young, becoming powdered, dark brown; odor and taste not recorded.

SPORES Dark brown, 4.5–6 µm in diameter, globose, warty.

ECOLOGY/FRUITING PATTERN Gregarious or in small groups; in soil and litter of conifer forests, montane, subalpine ecosystems; summer, fall.

OBSERVATIONS *quadrifidum:* Latin, meaning "four-forks." Also called *Geastrum coronatum.* Several species of earthstars develop rays that arch downward as they mature, thus allowing them to "stand" on their points. In this manner, the spore sac is lifted upward, high enough to catch more air currents, all the better to carry the spores into new, favorable environments. *Geastrum pectinatum* has radial grooves on the spore case just above the supporting stalk, along with a distinctly beaked and grooved pore mouth. *Geastrum fornicatum* has arched rays, but its pore mouth is torn and not well-defined; it is also larger than the aforementioned species.

ORDER
Phallales
FAMILY
Phallaceae
COMMON NAME
Stinkhorn
EDIBILITY
Inedible when mature

Phallus-shaped stalk with head; arising from soft, pinkish, gelatinous "egg"; head pitted, covered with greenish slime; odor offensive.

FRUITING BODIES **Head** conical; 4-5 cm tall x 2.5-3 cm wide; hanging freely around apex of stalk; small, whitish ring at apex; surface pitted, resembling honeycombed pattern of a morel mushroom; at maturity covered with olive green slime (gleba) that contains spores. **Stalk** 6-18 cm tall x 2-4 cm thick; white, spongy, more or less equal; hollow, surface rough; rising from primordial "egg." **Egg** roughly oval; pinkish when exposed; wrinkled, but not hairy; with mycelial strands at the base; 4-5 cm tall; enclosing young fruiting body within a gelatinous matrix; at maturity remains of egg persist at base of stalk as volva. **Flesh** of egg pinkish lavender, gelatinous; when mature, odor of slime offensive, like carrion; taste unrecorded.

SPORES Yellowish, 3-4.5 x 1.5-2 µm, embedded in slime, elliptical, smooth, no oil drops.

ECOLOGY/FRUITING PATTERN Common, particularly in gardens and parkways of Denver and other urban areas; usually gregarious; in soil among plantings, in grasses, under bushes; June through September; responding to warm, moist conditions.

OBSERVATIONS *impudicus:* meaning "shameless" (Latin). The offensive odor of these interesting fungi tends to give them a bad reputation with homeowners who find them in their well-tended flower beds. However, Stinkhorns are probably harmless, and in fact the mycelium does a good job of recycling organic materials in the soil for use by garden plants. Members of the order Phallales have a unique method of spore dispersal: The carrion odor of the slime on the top of the mature fruiting body attracts flies. When the flies crawl over the slime, the spores stick to their feet and are spread to other environments. The folk name for the egg, which is edible, is Witch's Egg.

ORDER
Nidulariales

FAMILY
Nidulariaceae

COMMON NAME
Common Bird's
Nest Fungus

EDIBILITY
Inedible

Tiny fungi resembling birds' nests; "nests" yellow to ochre, velvety on outside, smooth on inside; whitish "eggs" inside; attached to rotten wood, twigs.

FRUITING BODIES Tiny, 5–12 mm high x 5–10 mm wide; stalkless, attached directly to substrate; at first nearly round to cylindrical, velvety on outside, tawny yellow, with coarsely hairy lid; at maturity, lid disappears to reveal deep cup with nearly parallel to slightly flared sides, smooth pallid interior, and several whitish "eggs" or spore cases. **Spore cases** (peridioles) about 1–2 mm across, thin, lens-shaped; uniform, cream-colored, then white; each attached to cup by long, thin, cordlike strand.

SPORES White, 7–10 x 4–6 µm, elliptical, smooth, thick-walled.

ECOLOGY/FRUITING PATTERN One of the most common of the bird's nest fungi; in groups on stems, chips, and twigs; late summer and fall, often persisting for months; widely distributed throughout the Rockies, decomposing lignin-rich materials; not on soil or large logs.

OBSERVATIONS *laeve:* means "smooth" in Latin. The insides of the cups are smooth, as are the peridioles. The vase-shaped *Cyathus stercoreus* has a brownish to yellowish brown exterior that becomes blackish with age, with gray to black peridioles and large spores; it typically fruits on dung, manured ground, or sawdust. *Cyathus striatus* has shaggy brown exteriors; radially striated, shiny cup interiors; and blackish peridioles.

The tiny "nests" are called splash cups because of the spore dispersal mechanism, which depends on the splashing action of raindrops to disperse the peridioles. In some species, as the peridioles are ejected the cord attached to the peridioles wraps around nearby plants and holds the spore case in place until the spores are released.

Bird's nest fungi were economic predictors in some early peasant cultures, the number of coinlike eggs in a cup being related to the rise or fall in prices.

ORDER Tulostomatales
FAMILY Tulostomataceae
COMMON NAME Stalked Puffball
EDIBILITY Unknown

Pale gray, rounded spore case with thin, sandy coat that wears away above, leaving sandy basal disc below; eroded, fibrous central pore; grooved, brownish stalk.

FRUITING BODIES **Spore case** 1–2 cm thick x 1–1.5 cm high; subglobose; with sandy coat that wears away, leaving smooth to slightly roughened surface; lower third persistently sand-covered; pale grayish to pale brownish; pore area somewhat elevated; pore fibrous, lacerated or circular, not well-defined. **Stalk** 2–5 cm long x 3–4 mm thick; equal down to small bulb at base; scaly-rough over surface, longitudinally grooved, distinct collar at apex; surface brownish; interior white and with central cottony cylinder. **Flesh** powdery at maturity, reddish brown; odor mild, taste not recorded.

SPORES Rusty salmon, 4.5–6.8 µm in diameter, spherical or slightly oval, warty.

ECOLOGY/FRUITING PATTERN Widely distributed in northern and western United States; found in Colorado in arid locations in grasslands and semidesert shrublands; scattered to gregarious in sandy soil.

OBSERVATIONS *campestre:* Latin, meaning "fields" or "plains." The specific epithet was well chosen for this sandy survivor of arid conditions. Members of the order Tulostomatales develop underground, emerging at maturity by the efforts of their sturdy stalk, which pushes the spore sac upward. The outer wall of the spore case has a sandy layer that may break up or wear away, leaving the smoother, persistent covering for the spore sac. There is always a pore for release of spores, details of which help define various species. The specimens pictured were found at Colorado National Monument in Mesa County.

ORDER
Lycoperdales
FAMILY
Lycoperdaceae
EDIBILITY
Unknown

Small, flattened, globose, light gray puffball; skin papery with small tear or pore; resting on a sand case at base; partially buried or on top of loose, arid soil; on prairie.

FRUITING BODIES Spore case 1–2.5 cm across; spherical, often flattened or compressed; pore usually central, approximately round or torn in various manners; surface initially roughened by mycelial threads of outer skin (peridium) and adhering sand, these progressively weathering away to reveal more or less smooth, gray, papery surface of inner peridium. **Base** a firm sand case (sand covers lower one-fourth to one-third of spore case). **Stalk** absent. **Flesh** firm; white at first, soon olive to dark brown and powdery as spores mature.

SPORES Dark chocolate brown, 6–8 μm in diameter, globose, warty.

ECOLOGY/FRUITING PATTERN Developing underground in loose, dry soil in fall; exposed by wind throughout following months; usually found in spring as overmature fruiting bodies weathering out of soil; gregarious; fairly common in arid grassland and semidesert shrubland ecosystems of Colorado. There are reports of large fairy rings formed by these little puffballs.

OBSERVATIONS *subterranea:* under the ground (Latin). D. H. Mitchel, George Grimes, and Shirley Chapman of the Denver Botanic Gardens' Mycology Department elucidated the fascinating lifestyle of *Disciseda* species. They concluded that *Disciseda* species begin life as underground puffballs. As the fruiting body weathers out of the loose prairie soil, it is eventually flipped over, its previously sand-covered top becoming its base. Like a weighted harbor buoy, it is then able to disperse its spores from the pore on its top as it is wobbled about by the ever-present prairie wind. Sometimes dozens of fruiting bodies may be winnowed out of their locations, winding up on the powder-dry soil between clumps of grass.

Hypogeous Fungi

A diverse, loosely organized group, the hypogeous fungi all produce fruiting bodies that develop underground or just under the soil surface. This trufflelike growth habit is probably an adaptation to moisture-limiting conditions, and the reproductive success of the fungus depends on mycophagy by mammals and insects. Because airborne spore dispersal is not possible in the world of hypogeous fungi, odors are all-important. Animals smell the mature fruiting body, dig it up, and eat it on the spot or carry it away for storage. By this means the spores are eventually passed still viable through the animal's gut and are then spread far away from their hidden origins.

Hypogeous ascomycetes in the order Tuberales, which include the true truffles of gastronomic fame found in southern Europe, have fruiting bodies with marbled, channeled, or hollow interiors. They have been rarely reported in Colorado. However, hypogeous basidiomycetes, the so-called false truffles, have a rich mycoflora in the Rocky Mountains and are some of Colorado's most important fungi, forming valuable mycorrhizal relationships with forest trees. Many are related to common genera that develop on the surface of the ground, such as *Suillus, Russula,* and *Cortinarius,* perhaps having evolved from or given rise to them. The fruiting bodies of false truffles are often potatolike, the spore mass within or lining densely packed chambers. There may or may not be a rudimentary stalk or internal columella.

Truncocolumella citrina Zeller

ORDER
Hymenogastrales
FAMILY
Rhizopogonaceae
EDIBILITY
Unknown

Rounded, olive-yellow, pear- to egg-shaped fruiting body; branching, whitish internal stalk; matures underground; under conifers.

FRUITING BODIES 2–6 cm across; irregularly rounded or lobed; smooth, dry; lemon yellow to olive-yellow, staining dull orangish. **Stalk** stumplike, yellow, attached to basal rhizomorphs with a network of branches extending upward throughout spore mass. **Flesh** firm; spore mass pale yellow to olive-gray, chambered; odor mild, taste unpleasant.

SPORES Spore print not obtainable; 6.5–10 x 3.5–4.5 μm, elliptical, smooth.

ECOLOGY/FRUITING PATTERN Mycorrhizal with conifers, especially Douglas-fir; partially buried or in duff; solitary to gregarious; fairly common in summer and early fall; montane to lower subalpine ecosystems.

OBSERVATIONS *citrina: citrin* means "lemon yellow" in Latin. The identification of this colorful false truffle is facilitated by slicing the fruiting body and observing the branching rudimentary stalk-columella.

Members of the hypogeous genus *Truncocolumella* are believed to be related to the boletes, which fruit aboveground.

ORDER
Hymenogastrales

FAMILY
Rhizopogonaceae

EDIBILITY
Unknown

Rounded to oval, pale olive-yellow fruiting body; staining red-brown; finely chambered interior; stalk-columella absent; buried under needle bed; in lodgepole pine forests.

FRUITING BODIES Rounded to ovoid, with lobes or indentations; 2-6 cm across; white with cottony, fibrillose patches when young, soon scattered with brown mycelial threads appressed to pale olive to yellow-ochre surface, exposed areas reddish brown. **Stalk** absent. **Flesh** firm; interior of fruiting body white and soft when young, becoming pale olive, dark olive-brown at maturity; spore mass finely convoluted, sinuous, chambered throughout; staining pink to vinaceous where injured and deep reddish brown with KOH; odor mild to disagreeable with age, taste mild.

SPORES Spore print not obtainable; 8–10 x 3.2–4 μm, elongated-elliptical, smooth.

ECOLOGY/FRUITING PATTERN Solitary to caespitose; clusters of fruiting bodies buried under pine needle litter, at times close to surface and partially exposed at maturity; associated with lodgepole pine; montane ecosystems; late July through September.

OBSERVATIONS *rubescens:* Latin for becoming red. This may be the most common *Rhizopogon* species found in the Rocky Mountain region, where it can be abundant in some seasons in lodgepole pine forests. Other *Rhizopogon* species are differentiated by the color of the fresh fruiting bodies, color changes upon bruising, mycorrhizal associations, spore size, and other microscopic determinations. Typical of hypogeous fungi, the basidia of *Rhizopogon* species cannot forcibly discharge their spores; therefore, making a spore print is not possible.

There is a strong similarity between members of the hypogeous genus *Rhizopogon* and the aboveground-fruiting *Suillus,* a member of the Boletaceae family. Some believe that one genus has evolved from the other. Members of both genera are mycorrhizal with conifers and share spore characters, staining reactions, and other microscopic features.

ORDER
Hymenogastrales
FAMILY
Hymenogastraceae
EDIBILITY
Unknown

Sticky, olive-brown fruiting bodies resembling gilled fungi; fertile area contorted, reddish cinnamon, folded plates; short stalk extends into spore mass; near surface of soil under conifers.

FRUITING BODIES Cap 1–5 cm across; convex, flattening at center with age, at times with broad lobes; margins irregular, broadly wrinkled, remaining inrolled, never expanding or flaring; slimy when moist; smooth; dingy olive-yellow, darkening to deep dingy brown, often streaked. **Spore mass** deeply folded, contorted plates with small chambers; red–cinnamon brown. **Stalk** 1–4 cm long x 0.5–2 cm wide; at times rudimentary; equal; buff to brownish, tinged pinkish lilac where exposed to light; upper part with cottony-hairy fibers when young; extending into spore mass as narrow, unbranched columella. **Flesh** whitish, a thin zone just above columella; odor pungent, taste not recorded.

SPORES Spore print not obtainable; 14–16.5 x 8–9.5 µm, elliptical to oblong, warty-wrinkled.

ECOLOGY/FRUITING PATTERN One of the most common members of the family found in the Rocky Mountains; developing under soil and conifer litter or pushing through it; often gregarious to clustered under Engelmann spruce in Colorado's subalpine regions; mycorrhizal with conifers; July through August.

OBSERVATIONS *pingue:* meaning "fat" or "grease" in Latin. Because they have contorted plates instead of true gills, gastroid (like a gasteromycete) agaric mushrooms are often ignored as freaks. However, they exhibit a wonderful adaptation to living in harsh conditions with unpredictable moisture—in this case, the high mountains. Because they do not expose their fertile areas to the drying atmosphere but rather trap their spores within their gleba, hypogeous mushrooms depend on eventually rotting and having the elements spread their spores, or on being unearthed and eaten. Studies have shown that mushrooms serve as a major food source for many resident mammals, such as deer and squirrels, as well as insects. When dry, mushrooms such as the ones pictured here are stored by squirrels in huge caches for the winter. *Thaxterogaster pingue* is believed to be related to the mycorrhizal genus *Cortinarius*.

Jelly Fungi

The "jellies" are aptly named because their textures and often amorphous shapes sometimes resemble firm gelatin. Touch is a sense usually brought into play when one finds a colorful jelly fungus that looks like a gumdrop or a blob of jelly. The fruiting bodies are mostly water, and when they dry up, they

Guepiniopsis alpinus, a jelly fungus, not gumdrops

look like bits of varnish or paint stuck to the substrate. During active growth, their spores develop on the outer surfaces from specialized basidia that differ from those of most other basidiomycetes by being septate, multicelled, or divided in some manner. Even though these interesting basidia are visible only under a microscope, the jelly fungi as a group are usually not difficult to recognize in nature. There are at least four orders of jelly fungi reported in Colorado, two of which are represented here.

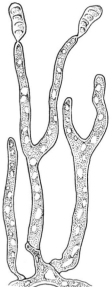

FIGURE 8 Basidium of a typical jelly fungus from the order Dacrymycetales

---

Auricularia auricula-judae (Bulliard) Schroeter

ORDER
Auriculariales
FAMILY
Auriculariaceae
COMMON NAMES
Tree Ear, Wood Ear
EDIBILITY
Edible

Human ear-shaped, brown, rubbery jelly fungus growing on dead conifer logs.

FRUITING BODIES Shaped like little ears or wrinkled shallow cups; edges smooth; 2–10 cm across; broadly attached directly to wood; upper surface brown to reddish brown, frosted with covering of fine hairs; undersurface reddish brown, strongly veined and ribbed, minutely hairy. **Flesh** thin, brown, rubbery; odor and taste mild.

SPORES White, 12–15 x 4–6 μm, sausage-shaped, smooth, from transversely septate basidia found on veined undersurface of fruiting body.

ECOLOGY/FRUITING PATTERN Gregarious on deadwood, often on subalpine fir logs; summer and fall; montane to subalpine ecosystems.

OBSERVATIONS *auricula-judae:* Latin for ear of Judah. Similarly colored cup fungi such as *Peziza* species are sometimes comparable in shape, but they usually grow on the ground and their texture is very brittle. A closely related cultivated species is sold in Chinese markets.

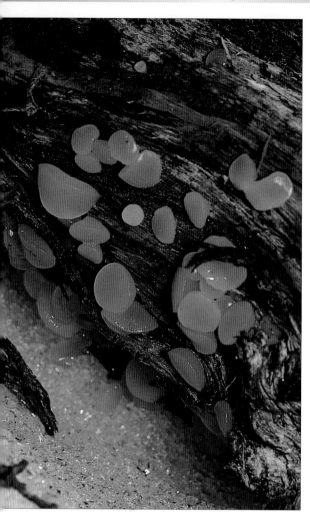

ORDER
Dacrymycetales
FAMILY
Dacrymycetaceae
EDIBILITY
Not recommended

Small, bright yellow-orange, conelike cups; attached to conifer wood by a point; jellylike consistency; in alpine regions near melting snowbanks.

FRUITING BODIES
Consisting of small, golden, gelatinous, cone-shaped fungi with concave tops; 0.5–1.5 cm across x about 1 cm high; moist and smooth when fresh. **Stalk** absent, attached to substrate by simple point. **Flesh** jellylike, gelatinous; orange; shriveled and dark rusty orange when dried; odor mild, taste not distinctive.

SPORES Pale yellowish, 15–18 x 5–6 μm, located in center of concavity, segmented, sausage-shaped, smooth.

ECOLOGY/FRUITING PATTERN Usually in groups of a dozen or more growing saprophytically out of the cracks of dead conifer logs or on twigs of living or dead conifers, sometimes fruiting right out of the snow; common in late May to June; subalpine ecosystems.

OBSERVATIONS *alpinus:* pertaining to alpine. A conspicuous member of the snowbank mycoflora of the Rocky Mountains, these colorful little fungi can brighten your viewpoint if you are closely examining the conifer twigs and logs alongside melting snowbanks in the high country. Although not poisonous, there is little to recommend them for the mycophagist.

As with other members of the order Dacrymycetales, *Guepiniopsis alpinus* spores are borne on long basidia that are divided into two arms, resembling microscopic tuning forks (Fig. 8). These basidiomycetes can be confused with cup fungi, even though the latter are ascomycetes. In the field, the gelatinous consistency and relatively thick flesh help distinguish these jelly fungi from cup fungi.

The type specimen of *Guepiniopsis alpinus* was found in southwestern Colorado.

acrid Having an intensely sharp or burning taste.

adnate (of gills) Broadly attached to the stalk over most of the gills' height.

adnexed (of gills) The gill edge curving gradually upward toward the stalk and the gills connecting to the stalk by a narrow portion of their height.

amanitins Deadly cyclopeptide toxins found in some mushrooms.

amyloid The blue-black to blue-gray color change of some spores and tissues when treated with Melzer's solution.

annulus A ring of tissue left on the stalk from the remains of a veil.

apiculus A short projection on basidiospores near the point where the spore is attached to the sterigma of the basidium; on ascospores, a short projection on each end.

appendiculate (of cap margin) Hung with pieces of tissue, such as the partial veil.

appressed Flattened to the surface of the cap or stalk, as in appressed fibrils or scales.

ascomycete Any fungus that produces asci and ascospores; member of the subdivision Ascomycotina.

ascus (pl. asci) A saclike cell that contains the spores in an ascomycete.

attached (of gills) Reaching the stalk and being attached to it.

basidiomycete Any fungus that produces basidia and basidiospores; member of the subdivision Basidiomycotina.

basidium (pl. basidia) The reproductive, often club-shaped cell of basidiomycetes on which basidiospores are formed following fusion of two nuclei and division of the resulting nucleus.

binomial The two-word, Latinized name given to each known species.

biodiversity An expression of the variety and value of life on earth. Fungal diversity is significant because of the large number of species, only a small portion of which are well known.

bolete A fleshy mushroom of the Boletaceae family with a tube layer on the undersurface of the cap.

broad (of gills) A relatively large distance between the gills' attachment to the cap and the gills' lower edge.

brown rot A type of wood rot in which the fungus degrades the cellulose but not the lignin, leaving a brown residue.

bruising Changing color when handled, rubbed, or otherwise injured.

buff Very pale yellow toned with gray.

button (mushroom) A young fruiting body with the veil intact and/or the cap not yet expanded.

caespitose Describes mushrooms in groups joined at their stalk bases.

campanulate (of cap) Bell-shaped.

cap The umbrellalike part of a fruiting body whose undersurface bears the hymenium on gills, teeth, tubes, veins, or smooth surfaces.

cellular (of cap or stalk surface) Composed of globose to saclike cells arranged in a single layer.

cellulose The principal polysaccharide in plant cell walls.

class The taxonomic rank above order and below division; suffix is *-mycetes.*

clavate (of stalk) Thickened like a club toward the base.

close (of gills) A relative term to describe spacing of gills; intermediate between subdistant and crowded.

conical (of cap) More or less cone-shaped.

conifer Cone-bearing, referring to trees with needles or scales, such as pines, firs, or junipers.

conk The common name of large, woody, hoof-shaped polypore growing on trees.

convex (of cap) Rounded, shaped like an inverted bowl.

coprine A toxin having an effect similar to antabuse; found in *Coprinus atramentarius.*

coprophilous Dung-loving; growing on dung or manure.

cortina (type of partial veil) A hairy, silky mass of filaments with the texture of a spider web.

crowded (of gills) So close together that spaces between them are hard to see.

cuticle The outer tissue covering the cap or stalk.

decurrent (of gills) Attached and running down the stalk.

decurved (of cap edge) Bent downward so that it points toward the stalk.

deliquescent (of gills) Autodigesting or liquifying at maturity, as in the genus *Coprinus.*

depressed (of cap) Having the central portion lower than the margin.

dextrinoid (of spores and tissues) Stained reddish brown by Melzer's solution.

disc The central part of the cap surface of a mushroom.

discomycete One of a group of ascomycetes possessing a microscopic palisade layer of asci on the exposed spore-bearing surfaces; member of the class Discomycetes.

distant (of gills) Having a wide space between adjacent gills.

division The major taxonomic order above class and below kingdom.

ecosystem A recognizable grouping of plants, fungi, animals, and environmental conditions, and the interactions among them.

egg The immature stage of *Amanitas* and stinkhorns; also the common name of the spore sacs in the splash cups of bird's nest fungi.

elliptical Having the outline of an ellipse.

equal (stalk shape) Having a constant diameter from top to base.

fairy ring Ring of mushrooms growing from the periphery of a radially spreading, underground mycelium.

family A taxonomic group of related genera; the rank above genus and below order; suffix is *-aceae.*

farinaceous Having an odor or taste of freshly ground meal; mealy.

FeSO₄ The chemical symbol for ferrous sulfate. A 10 percent aqueous solution is commonly used to test mushroom tissues for color changes.

fibril An aggregation of hyphae forming a threadlike filament.

fibrillose (of surface of cap or stalk) Having visible fibrils.

fibrous (of flesh of stalk or cap) Composed of stringlike, rather tough tissue.

filamentous (of hyphae) Threadlike; (of cap surface) threadlike cells forming outer surface.

flesh The inner tissue of the cap or stalk when viewed with the naked eye.

fleshy (of cap and stalk) Usually soft, decaying readily.

floccose (of cap or stalk) Having a cottony surface, resembling flannel.

forked (of gills and veins) Branching irregularly.

free (of gills) Not attached to the stalk.

friable Breaking up readily; describes a texture type of universal veil.

fruiting body The organized reproductive structure of a fungus that produces spores.

fungus (pl. fungi) A nonphotosynthesizing, spore-producing organism made up of hyphae that produce enzymes and absorb food from their environment.

gasteromycete One of a group of diverse basidiomycetes that develop spores inside spore cases and do not actively discharge their spores; member of the class Gasteromycetes.

genus A group of similar species; the taxonomic rank below family and above species.

germ pore The differentiated area on a spore through which the germ tube extends upon germination.

gills Platelike structures arranged radially on the underside of the mushroom cap on which the hymenium and spores are formed.

glandular dots Moist, sticky, resinous, dotlike structures on the stalk of some boletes.

gleba The spore-producing tissue, or spore mass, within the peridium of a gasteromycete.

globose Spherical, or nearly so.

glutinous (of surface of stalk or cap) Slimy, very sticky.

granulose Covered with granules, like grains of fine salt.

gregarious A pattern of fruiting in which many mushrooms grow close together but are not attached to each other.

gyromitrin A cellular, carcinogenic toxin produced by some false morels and others, breaking down to monomethylhydrazine (MMH), which is extremely toxic and volatile.

hardwood In the broad sense, denotes nonconifer trees such as aspen, cottonwood, willow, or alder.

homogeneous (of spores or tissues) The same throughout, not differentiated.

humus A type of soil; a mixture of decayed vegetation in a forest.

hygrophanous Appearing water-soaked when wet and then changing to a different (faded) color when moisture is lost.

hymenium The spore-bearing layer of a fruiting body.

hypha (pl. hyphae) A microscopic filament, the basic structural unit of the body of the mycelium and the fruiting body of a fungus.

hypogeous Developing and attaining maturity underground.

ibotenic acid-muscimol Toxic compounds responsible for inebriation syndrome, a type of mushroom poisoning.

incurved (of cap margin) Curved or bent inward.

inoperculate Without a lid; describes a group of discomycetes with ascospores discharged through a pore in the ascus.

inrolled (of cap margin) Curved in toward the gills and tucked under.

KOH The chemical symbol for potassium hydroxide. Usually a 2.5 percent aqueous solution is used for reviving tissues and a 25 percent solution for spot-testing for color changes.

lamellae Another name for gills.

lamellulae Shortened gills that reach only partway to the stalk.

latex A juice- or milklike fluid exuding from a cut or injured portion of some mushrooms, especially species of *Lactarius*.

LBM "Little Brown Mushroom," a term denoting unknown, small, brownish hard-to-differentiate mushrooms.

lichen A dual organism whose body is made up of a fungus (usually an ascomycete) and a blue-green algae or cyanobacterium.

lignicolous Wood-inhabiting.

lignin A major constituent of wood, very resistant but degraded by some basidiomycetes.

margin (of gills or cap) The edge; in the case of the cap, the area away from the disc toward and including the edge.

mealy (texture) Appearing as if covered with coarse meal; (taste) like that of freshly ground meal.

Melzer's solution A solution used to test spores and tissue; made by mixing 22 ml water, 20 g chloral hydrate, 0.5 g iodine, and 1.5 g potassium iodide; caution: poisonous.

membranous Resembling a membrane or thin skin.

micrometer One millionth of a meter, a micron, abbreviated as μm.

monomethylhydrazine (MMH) A mushroom toxin; see *gyromitrin*.

muscarine A mushroom toxin affecting the autonomic nervous system, causing perspiration-salivation-lacrymation syndrome.

mushroom A general term for the fleshy fruiting body of a fungus.

mycelium A collective term for a mass of hyphae or fungus filaments; the assimilative portion of a fungus.

mycoflora The fungi characteristic of an area.

mycologist A scientist who studies fungi.

mycology The science dealing with fungi.

mycophagist One who eats fungi.

mycorrhiza (pl. mycorrhizae) Fungus/roots; the symbiotic association of fungal mycelium and the root ends of trees or other plants.

narrow (of gills) A relatively small distance between the gills' attachment to the cap and the gills' lower edge.

non-amyloid (of spores and tissues) Remaining colorless or merely yellowish in Melzer's solution.

notched (of gills) Having a notch at the point of attachment to the stalk.

ochraceous Ochre-colored; dingy yellow to dull brownish yellow.

oil drops (of spores) Droplets of what appears to be oily material inside the cell when viewed under a microscope.

operculate Having a lid; describes a group of discomycetes that have asci with hinged lids at their apex through which spores are discharged.

order A taxonomic grouping of families; the rank above family and below class; suffix is *-ales*.

ornamentation (of spore surfaces) Having warts, ridges, lines, wrinkles; not smooth.

ovate Having an outline like the longitudinal shape of a hen's egg.

ovoid Pertaining to a solid, shaped like a hen's egg.

pallid Very pale, an indefinite whitish color.

parasitic Living in or on another living organism and obtaining nourishment from the association, usually to the detriment of the host.

partial veil A membranous, weblike, or glutinous veil that extends from the cap margin to the stalk, covering the young gills or tubes.

peridiole A small spore capsule produced by some gasteromycetes, examples being bird's nest fungi "eggs."

peridium The wall surrounding the spore case in gasteromycetes such as puffballs.

pileus The cap of a mushroom.

plage A depression or flat unornamented area on a spore surface, especially common in species of *Galerina*.

plane (of cap surface) Flat, not curved.

plano-convex (of cap surface) Convex with a flat disc.

polypore The common name for members of the Polyporaceae family with firmly attached, thin tube layers on leathery or woody fruiting bodies.

pores The mouths of tubes in boletes and polypores.

pruinose Appearing powdered, as if sprinkled with flour.

psilocybin/psilocin Hallucinogenic toxins found mainly in species of *Psilocybe* and *Panaeolus*.

radially arranged Radiating from a central point, such as pores radiating from the stalk like spokes of a wheel.

recurved (of cap margin or scales) Having an edge curved up and back.

resupinate (of fruiting body) Lying flat, crustlike on substrate with hymenium facing outward, lacking a stalk or well-defined cap.

reticulate (of stalk surface) Marked with a vein or netlike pattern.

reviving Resuming an earlier shape and function when moistened after drying; common in species of *Marasmius*.

rhizoid A rootlike structure attached to the stalk base.

rhizomorph A visible, rootlike bundle of mycelial hyphae, often penetrating the substrate; common in the *Armillaria mellea* group.

ring See *annulus*.

saclike (of volva) Shaped like a bag or sack around the base of the stalk.

saprophyte An organism that feeds on dead or decaying organic material and uses it for active growth.

scaber Rough, tufted hairs projecting from surface of stalk.

scaly (of surface of cap or stalk) Having small, flat, often tapered and pointed pieces of tissue.

sclerotium A fleshy mass of hyphae of definite structure serving as a resting stage for a fungus.

seceding (of gills) At first attached to stalk, at maturity becoming free.

separable (of gill or stalk) Easily separated from the cap.

sessile (of fruiting body) Stalkless, attached directly to the substrate.

sexual reproduction The fusion of nuclei of different mating types, followed by reduction division and recombination at some point in the life cycle.

sinuate (of gills) Having notched gills in which the gill edge becomes abruptly concave as it meets the stalk.

species A taxonomic group representing a population of individuals that have certain characteristics in common; usually considered capable of interbreeding.

spines See *teeth*.

spore The microscopic reproductive and dispersive unit of a fungus.

spore case The structure containing the spore mass in the gasteromycetes.

spore print The visible deposit of basidiospores made by placing a stalkless cap on white paper and covering it for a few hours.

stalk The structure supporting the cap or head of a fungus; also called a stipe.

stalk-columella The stalklike structure that supports and penetrates the gleba of some hypogeous fungi.

sterile Without reproductive spores; the opposite of fertile.

sterile base The sterile, chambered base below the gleba in certain gasteromycetes.

stipe The stalk of a fruiting body.

striated Describes a surface marked with lines, grooves, or ridges.

subdistant (of spacing of gills) Intermediate between close and widely spaced, nearly distant.

subdivision The taxonomic grouping above class and below division; suffix is *-mycotina*.

substrate The material on which the fruiting body is found and from which the fungus obtains its nourishment.

tawny Rich yellowish brown, the color of a lion.

taxonomy The systematic classification of organisms with emphasis on relationships.

teeth The pendant, spinelike, spore-bearing structures characteristic of the family Hydnaceae.

terrestrial Growing on the ground.

toadstool An ancient term for an inedible or poisonous stalked mushroom.

tomentum A covering of long, wooly, soft hairs.

translucent-striated (of cap margin) Having very thin, translucent flesh, allowing the gills to show through as striations.

truncated Chopped-off in appearance.

tubes Hollow, cylindrical structures lined with basidia and open at one end as a pore; characteristic of boletes and polypores.

type specimen A specimen or collection of fruiting bodies from which the original concept of a species or other taxonomic group is derived.

umbo A protrusion or knob on the disc of the cap.

undulate (of cap margin) Broadly wavy.

universal veil A layer of tissue completely surrounding the developing fruiting body, pieces of it sometimes remaining as scales or patches on the cap and/or as a volva on the stalk.

veil See *partial veil* and *universal veil*.

vinaceous Color name taken from that of red wine; closer to dull pinkish brown to dull grayish purple.

viscid Sticky or slimy to the touch.

volva Remnants of the universal veil left in various forms on or at the base of the stalk.

warts (surface feature of cap or stalk base) Small patches of universal veil remnants resembling warts; (surface of spores) small, rounded projections like warts.

white rot A type of wood rot produced by basidiomycetes that degrades both the cellulose and the lignin, leaving a whitish residue.

zonate Having zones of different textures or colors.

Suggested Reading

FIELD GUIDES USEFUL FOR COLORADO HABITATS

Arora, David. *Mushrooms Demystified.* 2nd ed. Berkeley, Calif.: Ten Speed Press, 1986.

———. *All That the Rain Promises and More ...A Hip Pocket Guide to Western Mushrooms.* Berkeley, Calif.: Ten Speed Press, 1991.

Bessette, Alan E., Orson K. Miller, Arleen R. Bessette, and Hope H. Miller. *Mushrooms of North America in Color: A Field Guide Companion to Seldom-Illustrated Fungi.* Syracuse, N.Y.: Syracuse University Press, 1995.

Horn, Bruce, Richard Kay, and Dean Abel. *A Guide to Kansas Mushrooms.* Lawrence: University Press of Kansas, 1993.

Lincoff, Gary H. *The Audubon Society Field Guide to North American Mushrooms.* New York: Alfred A. Knopf, 1981.

McKenny, Margaret, and Daniel E. Stuntz. *The New Savory Wild Mushroom.* 3rd ed. Revised by Joseph Ammirati. Seattle: University of Washington Press, 1987.

McKnight, Kent H., and Vera B. McKnight. *A Field Guide to Mushrooms of North America.* Boston: Houghton Mifflin, 1987.

Miller, O.K. *Mushrooms of North America.* New York: E.P. Dutton, 1973.

Phillips, Roger. *Mushrooms of North America.* Boston: Little, Brown, 1991.

Schalkwijk-Barendsen, Helene M.E. *Mushrooms of Western Canada.* Edmonton, Alta.: Lone Pine Publishing, 1991.

Smith, Alexander H., Helen V. Smith, and Nancy S. Weber. *How to Know the Gilled Mushrooms.* Dubuque, Iowa: Wm. C. Brown Company, 1979.

———. *How to Know the Non-Gilled Mushrooms.* 2nd ed. Dubuque, Iowa: Wm. C. Brown Company, 1981.

States, Jack S. *Mushrooms and Truffles of the Southwest.* Tucson: University of Arizona Press, 1990.

Tylutki, Edmund E. *Mushrooms of Idaho and the Pacific Northwest: Discomycetes.* Moscow: University Press of Idaho, 1979.

———. *Mushrooms of Idaho and the Pacific Northwest. Vol. 2: Non-Gilled Hymenomycetes.* Moscow: University Press of Idaho, 1987.

Weber, Nancy Smith. *A Morel Hunter's Companion.* Lansing, Mich.: Two Peninsula Press, 1988.

Wells, Mary H., and D.H. Mitchel. *Colorado Mushrooms.* Museum Pictorial No. 17. Denver: Denver Museum of Natural History, 1966.

BOOKS ABOUT MUSHROOM POISONING

Ammirati, Joseph. F., James A. Traquair, and Paul A. Horgen. *Poisonous Mushrooms of the Northern United States and Canada.* Minneapolis: University of Minnesota Press, 1985.

Benjamin, Denis R. *Mushrooms: Poisons and Panaceas.* New York: W.H. Freeman, 1995.

Lincoff, Gary, and D.H. Mitchel. *Toxic and Hallucinogenic Mushroom Poisoning: A Handbook for Physicians and Mushroom Hunters.* New York: Van Nostrand Reinhold, 1977.

Spoerke, David G., and Barry H. Rumack, eds. *Handbook of Mushroom Poisoning.* Boca Raton, Fla.: CRC Press, 1994.

BOOKS ON MYCOPHAGY

Bessette, Arleen Rainis, and Alan E. Bessette. *Taming the Wild Mushroom.* Austin: University of Texas Press, 1993.

Czarnecki, Jack. *A Cook's Book of Mushrooms.* New York: Artisan, 1995.

Fischer, David W., and Alan E. Bessette. *Edible Wild Mushrooms of North America.* Austin: University of Texas Press, 1992.

Rosenberg, Rita. *Mushrooms Wild and Tamed.* Tucson, Ariz.: Fisher Books, 1995.

OTHER REFERENCE BOOKS

Breitenbach, J., and F. Kränzlin. *Fungi of Switzerland.* 4 vols. Luzern, Switz.: Verlag Mykologia, 1984–1995.

Gilbertson, R.L., and L. Ryvarden. *North American Polypores.* 2 vols. Oslo, Nor.: Fungiflora A/S, 1986.

Hawksworth, D.L., P.M. Kirk, B.C. Sutton, and D.N. Pegler. *Ainsworth and Bisby's Dictionary of the Fungi.* 8th ed. Wallingford, U.K.: CAB International, 1995.

Hudson, Harry J. *Fungal Biology.* Cambridge, Eng.: Press Syndicate of the University of Cambridge, 1986.

Kendrick, Bryce. *The Fifth Kingdom.* 2nd ed. Newburyport, Mass.: Focus Information Group, 1992.

Largent, David, David Johnson, and Roy Watling. *How to Identify Mushrooms to Genus III: Microscopic Features.* Eureka, Calif.: Mad River Press, 1988.

Miller, O.K., and H.H. Miller. *Gasteromycetes: Morphological and Development Features with Keys to the Orders, Families and Genera.* Eureka, Calif.: Mad River Press, 1988.

Mutel, Cornelia F., and John C. Emerick. *From Grassland to Glacier: The Natural History of Colorado and the Surrounding Region.* Boulder, Colo.: Johnson Books, 1984.

Seaver, F.J. *The North American Cup-fungi (Operculates).* New York: Seaver, 1928.

Smith, Alexander H. *Mushrooms in Their Natural Habitat.* Portland, Ore.: Sawyer's, 1949.

Index

Bold entries indicate detailed accounts with photographs.

INDEX

DETAILED PARTS OF A MUSHROOM

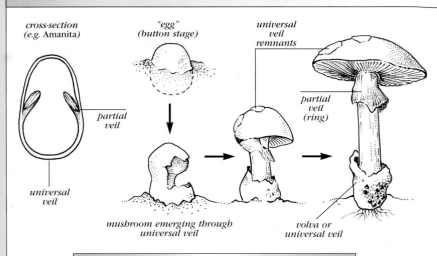

cross-section
(e.g. Amanita)

"egg"
(button stage)

universal
veil
remnants

partial
veil
(ring)

partial
veil

universal
veil

mushroom emerging through
universal veil

volva or
universal veil

GROWTH STAGES OF A GILLED MUSHROOM

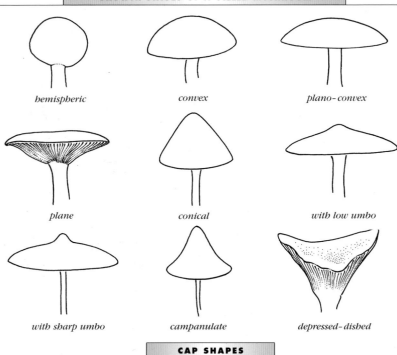

hemispheric

convex

plano-convex

plane

conical

with low umbo

with sharp umbo

campanulate

depressed-dished

CAP SHAPES

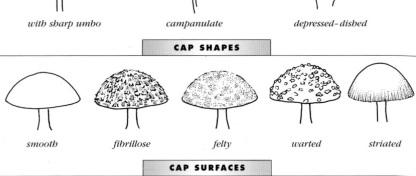

smooth

fibrillose

felty

warted

striated

CAP SURFACES

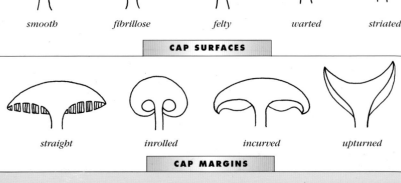

straight

inrolled

incurved

upturned

CAP MARGINS